IN PIAM MEMORIAM

STEPHANI PERSE
W.H.D. ROVSE

PERSICORVM
PRAETERITORVM
OMNIVM

PERSE

A History of the Perse School
1615-1976

S. J. D. Mitchell

THE OLEANDER PRESS OF CAMBRIDGE

THE OLEANDER PRESS
17 STANSGATE AVENUE
CAMBRIDGE CB2 2QZ
ENGLAND

THE OLEANDER PRESS
210 FIFTH AVENUE
NEW YORK, N.Y. 10010
U.S.A.

ISBN 0 902675 71 0

Contents

List of Illustrations

Foreword

The History of the Perse School written over fifty years ago by Sir John Gray ended just as the most remarkable period in the life of the school was beginning. This was the era of Dr. Rouse's Headmastership which not only made the school widely known but also significantly affected the course of English educational history by the successful innovations in teaching method which he and his gifted colleagues pioneered. The reputation for sound learning that Rouse gave the school has been maintained by his successors. It will be a source of interest to all concerned with education, as well as a source of pride to all of us who are associated with the Perse community, that Mr. Mitchell has been able to document and record this remarkable story.

Trinity College
Cambridge
May 1976

J. C. Polkinghorne
Chairman of the Governors
The Perse School

Preface

The author is glad to acknowledge the help he has received in preparing this history from a great number of books and from many people, mainly Old Perseans. A principal, and obvious, source of information has been the late Sir John Gray's *History of the Perse School* (Bowes & Bowes, 1922). Other books consulted are listed in the appendix, but a number of general books on education which have also been studied are not named.

Six Old Perseans whose help has been invaluable died before the book could be completed, and a special note of appreciation is due to their memory. Particular help was given by the Rt. Rev. Kenneth G. Thompson, lately Bishop of Sherwood. The others in this category who should be named were Dr. A. L. Peck, Mr. G. T. Salusbury, Mr P. J. Copping, Mr. A. C. Hawkins and Mr. D. M. Simmonds.

The list of others who have given a great deal of help is headed by Mr. and Mrs. Stanley Stubbs. Professor Eric Warmington, Dr. Frank Stubbings and Mr. Leslie Missen have made major contributions and others who have furnished important material include Spike Hughes, John Illsley, Cyril Peckett, Cyril Alliston, Leonard Amey, Humphrey Anthony, Alan Bottomley, Tony Billinghurst and Michael Goodchild. Mel Calman and Oliver Brown have made a most valuable contribution through their art work.

The author would place on record his particular gratitude to the Chairman of the Perse Governors, Professor J. C. Polkinghorne, other members of the Board, the Headmaster, Mr. A. E. Melville, the Committee of the Old Persean Society, and Messrs. Victor Sederman, Frank Elworthy, Keith Barry and Reuben Heffer. The two last named, by their practical interest and encouragement, have, more than any others, made this publication possible.

Considerations of space have meant the exclusion of two chapters, one covering the story of the Corps and Scouts in greater detail, the other concerning famous Old Perseans. The last-named may well be enlarged and published separately.

I

DR. PERSE AND HIS CHARITIES

In surveying the history of the Perse School one makes the acquaintance of some very remarkable personalities. None is more remarkable than the founder himself, Dr. Stephen Perse.

The name Perse, sometimes spelt Peirse or Peirce, is distinctively East Anglian, and a number of families of the name are associated with the marshland area of Norfolk, to the south and west of King's Lynn. Stephen was born in or about 1548 at Harpley, between Lynn and Fakenham. His father, John, moved when Stephen was about five to the neighbouring village of Great Massingham, and afterwards acquired property in Swaffham and Narford. Other branches of the family were established at the Walsinghams and Wiggenhalls, and at Northwold, near Stoke Ferry, the most eminent branch had secured a grant of arms which, with the pelican crest, granted in 1560, and most apt for its eventual purpose, was to become the Perse School's own coat.[1]

John Perse had, from small beginnings, achieved the status of the wealthiest inhabitant of Massingham, but he was never really rich and never had the rank of a gentleman. His son, on admission to Caius College, was described as *mediocris fortunae*. John was twice married, and Stephen's will remembered his step-sister's rather than his brother James' family. John left Stephen his signet ring — engraved with the family arms mentioned in the previous paragraph, to which he had no legal right — together with a good horse, rooms at the family home, and leases at Swaffham and Narford. James inherited the Massingham lands.

Stephen was educated at Norwich, probably at Norwich School, where the first Perse Master was afterwards Head, but possibly at a private school. He retained connections throughout his life with Norfolk and Norwich, and when he wished to study at Cambridge it was natural for him to choose Gonville and Caius College, which always had particular connections with his native county. He appears, however, to have migrated at one time to St. John's, but presently returned to Caius, where he spent the remainder of his life. He studied theology, was ordained, and became a Fellow, but presently 'changed both his sayd profession and his place to another fellowship, whereby he professed physick'. This was not an unusual career: both in the Middle Ages and down to the eighteenth and even the early nineteenth centuries men not infrequently took the double qualification in theology and medicine. Perhaps many of them were deeply moved, as well they might be, by the physical needs of ordinary people, often so frightful in that period as to suggest a greater urgency than their spiritual welfare. Or perhaps a young cleric turned doctor had in mind that the knowledge gained would enable him to survive during periods when his particular brand of faith was out of fashion.

There was indeed a special need for medical knowledge during the times of pestilence which were so frequent in that period; during the 16th and 17th centuries there were seven major outbreaks of the plague, and country vicars were able to help in some measure if they had small dispensaries. They would normally be physicians only, since the work of surgeons, involving the shedding of blood, was abhorrent to the clergy, and was left to the barbers[2].

Stephen was, it would appear, a good all-round scholar. His considerable skill as a classic is shown in the Latin verse he wrote in a volume published to welcome James I on his accession, and in the verses he wrote for his own tomb. But he was not a scholar in the bookish sense, for in the inventory of his goods at his death 'his library was appraised at less than half the value of his wearing apparel'. He must also have had a good grasp of accounts, since he served Caius as its bursar, from 1579 to 1593.

He never held any ecclesiastical preferment; so that his main career would appear to have been that of a doctor practising in the town of Cambridge as well as in the university. In this he made a great success, over some thirty years, and he also lectured in Physick in the University, being chosen to represent the faculty on the Caput, or executive council. He became popular in the town, and enjoyed good relations with other doctors, especially with the two most notable: Isaac Barrow (whose practice he may have taken over) and William Butler, who was James I's physician and a delightful eccentric, mentioned in Cooper's *Annals* in this context. In due course both of these were mentioned in his will; to Butler he gave a ring 'in token of my especial love'. The other Isaac Barrow, later Bishop of St. Asaph, was his godson; the most famous of the name, Newton's predecessor as Lucasian Professor and Master of Trinity, was no connection.

Stephen became so rich that he has been described as 'easily the most wealthy doctor who has worked in Cambridge'. We may well ask how he came to make such a fortune, amounting to £10,000 in all, which 'in those days was considered an enormous sum'[3]. Part of the answer certainly lay in his frugal habits, and the Caius *Annals* attribute his success to frugality: *Frugi erat homo et providus, unde longo temporis tractu haud exiguus divitiarum cumulus longe ultra communem Academicorum sortem ei accrevit.* This may be translated: He was a thrifty man, and one who looked to the future, and as a result he, over a long period of time, amassed a pile of riches which was not inconsiderable and far beyond the usual fortune of academics. The important word here seems to be *'providus'*; he had uncommon foresight and judgment and shrewdness.

He cannot, it would seem, have made his immense fortune merely by frugality, nor as a doctor, or a cleric, or a bursar. His money appears to have been made by an unusual astuteness as a man of business. He was a great speculator in land and property. His main source of income, however, came from a private practice as a money-lender. Yet he was by no means a usurer; for, while naturally he sought a fair return for his investments, his main object seems to have been to help young tradesmen and others in temporary financial difficulty. He must have felt keenly the need for this sort of help, especially needed in his time since a severe economic depression obtained throughout the country between 1596 and 1620. Indeed, he must have been the most well-disposed and benevolent of money-lenders, and was certainly, one feels, not guilty of the gross usury alleged against him in an unsuccessful Chancery petition brought in 1611-13, when records show that 'two yeomen of Haddenham' complained that he had demanded from them more than twice the original loan; they expressed surprise that he, 'being a learned man and a doctor skilful in the care of diseased bodies, should be so far forgetful of his own soul as upon his oath he brought forth and vomited such viperous and scandalous charges'.

We should remember the social importance of the money-lender at this period when, since there were no banks and building-societies, an expanding economy required a device to play the part of the modern mortgage, and thus the usurer was necessary to society and not a parasite preying upon its needs. The Middle Ages, through the Church, had always frowned on usury, but had in the end been compelled to 'turn a blind eye upon its catalytic operations, restricting its condemnations to oppressive rates of interest'[4].

An important section of Perse's will sought to continue his money-lending services in such a way as to benefit also his charitable foundations: he offered bequests to the corporations of Cambridge, Norwich, Bury St. Edmunds and King's Lynn, which would provide funds to finance loans to young tradesmen in those towns, at 5% — half the legal maximum — thus providing a useful service and at the same time securing an income for the new school. Both parties would benefit, just as the investor and the mortgagee both benefit from the work of a modern building-society. The wording in the will is inter-esting: the money was to be lent 'from time to time in parcels of £30 or £40 at the most, to several honest young men, tradesmen of those corporations, upon good security, for the use of which there should not be reserved above the rate of five for every hundred during one year; and that no sum so lent should remain in the hands of any one and the same person for longer than ten years'. However, none of the corporations was willing to take the risk necessarily involved.

Several of Stephen's family connections are interesting personalities. The most important by far, who became his principal trustee, was Martin Perse. The precise relationship of the two men has not been established, but Martin belonged to the Northwold branch and, although a younger son, became the head of the family, as his brothers left no heir. In due course he acquiesced in the use of the family arms over Stephen's tomb, and consequently they were adopted by the school. Martin became a rich and highly respected citizen of Cambridge, being successively a Freeman, an Alderman, Sheriff of the county and Mayor of the borough, in which last capacity he received Charles I on his first visit to the town. He died in 1636, a victim of the plague which that year was so bad as to cause the cancellation of Stourbridge Fair.

Martin married Stephen's half-sister and ward,[5] Katherine. She was the widow of William Becke (or Beck), a Caius lawyer who was descended, through his mother, from the Cottenham family of Pepys, related to the famous diarist. In 1610 William Becke bought the plot of land which was to become the Perse School, and sold it to Stephen in 1613. In compliment to his friend and relative, Becke named his son Perse; the name recurs, there being three Perse Beckes in the next two generations. The first of these was one of the first boys to enter the new school, and went on to become, at Caius, the first Perse scholar and the first Perse Fellow.

It is not difficult to visualise Dr. Stephen Perse as he must have been, and to appreciate what must have passed through his mind when he contemplated how best to dispose, in his will, of that considerable fortune. He obviously liked Cambridge, both the town and the University, and must have been distressed because relations between the two were so often strained. The University had not only held itself aloof from town life, but had acquired rights and privileges which caused constant friction with the townspeople. The law often allowed members of the University more generous treatment (because they were tried for offences in the Vice-Chancellor's court, not under civil law) and moreover the University had authority, naturally resented, over the townspeople, controlling weights and measures, issuing wine-licences (as it still does) and having the right to consign suspected prostitutes to the University Prison or 'Spinning-house'. Town versus Gown riots were frequent throughout the Middle Ages and relations were seriously strained during Perse's lifetime. Violence had flared up around 1615, the very year in which he made his will. The Town then petitioned the Crown for a new Charter conferring an extension of its privileges and reducing those of the University — which inevitably presented a counter-petition. Unfortunately, such ill-will was to continue for many years more, and there is, as later pages of this book will show, a recurring theme in Perse history of a Headmaster or a group of Governors falling foul of a body of townspeople because of their views, either in churchmanship or politics, or because they appeared to take the 'gown' view.

Dr. Perse clearly seems to have felt that the charity which it was in his power to bestow ought to try to bring Town and Gown together. As a college man working in the town he must have been keenly aware how the ancient feud aggravated the universal social problems of the time, when poverty, ignorance and vice were widespread and standards were falling. It is not clear whether he had himself remained unmarried or died a widower — he could have retained his Fellowship if widowed — but he was certainly childless, and his legatees were therefore to be the people he loved in Cambridge and elsewhere. A would-be benefactor in those days would find amply guidance available on how best to make his bequests. An obvious need which a rich man could fill was in the provision of a 'free' school, and this must have been the Doctor's chief intention. But it was not the only one. There were very many other ways in which a philanthropist could help his fellows and commemorate his name. As early as the fourteenth century the *Vision of Piers Plowman* had shown Truth admonishing the rich merchants that they could profit in the life hereafter by the use of their earthly

fortune to
> Repair hospitals,
> Help sick people,
> Mend bad roads,
> Build up bridges that had been broken down,
> Help maidens to marry or to make them nuns,
> Find food for prisoners and poor people,
> Put scholars to school or to some other craft,
> Help religious orders, and
> Ameliorate rents and taxes [6].

Ben Jonson, in *The Alchemist*, makes Sir Epicure Mammon declare that if he made money from the philosopher's stone he would 'employ it in all pious ways' including building schools, hospitals and 'now and then a church'.

Dr. Perse, therefore, had available to him many possible areas in which his wealth could be used, in a century which was to be notable for its charitable benefactions. Possible claims on his generosity had been enumerated in his own time by one Andrew Willet, Rector of Barley, near Royston, and apparently a personal friend of Stephen's. Willet was a hearty Anglican and a leading theological writer, the model for the Controversial Divine of Thomas Fuller's *Holy State*. His *Synopsis Papismi* — 'a general view of the Papacy' — was 'an armoury of weapons against the Papal theory'. In the 1614 edition — the book first appeared in 1592 — there is an interesting *Appendix on Protestant Charity*, which proclaims the impressive charitable achievements of the previous sixty years, declaring that more free schools and almshouses had been founded then than in the whole of the Middle Ages, and that Protestant philanthropy far exceeded the works of Catholicism. 'Such charitable works,' he declares, 'performed chiefly in London and in both Universities, do glitter as pearls, and the workers thereof shine as stars amongst us'.

Willet's catalogue is of interest because he specifies the Universities as an area from which charity came, and because he goes on to catalogue the main objects of charity in his time, and to name Perse's intended benefactions, a year before Perse made his will. From the standpoint of to-day it is interesting to observe that the greatest needs of the time were precisely those which the twentieth century still considers urgent and not fully catered for: education, the care of the poor and aged, roads and public health. Most benefactors in Stuart times remembered several of these, and any survey of education will recognise that bequests for almshouses, road-works and bridges were as often as not part of the wills of founders of schools. In the breadth of his charity, as well as in the distinctiveness of his school endowment, Stephen Perse will be seen to have been a man of generosity and vision typical of the best of his time, yet exceptional in many ways.

Before we consider in detail the provisions Perse made for his school, we should look at his other philanthropic bequests. At once a doctor and a clergyman, he cared passionately, one feels, for bodily health, social health and spiritual health. In addition, therefore, to founding his school and commemorating his name in his College, he remembered in his will the poor in the towns and villages known to him, and left money to improve roads and water-ways. He established six almshouses for parishioners of St. Edward's and St. Michael's, the churches adjacent to Caius. It is interesting that these were not for widows, but for 'poor aged people, single and unmarried persons, of the ages of 40 years apiece at the least'. He also left money to be distributed in the town; five pounds was to be spent on this, 'giving no one house above twelve pence'. Other sums were left for the poor of his native village, Harpley, of Great Massingham, where he spent much of his childhood, and 'to the maintenance of that charitable work intended to be performed and settled' at Willet's village of Barley. In the case of Barley, the bequest seems to have been intended to provide both almshouses and a school, in the Town House there, a building which still survives. The school came to an end in 1788, after which the trustees 'continued to pay £3 yearly, apparently without enquiring as to the purpose to which that money was devoted.' Under the revised Scheme of 1841 the annual payment was raised to £6, 'for the use of the poor scholars in the school at Barley'.

All Perse's bequests show his wide and compassionate interests. On the academic side, not only did Caius benefit, but there was also a sum of money for the University Library. Most interesting of all, since a doctor's concern for public health is shown, were bequests providing for an improved water supply and for the making up of roads through marshy land. The water scheme was in itself a rare instance — perhaps inspired by Perse himself — of cooperation between University and Town, for it was jointly initiated by the two bodies, to bring water from the Nine Wells springs near Shelford to what came to be called Hobson's Conduit. Both Perse and Hobson were directly concerned, but only later in the scheme, which began in 1610; Perse's contribution, as a bequest, came five years later and Hobson's only in 1630.

The new road which Perse provided for was what we now call Maids' Causeway; it was originally known as Barnwell Causeway, but in the eighteenth century was renamed after a group of almshouses established there for 'ancient maidens'. The whole approach road from the old village of Barnwell had led through marshy land, and the King's Ditch, the old town defence, and sundry other water-ways crossed it. The eastern section, from Barnwell Bridge, had been embanked under the will, of 1584, of Dr. Harvey, Master of Trinity Hall. Perse had already paid for further roadworks; his bequest was to continue the raised footpath as far as Jesus Lane and to extend the lane on the line of All Saints' Passage. A vestige of his causeway remains in the raised path on the south side of Maids' Causeway.[8] It is no doubt typical of the man that his will stipulated that the maintenance of the causeway and the river should be entrusted to 'my servant, Peter Thatcher'.

It is perhaps surprising that Perse did not, as part of his bequest, establish a hospital in Cambridge; it was left to Addenbrooke to do this in 1740. Yet in 1572, following the endowment of the first great London hospitals, a lead had been given to potential benefactors by the passing of an Act to encourage the founding of hospitals, as well as almshouses; the term 'hospital' included orphanages and asylums for the mentally deranged.

Perse's bequest to Caius provided for the erection of a complete new front court, to be known as Perse Court; this was demolished in 1868 to make way for Waterhouse's Tree Court. Stephen also endowed Perse Fellowships and 'close' scholarships from the school to the college; in doing this he obviously wished to link the two as Wykeham and Waynflete had done.[9] Worthy provision was made for the Doctor's own tomb in Caius Chapel, a photograph of which forms our frontispiece. It is an undoubted work of art, showing Perse in academic dress, kneeling at a prayer-desk in a tabernacle frame. There are elegiac verses in Latin and English, probably written for the purpose by Perse himself, and the family arms are shown. Later the college erected an effigy in the Court bearing the Doctor's name. The features, in both cases, are those of a kindly, shrewd and scholarly man, matching, it seems, the character we have suggested.

Of all his bequests, Perse's endowment of his school answered the most urgent need. In planning it he must have been well aware of the earlier history of public education in Cambridge, which, in spite of its standing as the site of a University, had been slow to provide a town school. Where towns like St. Albans and Winchester and, more locally, Ely and Bury St. Edmunds (the last two half the size of Cambridge) can point to a medieval free school, in Perse's time there was none in Cambridge. There are a number of reasons for this. One is that most of the early schools were ecclesiastical in origin, attached to abbeys, cathedrals or chantries. Another lies in the special circumstances arising from the jealousies of 'Town and Gown'.

The purpose of the early grammar schools, established as they were by church bodies, was to teach elementary Latin, known as 'Grammar', at a lower level for choristers and at a higher level for intending students of literature, philosophy and logic. The abbey schools usually catered for deserving boys in their localities. At the two universities, however, the colleges took a narrower view, usually limiting their teaching to their own personnel and not recognising any responsibility to the town boys. At Oxford, in spite of some friction with the town, Magdalen College established the fine school which still bears its name. At Cambridge four colleges had their own grammar schools, but none has survived in the full sense, though those of King's and St. John's continue as choir-schools and preparatory schools. King's College school is certainly the oldest Cambridge school, founded in 1443, but, with a few exceptions, it has never served the town. Trinity's school was closed in the nineteenth century.[10]

The school established by Jesus College had a life of only sixty-one years (1506-1567). Its closure, and changes in the status of the other college schools, followed the requirement of a Commission of 'Visitors' appointed in 1549, which ruled that 'money expended in any college on choristers, chantries . . . or grammar schools' should be converted to the support of the undergraduates. Trinity was called on forthwith to 'surrender the grammar schole' and absorb its pupils as senior students. In 1569 the Visitors positively prohibited the teaching of grammar in the Cambridge colleges, but for a time exempted Jesus and the choir-schools. In 1570 the exception in favour of Jesus was withdrawn, but the college had anticipated this and paid off its schoolmaster three years before. Only King's College School then offered the occasional possibility of 'grammar' education to town boys; there were certainly some cases of non-choristers being admitted to what had become primarily a choir-school, a notable example, at a later period, being that of James Essex, the architect (1722-84).

After the Reformation there was a shift of emphasis in the sphere of charity, many of the duties formerly discharged by the church being assumed by members of the new powerful merchant class or by guilds, livery companies and corporations connected with trade. The founders' object was still essentially a religious one, in that a bequest set up a kind of chantry to ensure that the founder — invariably styled 'pious'

— was remembered and prayers offered in his name by future generations. The earliest case of a school being founded by a corporation is that of Ipswich School, founded by the municipality at much the same time as Winchester College.

There were two great ages of charitable foundations. In the sixteenth century 185 schools were established. In the next half-century (1601-1651) the rate doubled, 186 being founded in that period.[11] The peak of the movement was reached in 1620. However, as will be seen, deterioration in the system began almost immediately, and was aggravated by the troubles of the Civil War and the Commonwealth. Numbers in the schools began to drop, abuses became common, and class-distinction began to show itself.

Dr. Stephen Perse's foundation therefore has to be seen as taking place at a critical point in scholastic history, at the peak of the age of pious founders, yet precisely when disillusionment and criticism of the grammar school system was beginning to mount.

Before Perse took definite action in the matter, there had been two attempts to establish a town school in Cambridge. In 1576 an abortive appeal for funds was made by the town authorities. No doubt they felt baulked by the unhelpful attitude of the university, but encouraged by the success achieved at Ipswich, and therefore formed a committee charged 'to devise and put into writing some good device for the erection of a grammer school within the (said) town, and how the charges of the same may be borne and raised'. The other proposal came from two successive members of the college then called Clare Hall. William Bridon, who died in 1590, is spoken of as the 'first projector of this excellent work'[12] ; he left a hundred marks 'towards founding a grammar school in Cambridge, or some other work for the encouragement of learning'. Thomas Cropley — evidently a friend of Bridon, who had left a legacy to one of his daughters — left a further hundred marks 'towards founding a free grammar school . . . and further directed that his gift should be combined to that of Mr. Bridon'. Cropley, 'a man of large property', also left sums of money for the poor in Cambridge and in Ely, where he was born. He had arms granted to him, and is buried in St. Edward's Church.

The amount of two hundred marks left jointly by Bridon and Cropley was clearly insufficient for the foundation of a school, but came to be thought of as opening a fund. The sum represented little more than two years' salaries to the Master and Usher of a school, according to the proposals in Perse's will. Perse's executors recognised the earlier benefaction as a useful donation; we read that they were 'to use the best meanes for the obtaining the two hundred markes' in question.

Stephen Perse died on 30 September, 1615; his will is dated three days earlier. The Executors appointed were Martin Perse, Valentine Carey, Master of Christ's and Dean of St. Paul's and later Bishop of Exeter, and Robert Spicer, Perse's own solicitor. After a short time, however, the two last named opted out, probably because Spicer was an old man and Carey often absent from Cambridge. They may have felt that the duties asked of them were beyond their powers; and it is also recorded that they did not get on well with Martin Perse, whom they found slow, overbearing and too tolerant to Stephen's debtors. A deed was executed on 17 November, 1615, in which the 'sole execution and performance of the trusts of the said will was committed to the said Martin Perse alone'. So he was left to carry the whole burden. One's impression is that, apart from the errors of judgment in the purchase of land of which we have to speak, he carried out his duties quite admirably and as his kinsman would have wished.

It was a difficult task to undertake. Not only were the bequests numerous and complicated. There were claims to be handled which members of the family, feeling themselves disinherited, had advanced. There was much to be done in winding up the medical practice and the money-lending business, and collecting such debts as could be recovered. Nearly a quarter of the money owing to the estate was written off as 'desperate debts'. The will had required that 'no sum be forborn to any of my debters (sic) which shall renew their securities, as by my will I have appointed, for above one year after such new security taken, but that speedy course be taken against such as do not come in to renew their securities and assurance, and also against such as having renewed their securities shall not make payment according to their days'.

Only when all this was settled could Martin give full attention to discharging the provisions of the will. Work on the College block, the Almshouses and the Causeway was put in hand without delay, and in these areas all was completed by early in 1617. Before action could be taken to establish the school it was necessary to ensure an income, as required by Perse, by an approach to the East Anglian towns named in the will in connection with the loan scheme. When they all refused, Martin reported his failure to the Master and Fellows; an indenture made between them and dated 27 October 1616 records that the £5000 in question 'had been offered to the Corporations specified in the (said) will but (that) the said Corporations had neither given the security required . . . nor returned any answers, whereby delay of the good work intended by the (said) will had arisen'.

The will had specified that if the Corporations refused the loan an investment in land was to be made. This appears to have been a death-bed addition, when Perse appreciated that his first scheme might miscarry. Martin therefore took personal responsibility for securing some suitable property, and he undertook in the indenture with the Caius authorities that 'at or before the Feast of St. Michael the Archangel then next (i.e., September, 1617) he would pass over or assure or cause to be assured from the said Corporations or himself or his heirs or assigns so much lands as should be of the yearly value of £250 . . . for the performance of the said good uses, and would before the same Feast erect and build up or cause to be erected and built up and made the Free School, Almshouses and Causeway mentioned in the said will'.²

However, it took longer than the suggested eleven months to achieve this. Martin's undertaking implies that he first had to make further approach to the East Anglian towns, and, when they finally refused, he had to look for a suitable land investment — which proved hard to find. Much in contrast with Stephen's business astuteness, Martin's judgment as a land speculator was sadly at fault. His principal purchase was an estate at Frating, a few miles to the east of Colchester, which, remaining Perse property until 1913, was to prove an embarrassment rather than an asset. He acquired also some other estates, notably one at Bassingbourn, which had belonged to no less a person than Oliver Cromwell's widowed mother. For several years he personally made up a deficiency.

The Frating property was bought by an indenture of bargain and sale enrolled in Chancery and bearing the date 25 June, 1618, the vendor being Sir Thomas Bendishe of Steeple Bumpstead. The estate was conveyed to the Master and Fellows of Caius — even before completion of the purchase — by an indenture dated 6 March, 1618, by which they were 'to dispose (it) in the performance of the good uses expressed in Stephen Perse's will'.

The foundation of the school was obviously the main provision of the will, in the discharge of which most care had to be exercised. The site was already available, having been provided by Stephen himself through the purchase of the 'garden grounds parcell of the Fryars' from his brother-in-law. Thus the new foundation had something in common with other great schools in that it was established on land which had belonged to a religious Order. The Augustinians, moreover, had been distinguished as reforming thinkers in the pre-Reformation period. Their Cambridge Friary occupied a large site, bounded by what to-day are called Bene't Street, Wheeler Street, Corn Exchange Street and Downing/Pembroke Streets. The plot acquired by Perse fronted on to what was then called Lorteburn or Lithburn Lane. The burn in question was one of a number of brooks which at the time drained into the King's Ditch, the ancient moat-like defence of the town. The name had taken various forms since the fourteenth century, some using, inappropriately, it would appear, the element 'burgh' or 'bury' and thus suggesting London's Lothbury. By 1750 the street had acquired from its newest building the honourable title of Free School Lane. It is perhaps significant that it was never called Perse Lane, showing (as other references show) that the school during its first period was not usually called after its founder but known as the Cambridge Free School.

The property had formerly belonged, as it happened, to the Regius Professor of Physic, who had lived in the former refectory, opposite St. Benet's. It is consequently likely that Stephen, as a student and as a practising doctor, had visited what was to become the site of the school. Katherine Becke inherited the old refectory, through Perse's will, and she and her husband, Martin Perse, lived there until 1632 — as Gray puts it, 'watching the little seedling planted by their kinsman pass safely through the critical stages of these early days'. The Perse coat of arms, carved 'over ye chimney-piece and on ye wainscot' remained in later years.

The plot was more than adequate for its new use, and some adjustments, reducing its extent at the northern end, were made forthwith. The Horne, or Antelope, which adjoined the old refectory, was sold, and other parts of the property were leased out, while, to provide the full area required, some leases were 'purchased in' as required by Perse's will. The Horne itself Stephen had bought from his friend Isaac Barrow.

In the course of the two ensuing centuries there was some adjustment also in the properties owned by the Foundation outside Cambridge. The Bassingbourn estate was exchanged for land at West Dereham which had been left to Caius by Dr. John Lightwine (or Lightman) in 1723. Other land, at Lawshall, Suffolk (from 1736), at Great Bentley, Essex (1830) and elsewhere in Essex (1824, 1834 and 1836) was bought 'in trust for the uses intents and purposes mentioned expressed and declared by the will of Stephen Perse'.

II

THE SCHOOL'S FIRST FIFTY YEARS: GEORGE GRIFFITH

Perse had himself, no doubt with Colet's[13] rules in mind, since these were usually taken as a guide by founders, worked out many of the requirements for the building and for the organisation of his school, and put his ideas on paper. He had provided that the Master and Usher to be appointed must be graduates of Cambridge; for both posts former pupils of the school were to be preferred — though, in the event, the preference tended to go to Caius men. The Master's stipend was fixed at £40 per annum and the Usher's at £20. These were fair salaries at the time, rather more than was offered in some contemporary schools. It should, however, be remembered that the provision for a hundred free scholars made it a large school for the time, and that, on the other hand, further fees could be earned by teaching non-foundationers and by taking in boarders.

Martin, anxious no doubt to do exactly what Stephen wished, 'framed Ordinances for the conduct and management of the said Free Grammar School'. These were prepared at the very outset of the proceedings, while Carey and Spicer were still serving as Executors, and before any building was started.[3] The Justices of Assize duly approved the Ordinances, which were 'reduced into writing' and signed by the three Executors on or about the 19th February 1623.

Of the nineteen Ordinances space allows us to quote only the most interesting; the others give detailed instructions which are not especially quotable:

1. There shall a hundred scholars born in Cambridge Barnwell Chesterton and Trumpington be taught in Dr. Perse's Free School in Cambridge freely according to Dr. Perse's will which shall be called the Free Scholars.
2. They shall be carefully and diligently taught while they remain there as well in good manners as in all other instruction and learning fit to be learned in a Grammar School neither shall the Master or

Usher or any for them exact anything of their parents or friends for their teaching.

3. Neither shall there be any more or any other taught in the said free school besides the free scholars except the Master and Usher do take to them such further sufficient help as the Executors for the time and after Dr. Perse's Supervisors shall think fit.[14]

8. And if any of the Free Scholars shall be absent a whole month together from the school they shall lose his or their places and others shall be chosen thereunto except their absence be by reason of sickness or some other cause as shall be allowed by the said Executors or one of them or after the decease of the said Executors by the said Supervisors or three of them.

9. And when there is any Scholar's place void a poor man's child shall be preferred to it before a rich so that he makes suit for it in time.

12. The Schoolmaster or Usher shall call the scholars to prayers every morning half an hour after six in the morning and at five in the afternoon.

13. The Schoolmaster and Usher that shall be from time to time chosen into the school shall be sufficient scholars for the place and of good government and qualified by their degrees according to Dr. Perse's will and if the Schoolmaster or Usher which shall be so chosen do hold an ecclesiastical living or Fellowship in any College when he is chosen to the said school they shall give over their ecclesiastical preferment or Fellowship within one month after he or they shall enjoy their places in the Free School or else their places in the Free School shall be void.

17. And if the Master or Usher at any time hereafter shall be found to be usual frequenters of taverns or alehouses and be found to be given to that evil vice of drinking and be admonished thereof twice by the said Executors during their lives and after their deaths by the said Supervisors and they be afterwards found faulty therein their places in the said school shall be then void and others better governed chosen in their steads.

18. (part) The Master or Usher shall cause prayers to be used the time that they come together again to school in which some mention shall be made of the Founder of the said school with giving thanks for the same.

It is to be noted that the Ordinances limit the catchment area to Cambridge and the three adjoining villages; no educational test was proposed for prospective pupils, who needed only to produce evidence of birth in the prescribed area and of baptism.   Ordinances 2 and 9

The School in Free School Lane 1840

seem to reflect Perse philosophy. Ordinance 8 is a strict one not always insisted on in later years.[15]   Ordinance 13 gave rise to scandals when, as not infrequently happened, it was disobeyed. Ordinances 3, 8 and 17 mention the important provision that, after Martin's death, the Master and four Senior Fellows of Caius would become Supervisors of the Perse Trust.

The building of the school was commenced in February 1617.[12] The design of the buildings was typical of schools of the time, and might at the same time be thought to owe something to the traditional lay-out of the Cambridge Colleges. The plan formed three sides of a quadrangle, facing the lane, with a curtain-wall containing a formal gateway surmounted by the Perse family arms (carved in stone), which Stephen had assumed, or Martin had, at this point, allowed to the foundation.

There was one really fine room, the hall or 'Big School' which is the only part still surviving. As will be seen, the two later buildings designedly continued the idea thus established, of making the hall an architectural feature, and the centre of the community life. The great feature in all three halls proved to be the roof; at Free School Lane it has five hammerbeam trusses, springing from moulded stone corbels.

There are moulded pendants between the arched braces; the spandrels are filled with pierced scroll-work and the bays are ceiled in plaster at collar-beam level. Apart from the roof, there was no attempt at decoration. The original windows, which have not survived, were no doubt fitted with stone mullions and filled with thick diamond-shaped panes of glaṣs. Part of the original brickwork of the walls, 1½ feet thick, can still be seen, but the exterior is concealed by the University laboratory which has incorporated the hall.

The two wings contained the staff 'lodging chambers', the Master living in the north wing and the Usher in the south; however, in the eighteenth century the Master moved into the south.[16] Both wings included attics, and there were cellars under the hall, which were no doubt used by the Master and Usher. At times when the number of pupils was small teaching took place in the Master's study, on the first floor. To the north, extending to the old refectory, was a garden, which included a summer-house and a pump. To the south, 'on the fore-front', were 'six several low Tenements of one room apiece', the Almshouses; these faced the King's Ditch, which ran on the north side of Pembroke Lane (now Pembroke Street). The plan on p.44 shows how the Ditch had by Victorian times been piped underground, to emerge beyond the almshouses, where the old University Botanic gardens created a frogs' pool. The plan, with the photographs, shows how the whole site appeared in 1856, after the additions of 1841. A description of the school at that period will be found in Chapters 4 and 5.

Latin was the main basis of all teaching in grammar schools, and it was usually laid down that 'the boys shall constantly talk in Latin'. The oral method foreshadows the Direct Method for which the Perse was to become famous under Dr. Rouse, who justly claimed that he was reviving the ancient system. Greek was added in the top form, and a few schools — not the Perse — also taught Hebrew.[17] Mathematics, French and other subjects later thought essential to the curriculum were not taught in school for another century.

Some boys left school when they were twelve years old, or before they were fifteen, to become apprenticed to tradesmen, but a high proportion went on to the University, where Perseans attained a very good standard in degree courses. The poorer boys going to the University would often be sizars, a title which in those days meant that part of the fees would be met by the student's working as a college servant. Other boys used to pay their fees 'in kind' by offering wares from the family shop. Piele's *Biographical Register of Christ's College* records how a Persean student's bill was in part paid 'in wares' in 1627-28.

There was no provision whatever for physical education or for games. Cambridge was, however, fortunate even at this period in having more open spaces than most towns, and particularly so in having available Parker's Piece, a unique public playground, which was acquired by the town authorities in 1613, as an exchange with Trinity College for 'Trinity Backs'. The Piece was to figure prominently in Perse history.

Dr. Perse's school was ready to open by March 1618. The first Master was Thomas Lovering, who had been head of King's College School. He must be reckoned as one of the three or four really first rate heads the school has had, for under him a promising start was made, and pupils from outside the immediate region — from as far away as Northumberland and Cork — were attracted as non-foundationers. Clearly it was never intended that the school should be purely for local boys, despite the precise wording of the Ordinances.

The first Persean to become nationally known entered the school within a few years of its inception. This was Jeremy Taylor, who has been called 'the saintly genius' and 'the Shakespeare of divines'. Details of his early life are obscure; his father was certainly church-warden of Holy Trinity church, and was probably a barber in Market Street. Jeremy became a sizar at Caius in 1626, at the age of 13. He did very well there, and became a Fellow. Such was his intellectual brilliance that it soon attracted the attention of Laud, to whose doctrines he subscribed. We read that the Archbishop, 'thinking it for the advantage of the hierarchy that he should have more time for study and improvement than a continued course of preaching would allow', procured him a Fellowship at All Souls'. Hearing him preach at St. Paul's cathedral, Laud had found 'his discourse beyond exception and even beyond imitation'; and it was as a preacher and writer of the most beautiful prose that he made his name. 'Though he was a contemporary of Milton, his prose is popular and modern; it can be read easily when Milton's must be studied'.[18] As a theologian he also exerted great influence, John Wesley being among those who have been greatly influenced.

During the Civil War, having espoused the Royalist cause, Taylor retired to Golden Grove, near Carmarthen, where he wrote much of his great work. Among his books should be mentioned *The Great Exemplar*, a delightful life of Christ, selections from which formed a text-book used in the school after 1910, in which year Robert Parker-Smith prepared a volume published by Heffer's. Other important books were *A Discourse on Friendship*, *A Discourse on Confirmation* (a

NON MAGNA LOQ VIMVR, SED VIVIMVS:
NIHIL OPINIONIS GRATIA. OMNIA
CONSCENTIÆ FACIAM

Jeremy Taylor

copy of which is in the school archives), *Holy Living and Holy Dying*
and *The Liberty of Prophesying*. The last-named is a plea for moderation
and toleration, and as such an expression of an attitude which we may
feel Stephen Perse himself would have approved.

An old Persean, the Rev. Trevor Hughes, a distinguished Wesleyan
minister and former Principal of Westminster Training College, has
written a study entitled *The Piety of Jeremy Taylor*. In it he remarks
that *Holy Living and Holy Dying* was one of the few books that he
took with him on war service overseas during the critical days of the
Second World War.

Also under Lovering, there were as pupils of the school two
members of the Pepys family, cousins of Samuel, or, to be precise,
sons of his great-uncle, Talbot Pepys of Impington. They were both
members of Christ's College and of the Middle Temple. Roger Pepys
became Recorder of Cambridge (1669) and Member of Parliament for
the town in the Long Parliament. He was censured by Judge Keeling at
Cambridge Assizes, in 1664/5, for speaking disrespectfully of the Lord
Chief Justice, and was removed from the Recordership, but was
subsequently restored, holding office until 1685. John, his brother,
became a Fellow of Trinity Hall; he was a Royalist in the Civil War
but survived the Commonwealth.

Altogether, Lovering's record will bear comparison, when due
allowance is made, with the other great eras of Perse history. Of some
hundred of his pupils who proceeded to Cambridge colleges, fifteen
became Fellows, among then Jeremy Taylor, and the son and stepson of
Martin Perse.

For a time Lovering employed one Peter Burgis, whose subsequent
career is of interest. Burgis does not appear to have been an official
Usher, but served, as Gray surmises, as 'a further sufficient help' in
accordance with Ordinance 3, assisting in the teaching of non-
foundationers.

In 1630 Burgis was appointed as Master of Saffron Walden Grammar
School; he wrote of how, 'being employed at Cambridge in the Free
School there, the town of Walden sought me, and at their entreaty I
came over and was chosen by general consent'. Like Stephen Perse, he
had taken Orders (in 1629) and also, having studied physick, was
licensed to practise medicine in 1634. However, about 1637 a group of
Walden people whose enmity he had somehow incurred tried to get
him ejected from his post. At first they asserted that he was a Puritan
and complained that they knew 'no so noxious a pestilence to Church
and Kingdom as a Puritan schoolmaster'. When he showed that he was

'conformable' his adversaries changed their ground and accused him of being a Papist and Arminian' and finally appealed to the Chancellor of London 'to put him out for insufficiency'. Burgis then made representations to the Archbishop himself, pointing out that there could be no question of 'insufficiency' since 'I have sent more scholars up to Cambridge in my short time than were sent in thirty years before, and the school is as well attended as the oldest man in Walden can remember it'.[19]

History was to repeat itself rather closely in the Victorian period, when a Perse headmaster dismissed one of his staff, arguing first on religious grounds and subsequently on grounds of what proved to be dubious 'insufficiency'.

After holding office for eighteen years, Lovering left, like a number of his successors to become Master of a better-known school, no doubt offering a better salary. He went to Norwich Grammar School, where Stephen Perse was probably educated. The appointment of the next Perse Master was one of the first duties discharged by the Master and four senior Fellows of Caius when they became Supervisors of the Trust on the death of Martin Perse.

They made a bad and ominous beginning; ignoring Ordinance 13, which forebade the appointment of college Fellows as school staff, they appointed the Tutor and Dean of Caius, one Richard Watson, 'a vain and conceited man' who proved a bad and, inevitably, neglectful head. The school soon lost the reputation it was earning, boys were no longer attracted from outside the area and few Perse scholars went to the University, while one-third of the free places were unfilled. It seems that Watson's religious views, rather than the school's lack of success, caused his resignation. He was 'a most zealous man for the Church of England' and in 1642 preached a sermon in Great St. Mary's which caused offence in Presbyterian circles. He fled overseas, but after the Restoration returned, to become Chaplain to James, Duke of York.

Fortunately the next Perse Master was a good one, who was not only not a pluralist but was also the first Old Persean to hold office — which would have pleased the Founder, who had directed that preference was to be given to suitable old scholars. It was well that a man of character was in charge during the Civil War and the Commonwealth, both of which he weathered, serving from 1641 until 1652. He was Thomas Crabbe, a connection of the Suffolk family which produced George Crabbe, the poet. During the period Cambridge was strongly Cromwellian, but Crabbe, although known to have Royalist sympathies, kept his place by the exercise of tact and discretion. The school continued throughout the war; in fact, one boy came, in 1641, as a refugee from Ireland: *in Angliam fugiens, in publicum Cantabrigiense gymnasium receptus*.

A period of great difficulty followed the war. It had not been possible to collect the Frating rents during the war, and afterwards the tenants, who were heavily taxed, declared themselves unable to pay. Staff salaries were halved. Later, however, backpay was made up, and the school survived to regain much of its former reputation. There was, however, internal friction when the Parliament appointed an unsympathetic Puritan as Master of Caius and ex-officio Chairman of the Perse trustees. This was William Dell, who had revolutionary ideas on education, which he propounded in a pamphlet, *The Right Reformation of Learning*. Some ideas of his were remarkably advanced, especially the proposal that University culture ought to be within the reach of all the people in the larger towns, which foreshadowed the University Extension Movement. As to the school curriculum, he advocated the abolition of all Classical teaching, which he thought unsuitable for Christian schools, and proposed that English should be used in all teaching and that the Scriptures, with some mathematics, should be the basis of instruction. Even for his age, he was thought to be a crank — a contemporary comment calls him 'a very peculiar and unsettled man' — but for a time he had his way; and the philosophy he held was to be repeated in the reforms and pseudo-reforms of later generations.

There now comes into the story the oddest and most unworthy of all Perse pedagogues, one Robert Crayford. He had been Usher for a number of years during the war period, when he had behaved with moderation and discharged his duties satisfactorily. On Crabbe's departure he acted as Master for one term, drawing an additional fee of £14. When, however, a new Master was appointed over his head, his resentment led him to behave disgracefully. The new man, George Griffith, was appointed in defiance of the anti-pluralism rules, for he was a Fellow of Queens', and Crayford must have been incensed because the rules had been quoted as a reason for not promoting him, and his other post was the much less remunerative one of curate of Haslingfield. He showed his pique immediately, by intruding into the school, in defiance of Griffith, seven private pupils, ineligible for free places, and became grossly insubordinate to his new superior.

The climax was reached when Crayford took to assaulting both Griffith and some of the boys. No history of the Perse can fail to quote the quaintly-worded complaint made against him by one of the

Governors, that he used the 'scandalous, opprobrious and reproachful words following to Griffith, to witt, You are a stinkinge knave: you come to steale away my due: I will take you a kicke on the britch and tred in your feete'. Still more striking are the stories of how he misused two of the pupils.

One, we are told, 'is to this day, by the cruell usage of Crayford, soe much disabled in his speech and also in his memorie that his father, to his great greife, was necessitated to divert him from the way of a scholler to a serviler imployment'.

The other was 'one Thomas Peters, whom ye said Robert Crayford wrung by both his eares in the most violent manner that one of his eares was most cruelly torn both skinne and grissle and almost went from his head: ye said Thomas Peters going home to his mother Katharine Peters house in Cambridge with his eare so torne and bleedinge to her great affrightment, the blood running down ye body of the said Thomas Peters from his head unto his feet'.

Eventually Crayford was dismissed, and an expensive lawsuit, lasting over two years, followed, which the Trustees eventually abandoned to effect a compromise whereby, although he was not reinstated, the Usher was allowed to occupy his official house for a further year, after which he became Rector of East Grinstead.

The publicity given to all this did the school a great deal of harm, but Griffith outlived it, retained his place after the Restoration, and went on for some years to prove himself a very competent Master. He held office for thirty-four years in all, and successfully rode out further crises, including enforced closures during outbreaks of plague in 1665 and 1666. Luckily he had some independent means, which enabled him to survive a further halving of salary. Under his direction the school once more attracted pupils from far afield, and a good number of Perseans passed through the University, fifteen in his time becoming Fellows of colleges. He would appear to have been a good disciplinarian; the Sidney register speaks of one John Heath as having been educated 'sub ferula magistri Griffith' — but clearly he avoided the excesses of violence of his one-time colleague.

When he died, in November, 1686 (his will was proved the following February) he left £100 'to be by the Trustees employed to the best advantage for a supplement to the revenues of Dr. Stephen Perse's Free School in Cambridge' and also certain of his 'goods and utensils of household stuff' — representing an income of some £50 — for the use of the succeeding Masters. Harraden[20] says that 'the Master's and Usher's salaries have received a small augmentation by the

donation of Mr. Griffith(s)'. He is, very properly, remembered in the
school prayers. Incidentally, he bore arms, which appear on his
tombstone in St. Edward's church — gules a chevron ermine between
three men's heads cooped proper.

The most notable of Griffith's pupils was Sir Robert Tabor (1642-
81), whose uncle, James Tabor, had been one of the first Perse pupils,
in Lovering's day. After leaving school, Robert was apprenticed to a
Cambridge apothecary — almost certainly the well-known Peter Dent,
who appears to have owned the business continued today by Bernard
Coulson, an Old Persean, who had in his possession some pharmaceutical
relics of great interest, probably dating from Dent's time, which were
lost in the bombing of 1942. Dent is buried in St. Sepulchre's
churchyard.

It was during the period of his apprenticeship that Tabor discovered
the medical method which was to make him famous, the administration in
cases of fever of cinchona bark, the crude drug from which quinine is
extracted. He tested his ideas by moving from Cambridge to the Essex
marshlands, where fever was prevalent, and discovered that the secret
of success was to administer the drug in smaller doses at frequent
intervals. The opportunity of proving the value of his discovery came
in 1678, when he managed by its use to save the life of King Charles
II, who in gratitude knighted him.[21] His reputation spreading to the
Continent, King Louis XIV sent for him to attend the Dauphin, and
he later became medical adviser to the Queen Consort of Spain. His
son, perhaps regrettably, did not come to the Perse, but entered the
army, where he became known as 'Handsome Tabor'.

Among the several Ushers who served under Griffith was Henry Rix
(Usher from 1661 to 1668). He was the son of a Cambridge brewer
and an Old Persean, and when he left he became successively Master
of Saffron Walden Grammar School and Newport Grammar School.[17]

III

THE AGE OF CORRUPTION AND APATHY

The next chapter in the school's history — constituting its second period — is entitled by Gray 'Decline and Fall'. The title is apt, and altogether the century, 1687-1787, saw many events to the discredit of the foundation which had begun its life with so much promise. There were continual financial difficulties, leading to salary cuts, and a succession of weak and often irresponsible Masters. Weakest of all was Edward Sparkes, who followed Griffith and was witness to his will. Of him Gray writes that, 'being utterly devoid of ambition, he was content to remain as he was, to obtain what salary he could and to do the least possible required for the earning of it'. One finds with shame that this man was an Old Persean, a Perse scholar of Caius, and had been promoted from the post of Usher.

Under Sparkes, and others like him, the school's fortunes declined, and King's College school took the lead. The establishment of Charity schools removed many potential pupils, and especially those of the working-class who were looking for a utilitarian education. Harraden records that at this period several Charity schools had come into existence in Cambridge, 'for instructing girls and boys in reading, writing and arithmetic' and goes on that 'the first promoter of these was the celebrated Wm. Whiston in the year 1703, being the Lancastrian Professor of mathematics in the University'.[20]

At the end of Sparkes' mastership very few Perseans were proceeding to the University, and the number of boys in the school had dropped, in 1731, to as few as ten. About 1730 James Essex, already mentioned, attended King's College school, obviously in preference to the Perse. In view of the small number of pupils, the hall and other rooms were actually let out as an organ-builder's workshop; one wonders how Stephen Perse would have felt had he known how his benefaction was abused![22] The school buildings being out of use, a fee of one guinea was paid in 1730 to one Jacob Butler of Barnwell Abbey 'for pleading yt ye Free School should not be assessed to ye rates'.

Pluralism was the rule in the eighteenth century, in the church and, in spite of Ordinance 13, in Free School Lane. The supreme pluralist was Henry Goodall (Master, 1732-50) who, in addition, was a Fellow of Caius, Chaplain to the Bishop (who was the Master of Caius), Archdeacon of Suffolk and incumbent of three livings. In his time the school was left entirely to the Ushers, who were, luckily, not without conscience and ability. In spite of all the abuse, a few clever boys still went to the University, one, Robert Cory, achieving the distinction of being the first Old Persean to become Master of a Cambridge college and to gain a Professorship. The credit for his early education must obviously go to the two Perse Masters who, in contrast to the usual rule, did their work honestly. These were John White (1755-66) and William Bond (White's Usher and successor).

Cory became a Fellow of Emmanuel in 1782 and was Master from 1797 to 1835. He was Knightsbridge Professor of Moral Philosophy from 1809 to 1813. In the Memoirs of John Barber Scott, who entered the college as a Fellow-Commoner in 1811, Cory is described as 'timid, unused to the world, troublesomely conscientious, but very kindly disposed'.[23] Incidentally, the College still possesses a pair of bowls woods marked R.T.C. which probably belonged to him. The Bowtell manuscripts include a comment that 'Jeremy Taylor . . . and Dr. Cory, the present worthy master of Emm. Coll., rank among the distinguished scholars of the foundation'.[12]

One of the Ushers who managed the school for Goodall was Charles Davy (1747-51) who later in life wrote several books on educational theory, which gave him a place in the *Dictionary of National Biography*. His views had something in common with those of Dell, though he did not advocate zealous devotion to the Scriptures. In his *Letters addressed chiefly to a young Gentleman* he advocates a reform in curriculum by abandoning the classics and concentrating on mathematics and such scientific studies as were possible. The Master from 1766 to 1767 was Samuel Reeve, who twenty years later achieved notoriety when, while Senior Proctor, he hanged himself in a lumber-room at Caius, his body not being found for four months.

After the death of the organ builder the school premises were let to the highest bidder, any teaching being done in the rooms of the Usher at the school or in Caius. One tenant was a highly eccentric character, a solicitor named Jemmy Gordon, who (around 1780) led a profligate life there, but in due course met his proper due, becoming a beggar. He would roam the town dressed in the tarnished uniform of a

Robert Townson Cory. The first Old Persean to become a Professor and Master of a College; Master of Emmanuel, 1797-1835

general or admiral which he had scrounged from some old-clothes shop.

The lowest point in the school's fortunes was reached in the last quarter of the century, when 'it almost appeared as if the Perse benefaction was destined to come to a dismal end'. By 1785 there were no pupils at all, and the junior Fellows of Caius held the posts of Master and Usher as sinecures. A similar state of corruption existed in very many schools throughout the country.[24] By 1818 Nicholas Carlisle, in *A Concise Description of the Endowed Grammar Schools of England and Wales*, had cause to observe sadly in his preface: 'It is painful that many of our numerous and ample endowments have fallen to decay by the negligence of ignorant and unprincipled trustees'. This summed up the national situation. Many schools disappeared in the period between 1780 and 1860, and those which survived were rescued either by a strong-minded headmaster or because some public-spirited citizen exposed what, in modern slang, had become a racket.

Two instances may be quoted. At Shrewsbury the famous Samuel Butler, becoming Headmaster in 1798, found 'scarcely a single boy . . . no regular school, or discipline, had been established there for twenty years'. At Newport a Commission of Enquiry, set up, surprisingly early, in 1742, discovered that the Headmaster had received all the income payable to the foundation, but had paid out dues in the proportion laid down in the Foundress' will. The Visitor (the Master of Caius) had not been in the school for eight years. The Commission ordered the repayment of all but the agreed salary and expenses.

Cambridge provided an example of how an abuse was righted through publicity in the local press. A letter in the *Cambridge Chronicle* in 1787, signed 'An Inhabitant of Cambridge', enquired how the Free Grammar School was organised. In reply 'A Gownsman', who was at pains to point out that he was not a member of Caius College, asserted 'that the school was kept open as long as any boys were sent for education; that the masters are, and always have been, ready to admit scholars agreeable to the Will of the Founder; and that the parents of children properly qualified have only themselves to blame if they do not reap the advantages of that beneficent foundation.' The final letter of the series, signed by 'One educated in the school', insisted that the decline of the school was caused by the slackness of the masters, and tells how 'the boys attending hours before the Master came, and when he did come staying so short a time, reduced the school to so small a number that the Master gave up attending at school and ordered the boys to his rooms in College'. This letter provoked the Master and Fellows to announce the reopening of the school. For six or seven years there was a revival, but it did not last, and in 1794 the sinecure of Caius Fellows was resumed.

The Master from 1789 to 1791, during the period of revival, was Charles Davy, whose father had achieved some note because, as a nominal Usher, he had advocated a reform in the curriculum. The son made a serious effort to bring in a scheme of teaching on the lines his father had proposed. Although he was in Orders, he was essentially a scientist and mathematician. However, he received little support from the Supervisors, either financially or morally, and he and his Usher resigned together, possibly in protest. In the next three years two further Masters, John Borton and John Cobbold, kept the school just alive. Borton was quoted in the Chancery Enquiry of 1836 as having been wrongly appointed, being only a B.A. Cobbold seems to have had some skill, since a pupil of his proceeded to Caius, the first for over a hundred years. Cobbold, however, went on after a year to become Headmaster of Nuneaton School.

Numbers soon dwindled again, and after 1794 the school existed in name only until 1812. During this period seven Fellows of Caius in succession held the title of Master, without doing anything to earn the salary attached. Three of the seven are of interest, though not for their efforts in the name of the Perse.

The first of these was certainly the most eminent man ever to have held office at the Perse. This was William Wilkins, the famous architect of the Greek Revival, who held the sinecure Mastership from 1804 to 1805, like Borton illegally, since his degree was B.A. From 1800 he had been travelling in Europe to study its buildings, having gained West's Travelling bachelor Studentship and been elected to a Fellowship, embracing the Perse mastership, while still abroad. On his return, while still nominally in charge of the school, he began to design buildings in Cambridge, securing his first success when appointed to design Downing College in 1804. He later built the bridge, screen, hall and Provost's Lodge at King's, New Court at Trinity and the chapel and main court of Corpus Christi. His designs for the University Library and the Fitzwilliam Museum were rejected, but he became nationally famous through designing Haileybury College, the National Gallery, St. George's Hospital and University College, London. University College was probably his greatest work, and Downing is important as virtually a trial exercise from which it developed. He is buried at Corpus, where a memorial plaque speaks of how

Ingenium et sollertiam testantur multa Londini et Cantabrigiae
aedificia publica.

The second interesting sinecure head was Daniel Gwilt, who, as a former pupil of Newport Grammar School, forms a further link with that foundation. He became well known as a supporter of agricultural improvements.

The other noteworthy personality in this list was George Grigby (Master, 1799-1802) who had the unusual distinction of having taken Holy Orders (he was Dean of Caius in 1798) and subsequently, after leaving the Perse sinecure, became a soldier in the Peninsular War. He was a Captain in the 11th Foot and met his death, with 233 men of his regiment, when the transport taking them to Cadiz was in collision off Falmouth and all were drowned. Grigby's giving up an academic and ecclesiastical career to join the Army was not only unusual but 'must have seemed, according to the standards of the time, most improper. It is the more peculiar in that there was little patriotic fervour at the time of the Napoleonic wars; the Commander-in-Chief even claimed that a military career at that time was less popular during hostilities than during peace. The lack of enthusiasm is rather well illustrated by the fact that Grigby was the only Caius man to die in over twenty years of war'[25] — and apparently the only one with any Perse connection.

Grigby appears to have published a trigonometrical treatise in 1807, which is 'in the style one might expect from a don turned soldier, though a university connection is not mentioned'.

Throughout the country feeling against the endowed schools continued to grow. The reforms of the period had the paradoxical effect of creating new distinctions in education, in that the fee-paying boarding 'public' school changed its character, and new foundations, like Cheltenham College, were added, while at the same time there was a demand that grammar schools should provide something analogous for the middle classes, as was done at Harrow, Oundle and Rugby, where separate new foundations catered for local boys. There was public outcry when an old 'free' school became a 'public' school for 'foreigners' while the poorer boys, requiring a practical or commercial education, were excluded. In many cases there was conflict between church and non-conformity, and in Oxford and Cambridge the old 'Town and Gown' struggle received new impetus. At the same time, to answer the new demand, there was rapid development, all over the country, in what we would today call the private sector of education. Private schools were set up, either in imitation of the 'public' schools or to provide commercial instruction for the middle class. The fraudulent schools of the first type are enshrined in literature in the Lowood Asylum of *Jane Eyre* and the Dotheboys Hall of *Nicholas Nickleby*. Such schools were often merely a means of making a living for their owners, and many were short-lived — though often enough the promoters may have been inspired by the purest philanthropic motives or by the misguided zeal of a Gradgrind.

In Cambridge, in addition to the Charity schools which continued to be set up, there were a number of private schools, both day-schools and boarding establishments; parents living at some distance may well have felt that there would be a certain cachet in having a child at school in a university town. Most of these were in private houses, and many were kept by clergymen or graduates who were also tutoring undergraduates. A school in Green Street was kept by the father of Edward Palmer, who is mentioned in the next chapter. In the mid-eighteenth century, one Mrs Wigmore kept a flourishing private boarding-school on the site of the Arts School in Bene't Street, which is mentioned by Cole the antiquary. There was no copyright on the title Cambridge Grammar School, and the Perse was known usually as the Free (or Public) Grammar School, still never by its founder's name. In 1779 and again in 1876 a private promoter called his establishment, simply and grandly, The Grammar School. During the period when the Perse was in eclipse this had an obvious appeal to clients. The 1779 proprietor was Rev. Edward Waterson,[26] who, curiously, in his advertisements in the *Cambridge Chronicle*, on 29 May 1779, 1 January 1780, and 13 January 1781, gave no address — which led Dr. Venn[27] and others to assume that his school was the Perse.

Waterson's 1780 advertisement may be quoted, as showing a typical scheme: 'The Rev. Edward Waterson, M.A., of St. John's College, Master of the Grammar School, Cambridge, begs leave to acquaint the public that he now boards young Gentlemen for 20 guineas per annum and two guineas entrance, and instructs them in English, Latin, Greek, French and Italian languages. Writing and arithmetic in all branches, navigation, mensuration etc. Masters attend to teach drawing, dancing and music.'

The best known of Waterson's pupils was Henry Gunning, author of the famous *Reminiscences of the University, Town and County of Cambridge*. When the Cambridge school closed down, on its principal's departure — as the 1781 advertisement stated — to 'the vicarage of Sleaford in Lincolnshire, with the chaplaincy of the hospital and the mastership of the Free Grammar School in that town', Gunning went with him.

In 1808 another school was established, calling itself 'a new Free School for Cambridge'; it was in St. Peter's parish and was described by Harraden as 'founded upon the plan of Dr. Bell and Mr. Lancaster, for the education of the poor of this town and the adjacent villages'. This appears to have been a different type of school, whose foundation suggested philanthropic motives. In any case, the very formation of schools of either kind implied criticism of the way in which the Perse endowment was being handled.

At the end of the eighteenth century King's College School also suffered a decline, but it never closed down completely. It still gave instruction to the sixteen choristers on the college foundation, though after about 1740 that instruction appears to have been of a most elementary nature. The Mastership was invariably bestowed on a junior Fellow.

For a long time after 1794 the Trustees of the Perse accepted the situation complacently, disregarding all criticism and allowing the numbers in the school to drop. While themselves enjoying the proceeds of the endowment, they continued to pay the teachers what had become pitifully inadequate salaries. In 1812 they took action to raise the Master's salary, from £53 10s. to £120; but this was still poor in comparison with salaries offered by some other schools, and it was achieved by drastically reducing the scope of the foundation, abolishing the post of Usher and limiting the number of official scholars to sixteen. At first the Master was again allowed to take in fee-paying non-foundationers, as had been customary in the early days, but, although it made the school 'public' according to the then accepted definition, this concession was soon withdrawn.

The arrangement thus obtaining meant, of course, that unless a quite exceptional man was in control the school was virtually condemned to stagnation, with a mere sixteen pupils. The Master now appointed, John Wilson, formerly Chaplain of Trinity, was so uninspiring a teacher that in the thirteen years of his mastership only one boy seems to have proceeded to the University. There appeared to be no hope of recovering the old prestige. Moreover, the Trustees made no attempt to improve the facilities and allowed Wilson to continue in his feeble way.

The old buildings in Free School Lane were never again used, in their entirety, as a school. In 1816 the University received the Fitzwilliam Bequest, under which an art museum was to be built.

'*Big School' when used as the Fitzwilliam Museum 1816-1842*

Looking for temporary accommodation, the Syndicate appointed chose to 'enter into an agreement with the Trustees of the Free School for the use of that building' and took over the greater part of the school-house, including the Hall and the north wing (which had become the Usher's house). The architect making the necessary modifications was, by a nice twist of fate, no other than William Wilkins, who had £1,000 to £1,300 allowed for the work. So it came about that he actually worked for a time in the building of which he had earlier been the nominal head. The very limited purposes of the school were sufficiently catered for by the south wing.

The agreement with the University Museums Syndicate, made on 17 May 1816, states that accommodation was included (in the north wing) for a resident Curator. The Syndics were to build a new school-room and 'offices for the Master' and the Trustees would, 'in consideration of the improvements made in the said offices, pay to the Syndics the sum of £300 if they should regain possession of the (said) premises within six years, or £250 after seven years, or £200 after eight years, and so on for twelve years, afterwards receiving a rent of £50 yearly'. In January 1817, it was agreed that the north wing should not be used by the Curator but be fitted up for the reception of books and pictures, with further provision for the University to pay for the expenses should the school regain possession.

In 1833, when the scandal of the Trustees' mismanagement began to boil up against them, the University paid the college £400 for the rent of the premises and agreed to pay a further £230 on giving them up. In 1834 a definite request was made to the University to give the buildings up, and in 1842 they were returned to the Trustees. The Museum had thus been housed in the Perse building for twenty-five years, almost a generation.

Incidentally, in their earlier discussions, in June 1816, the Museum Syndics decided that 'the most eligible site' for the permanent building was 'the land extending from the east end of King's chapel to King's Lane'. Mercifully this recommendation was not followed.

All this time the fund had a large surplus which could have been used to help the school, but which was turned instead, as permitted by Perse's will, 'in such charitable uses as my Executors for their times and after my Supervisors shall think fit'. The so-called charitable uses were mainly internal to Caius College, and amounted to grants unconnected with charity. Indeed, the use of the buildings by the museum in itself was a measure of the Trustees' cynical lack of interest in the school.

IV

BAILEY AND MASON: THE CHANCERY PROCEEDINGS

The situation improved when, on the resignation of Wilson in 1825, another Trinity man was appointed, this time a man of character who by his energy and enthusiasm restored much of the school's reputation, though not its material success. This was James Bailey, one of the most remarkable men who have served the Perse, and one of the finest scholars, having taken high honours and won the Browne medal and the Members' Latin Essay prize. Yet in spite of his brilliance he had been unable to find a congenial post, and had been obliged, like many a struggling man of the period, to 'tout' for patronage. This had led to an interesting connection with Sir Walter Scott, whose advice he sought. The four letters which have been preserved, in the Fitzwilliam Museum, are much to Scott's credit, since he twice sent Bailey cheques, one for twenty pounds, another for twenty guineas, 'which I entreat you to consider as your own until your better fortune shall enable you to accommodate in the same manner any young man of genius in temporary distress'.

On his appointment to the Perse, Bailey took immense pains to make the school both attractive and efficient. His own experience of schoolmasters was not flattering: having run away from Giggleswick and from another school, he wrote that 'if my own son had run away from a third school I should have endeavoured to heal the matter up, but would not have thought a bit the worse of him for it'.

It took Bailey three years to introduce the reforms he had in mind. On 9 January 1829, a very full statement of what was intended appeared in the *Cambridge Chronicle*:

The Headmaster of the Perse Free Grammar School begs leave to caution the inhabitants of Cambridge and the vicinity against a report, which he believes to be prevalent to a certain extent, that none but free scholars are admissible to this school. The number of free scholars on this foundation is sixteen. The Day Scholars are

35

limited to no particular number. Of the pupils who went to the University from this school in the October term two out of three were Day scholars.

Evidently, then, Bailey had persuaded the Trustees once again to alter the conditions in the school, thus allowing him to compete, as Wilson had not done, with the various private schools. He had also persuaded them to allow a variation of the curriculum and to employ additional staff. The newspaper announcement goes on to announce that mathematics, French and possibly Italian are now taught, the languages on an optional basis. In a further notice, on 22 January 1830, he announced that 'a French master will attend weekly' and that Day scholars, 'if qualified by the conditions expressed in the Founder's will, succeed to vacancies on the foundation according to seniority'.

Bailey was obviously struggling, not only to make a success of the school, but to make a reasonable living for himself. His salary, though raised to £450, was still below that offered elsewhere, and well below what his talents deserved. Moreover, it appears that he had to pay his assistants out of his own pocket. Eventually both he and his Usher found themselves in financial difficulties, the Usher escaping going to prison as a debtor only by the intervention of the Master of Caius. In addition, Bailey had to live through a period when the foundation, and inevitably its headmaster, came under heavy public criticism, which led to a suit in Chancery. He was an outspoken critic of the many things of which he disapproved. Perhaps this explains his earlier failure to secure a University post. It seems also to explain how he came to be known in the town as 'Beast Bailey' — under which name he appears in the diaries of Joseph Romilly.[28] It has, however, been suggested that possibly the name arose from his having written a pamphlet on the 'Beast' in the Book of the Revelation.

In the end Bailey seems to have worried himself into a stomach ulcer. His health deteriorated; 'the root of the mischief was in the digestive organs,' he wrote, and he feared that the complaint 'might become general, which previously required the scenery of a school to elicit it'. He therefore applied, in 1833, with obvious reluctance, for a pension, and went to London to live in conditions of poverty. A letter written from a Peckham address speaks quite pathetically of the difficulties of trying to do some literary work 'without snatching my books from the gripe of the pawnbroker'.

Bailey's declining years were somewhat alleviated by the grant of a Civil List pension of £100 a year, in recognition of his quite considerable services to classical studies. Romilly[28] was 'quite delighted with this unexpected good fortune of the poor fellow at last'. His Perse pension was £75, and he should have been able to make ends meet, but, observed Romilly, 'Beast Bailey ought to be able to get on . . . but he has no management'. He also characterised him as being 'utterly devoid of worldly wisdom'. But he never recovered and continued his 'queer way of living' until he died in 1864. His son had a similar temperament and in 1871 wrote to Trinity offering the Scott letters to them as a means of raising money.

The man had many merits as a teacher and headmaster. He built the numbers at the Perse up to fifty, and in his last year as Master eight boys out of twelve in the top class went to the University, seven graduating with honours. Moreover, it now began to appear that the fortunes of the school had passed their lowest point. It had been a long period of decline, but at last there was a feeling of revival and an appreciation of the challenge to be met. Venn,[27] writing in 1890, puts the situation vividly:

> Between the years 1623 and 1678 there are no fewer than seventy names of lads entering Caius College from the Perse School: of these twenty have been recorded as Fellows of the College. But from 1678 to 1833 only two or three students are recorded, and these in no way distinguished themselves. It would be interesting to account for this extraordinary falling-off.

No doubt the record of these pages does account for it, and for much besides. Yet, although the worst period of Perse history seems to be over, the next section will show that troubled times were still to come.

The Perse foundation finally emerged from its odious obscurity because of the political events of the early nineteenth century, which led public opinion to demand reforms. There were many other schools, up and down the country, whose situation was similar, and many a pious bequest had long been abused. Dickens in *Nicholas Nickleby* and *Hard Times* provides examples of how the scandals came to be embodied in literature. Perhaps the most instructive literary passage is in George Eliot's *Mill on the Floss*.

In 1833 an Information was filed in Chancery against the Perse Trustees, which called for an investigation into the way in which the wills of Perse and Griffith had been and were being misapplied. This explicitly demanded that the Master and senior Fellows of Caius should be ordered to refund all monies received by them since 1804, and should be deprived of future control of the Trust funds. While the case was still awaiting its hearing a pamphlet was published and circulated in Cambridge which presented the main substance of the charges made. The pamphlet, bearing the address 'Downing Terrace' and the date 17 December 1835, was entitled 'A Letter to the Burgesses of Cambridge' nominally addressed to Gamaliel Thorn, Esq., by Lancelot Probe. It is not known who the persons were who were concealed by the pseudonyms. A part of the material was concerned with the approaching municipal elections, but the important part lay in the 'Appendix relative to the Perse Free School', to which it is appropriate to refer at some length: [3]

After surveying the history of the school's foundation, speaking incorrectly of Stephen as 'a native of the once proud, but now politically degraded, city of Norwich', the letter lists the estates bought by the Trustees, which we have already detailed, adding that 'large investments have been made in the public funds: so that the clear annual income of the Trust (after allowing for a recent reduction in the rents) is about £2,000, or eight times the amount of the original endowment'. It goes on to detail the ways in which the funds had, in recent years, been misapplied, since 'on general principles the objects of the charitable trusts ought to receive any benefit which may arise from the increase, or suffer any loss from the decrease, of the trust proportionately'. In the next section of the document, 'in order to show how proportion has been violated in this case', the expenditure of the Trust is set out to show in one column what the Founder had proposed and in another what the Trustees had in fact received in 1829 and what the school, the almsfolk, and other beneficiaries were allowed. The figures show that the Master and Fellows, while neglecting the school, had raised their own emoluments from £9 p.a. to £840. 'The coolness with which the Master and four senior Fellows raised their own stipends . . . must excite in the breasts of the old Corporators (sc. of Cambridge borough) a conscious sense of their inferiority in the practice of that charity which begins at home'. Moreover, new beneficiaries in the college had been added: 'Dr. Perse in his will gives nothing to the Dean, the Steward, the Conduct, the College Registrar, or the Gardener; but his faithful Trustees have no scruple in extending to these meritorious personages the benefit of his munificence, and in 1799 the sum of £800 was paid out of the trust-fund towards the sum expended by the college in repairs and new buildings, and in a contribution to government for the internal defence of the country!'

The letter then expressed astonishment 'that the malversation . . . should have been as long permitted . . . I can only account for it by the want of suspicion on the part of the public and the profound secrecy in which all matters of the kind have been kept in Cambridge'. Dr. Perse himself had not 'placed a foolish confidence in the character of the Trustees', but had provided for an audit of accounts, which were then to be presented to the Vice-chancellor and Esquire-bedells. 'This has never been done within memory and the accounts (kept infinitely worse than churchwardens' or constables' accounts are usually kept in country villages) are audited by the Trustees themselves — with what care will appear from the facts': two cases of gross error, always in the favour of the trustees, are quoted in illustration.

The steady decline of the school is remarked, and the various irregularities are detailed, including the use of the building for the Fitzwilliam Museum, the charges introduced into a nominally free school, and the disregard of Ordinance 13: 'out of twenty-eight schoolmasters twenty-three of them have been Fellows of Caius, as have thirty-two out of thirty-nine ushers'. The pamphlet concludes by asserting that, 'although Dr. Perse's trust is of more importance than any other (for assuredly education is the greatest blessing a munificent benefactor can bestow on a town),' there were other charities in Cambridge which required investigation. An appendix summarises the letter as showing 'in a most striking manner the ill effects of irresponsible power and that men of high personal character are not always sufficiently regardful of public duties'.

The legal action came on for trial in the Rolls Court in 1836, with judgment in 1837. The Relators are reported as 'praying for better regulations of Perse's Free Grammar School in the town of Cambridge and for an account of the funds vested in (the defendants) by the will of Dr. Stephen Perse'. Evidence was given that the value of the estate 'had increased very much, so that the rents were about £1,200 and there was an accumulated residue of £5,000 which if invested should produce an income of nearly £2,000 altogether'. Counsel for the Relators, said to be 'extremely respectable inhabitants and tradesmen of Cambridge', argued that the public interest required the defendants to account for their disposal of the funds, and 'concluded by urging ... that his Lordship should refer the scheme in future as a government charity and should declare the principle on which the scheme should be made'.

Counsel for the defendants 'cited many cases to show that the defendants were not answerable as Trustees for acts of their predecessors. They were a fluctuating body and not bound to account to the Relators; and (that) they were entitled to disperse surplus trust funds'. The Master of Caius (the Rev. Martin Davy) had admitted certain irregularities, such as the appointment of Borden and Wilkins without a master's degree and a mistake over the revenue figures. He had insisted, however, that he did not know anything about the situation before 1812. But since 1812 he could not say 'whether Masters caused the boys to sit upon the stairs outside their rooms in college to wait for them or did not live in the schoolhouse or go there to teach'. The University, since vacating the rooms used as a museum, had paid for their restoration; the remaining part of the school was 'unfit for 100 boys but adequate for numbers then attending'.

Judgment was to the effect that Perse's principal benefaction was undoubtedly to the school and that a new Scheme for its administration must be drawn up, which might well revise the curriculum. It was not, however, judged possible, in view of Perse's clear intention, to remove the College officers from their trusteeship, nor was it feasible to require the repayment of funds wrongly dispersed, since others equally culpable were then dead.

A nice touch of irony appeared in that the Master of the Rolls at this time was Lord Langdale, formerly Justice Bickersteth, who had been one of the four senior Fellows of Caius and as such a Trustee of the Perse at the time of its most scandalous mismanagement. When the Court of Chancery proceedings began in 1883 he had voluntarily returned nearly £800 to the College, feeling that in the light of the evidence then adduced he was not entitled to the money; the Caius accounts record this payment of conscience money as simply 'Received of Mr. Bickersteth'. Naturally, 'Mr. Probe' noted this, and recorded it as 'an incident worthy of especial notice'.

The Revised Scheme arising from the enquiry was published in an Order dated 31 July 1841. Many of the original regulations (from the first Ordinances) were repeated, and the number of scholars was kept at one hundred, drawn from the area originally specified; but there were detailed directions for choosing them and a definition of age-limits, much as is usual today, with scholars entering at 'ten plus' and remaining until 18. Fee-payers from outside were allowed, thus regularising what had been a recurring matter of contention. The Master and Usher, and an assistant if one were needed, were more realistically salaried. To ensure that the finances were in future controlled, new regulations appointed a Registrar, independent of the Trustees, to receive rents and dividends and keep acccounts. It was laid down that there should be an annual Audit and Dinner (£20 was allocated for the Dinner); the occasion was to be kept as 'Dr. Perse's Day' and to be a school holiday.

From now on the record of Caius College is unblemished; as the programme now issued for the annual Perse feast records:

Caius, as Trustees, maintains the Almshouses — rebuilt in Newnham Road in 1890 — and contributes to the maintenance of the 'sufficient Causey from the further end of Jesus Lane to the hither end of Barnwell' and of the 'banks and currents of the New River brought into Cambridge'; sums are paid yearly to 'the Master Cooke, the Under Cooke, the Butler and the Porter'; the Vice-chancellor signs the Trust 'accompt to be yearlie kept'; the Vice-chancellor and 'Esquire Beadles' are invited (with appropriate remuneration) to an annual dinner; and provision is made at the dinner for what Stephen wished to be 'an exceeding in diett among the schollers of the Colledge'. An annual Perse Sermon is preached in Dr. Perse's memory — originally on his obit day, but, since the Report, on his 'Mortuary or Commemoration Day', which is the 14th December or 'if the same be a Sunday on the Saturday immediately succeeding or the Monday immediately succeeding' — and is followed by the Commemoration Dinner.

Other regulations laid down in the Report specify that the school shall be provided with pens, ink, fuel and lighting, and £10 was to be made available for prizes and 20 guineas for examiners' fees. The paying scholars were to pay 20s. to the Perse School Book and a further 10s. half-yearly. The school hours now became 7 a.m. to 5 p.m., with breaks at 8-9 a.m. and 12 noon-2 p.m.; only the morning session would be worked on Saturdays.

An obviously prime requirement for the effective working of the new Scheme was the rebuilding and enlarging of the premises. In 1841 we read that 'The Perse Free School and the houses of the Master and Usher have been already rebuilt in pursuance of direction'. In fact, the work was not finished until 1842. After the Fitzwilliam collection had been moved out (in 1842), other new accommodation was added, built in the characteristic white brick of the period, but of a good standard of workmanship. The most important addition was a further large school-room, at right-angles to the Big School, built in deliberate imitation of the Jacobean structure, even to a repetition of the roof truss and ceiling apertures. It has three and a half bays, as against the five of the great hall. The new room ran to the full extent of the site, and consequently its end wall is not square, but at an angle, as shown on the plan. Doors communicated with the Big School, and a stairway close by led down to the playground. At the south-east end of the old hall a smaller extension was made, and at the north-west angle a

'Big School': The Hall of the School in Free School Lane: 1890. Note the Fellowship Board, Honours Shields, gas jets and bell-rope

The Junior School of the School in Free School Lane looking East

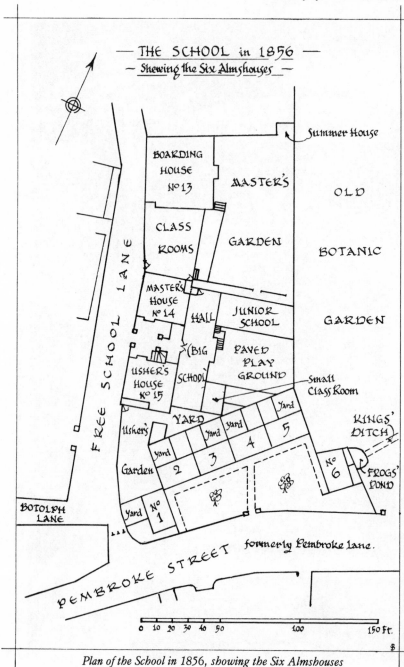

— THE SCHOOL in 1856 —
— Shewing the Six Almshouses —

Summer House

BOARDING HOUSE Nº 13

MASTER'S

OLD

CLASS ROOMS

GARDEN

BOTANIC

FREE SCHOOL LANE

MASTER'S HOUSE Nº 14

HALL

JUNIOR SCHOOL

GARDEN

(BIG SCHOOL

PAVED PLAY GROUND

USHER'S HOUSE Nº 15

Small Class Room

KINGS' DITCH

YARD

Usher's

Yard

Yard

Yard

Yard

5

Garden

2

3

4

Nº 6

FROGS' POND

BOTOLPH LANE

Yard

Nº 1

PEMBROKE STREET   formerly Pembroke lane.

0 10 20 30 40 50   100   150 Ft.

Plan of the School in 1856, showing the Six Almshouses

doorway was cut allowing access to further classrooms made out of the Master's house, which had become the Usher's, the Master moving to the south wing.[16] The south wall was largely rebuilt.

Today the two main rooms survive, forming an attractive setting for the Whipple Science Museum. Modern laboratories surround them, and the sites of the two houses and of the entrance courtyard have been taken by the Hopkinson laboratory building of 1899, with its cupola which appears to have been deliberately designed to echo the Jacobean spirit of the old hall it engulfs and masks from the road.

The buildings continued in use for a further forty-six years, although it was obviously a restricted site, with only the small paved playground, and although the sale of the adjacent area for University laboratories made any extension impracticable. The immediate effect of the extensions and the new organisation was that the number of boys rose immediately from twenty or so to the full one hundred. Some additional Regulations were made in 1847.

Bailey, despite having been a defendant in the lawsuit, survived its worries: he was in effect exonerated and no order for costs was made against him, but the strain of the case and subsequent public inquisitiveness must have contributed to his break-down. His successor, appointed in 1837, was Peter Mason, another rather peculiar man. However, under his management the school for a time achieved renewed success; there were again many boys going on to the University, and five, including Mason's own son, obtained Fellowships. The curriculum at the time was a very limited one, almost exclusively mathematical, with in addition only some weak classical teaching, a little English and Geography, but no modern languages and no science, music or art.

Mason had some admirable qualities. A writer in the *Pelican* for June 1905, remembers that he 'was unquestionably a good teacher and scholar (he graduated as Third Wrangler). Every boy felt and knew that as soon as he developed the slightest spark of mathematical taste he found in his headmaster a fine friend, a teacher, and, more, a worker with him, absolutely untiring in his efforts to clear away difficulties and encourage him to make big his aims'. The difficulties which led to another sad and scandalous episode in the school's history arose from his remaining in office long after he should have retired, when increasing ill-health and a feeling of discouragement made him lose heart, and, to add to his difficulties, his wife took to drink and, as Romilly puts it, he 'parted from her'. Incidentally, he cannot have been very prepossessing personally, as Romilly calls him 'the beautiful schoolmaster' in obvious sarcasm and John Lewis Roget, Romilly's cousin, calls him 'excessively ugly'.[28]

The situation in Mason's last years was such that, except for the salary quoted, George Eliot, in *The Mill on the Floss*, could have been writing of him as 'a headmaster, toothless, dim-eyed and deaf, whose erudite indistinctness and inattention were engrossed at the rate of £300 a head — a ripe scholar, doubtless, when first appointed; but all ripeness beneath the sun has a further stage less esteemed in the market'. The work suffered further from the fact that the Usher of the time, who was often left in sole charge, was as disloyal as he was incompetent. Consequently a serious state of indiscipline came about, which led to a public protest and vitriolic letters in the local press. The situation became intolerable when the Usher, an Irishman named James McDowall, came to blows with another master in front of a class. The Trustees had then to intervene. In 1864 the state of the school led them to treat Mason as Bailey had been treated in the previous generation: he was compulsorily retired on pension. His tenure of office had extended to twenty-seven years, which could fairly be described as 'The Troublesome Reign of Peter Mason'.

An Old Persean, the Rev. T. B. Nichols, writing in the *Pelican* of 1910, has described Mason's attempts to enforce some discipline: 'As often as not, he did not come into the school at all, and when he did it was mainly for the purpose of a little exercise in going round and caning the boys on one of the back rows, where he had plenty of swing for his arm. I well remember the rush of those luckless boys, about eleven in the morning, for permission to 'leave the room'.'

Mason's son, also Peter, who went through the school and on to St. John's, is an interesting character. He graduated as Eleventh Wrangler and became a Fellow. His honours shield is one of the oldest on display in the school, and the college has his portrait, painted by Brock.[29] He took up the study of Hebrew.

The most outstanding Persean of the time was Edward Henry Palmer, a fascinating character, who showed an amazing flair for languages while he was still at school, and went on to achieve a unique reputation. The son of a schoolmaster who died very young, he left school early on account of ill-health, but made a complete recovery from the tuberculosis which threatened him.

He began his linguistic studies with Romany, which he taught himself by going into the country and talking with gypsies and travelling tinkers, in due course making his own Romany dictionary. He extended his studies to other languages, which he learned by the same method. He was said to have learned German in three weeks, and while still a young man he completely mastered 'the whole groups of the Latin, Scandinavian and Teutonic languages and their dialects; he knew Welsh; he had begun the Slavonic languages and knew some Russian and a little Polish'. But it was the Oriental languages that most enthralled him, and he became the acknowledged Oriental scholar of his country.

Palmer became a Fellow of St. John's and, in 1871, Lord Almoner's Professor of Arabic. He made his name, however, not only as a linguist but in many other ways, and above all as a man of action. As a writer he achieved distinction both in the serious spheres of translation and journalism — he was leader-writer to a London newspaper — and as a humorous poet. His first essay in this, entitled *The Hole in the Wall*, and called 'a merrie metrical and monastical Romance' in imitation of the *Ingoldsby Legends*, was written when he was seventeen, and two copies are among the school archives. He was also a qualified barrister, a competent geographer and, by way of hobby, a brilliant conjuror.

He won his greatest distinction, as has been said, as a man of action. He was sent by the Government on three occasions 'to arrange matters' with the Arabs, following the rebellion of Arabi. By great presence of mind, audacity, pluck and personality, he several times escaped death at the hands of treacherous guides and robbers. In the end, though he was murdered, being given the option of being shot or jumping over a precipice — and choosing to jump — he achieved what he set out to do. We read that 'at the bidding of one man, many thousand wild Arabs laid down their arms, the rebellion was still-born and the Suez canal was saved from destruction'. The victory of Sir Garnet Wolseley at Tel-el-Kebir followed, made possible by his work. The audacity of Palmer's last ride through the desert, as told by his friend and biographer Walter Besant, makes a wonderfully thrilling story, in some ways anticipating the more famous exploits of Lawrence.

Besant sums up the life of this Persean, who received a hero's burial in St. Paul's, by suggesting that it shows how a brave boy may 'win his way from obscurity to honour by indomitable courage and persistence, and how the mortal remains of a quiet scholar and man of books find a place beside the bones of Wellington and Nelson'.

There emerges from Besant's account of Palmer's schooldays, and from other contemporary writings, that the Perse at this time lacked much of what came to be called the public-school spirit and *esprit de corps*. 'There was no organisation of games, no school eleven, no

Edward Henry Palmer

school anything. Once outside the door of that big school the units fell to pieces for want of social cement, each going his own way to his house or to companions of his own choosing. A shy, self-conscious boy gained nothing but intellectual advantages — only part of what a school can give'. One is bound to reflect that Besant wrote some twenty years after Arnold's reforms at Rugby and at a time when many comparable schools had already begun to make a reputation for activities outside the class-room.

V

REVIVAL: THE TAUNTON COMMISSION AND HEPPENSTALL

In the 'sixties and 'seventies education began to come under close public scrutiny. There was strong feeling throughout the country that endowed schools like the Perse should reform their curriculum in a practical way; still more, that they should be brought under the control, in some measure, of municipal authority. The rise of Non-conformity and of the Liberal party, and the critical attitude of 'organised labour', led to a feeling that the ancient schools had become a prerogative of the privileged, and that the intentions of the founders were not being carried out. In Cambridge the town versus gown feud broke out again, taking on also the character of Liberal/Non-conformist versus Church/Establishment.

A series of public enquiries, on a national scale, took place. In 1858 the Popular Education (or Newcastle) Committee made an investigation, and in 1861 a Royal Commission under Lord Clarendon considered the cases of the nine best-known endowed schools. In this same year the Cambridge Borough Council appointed a Committee — to consider the Perse discipline scandal,[30] in the first place — which agitated for municipal representation on the Board of Trustees, but achieved nothing. In 1864 came the Public Schools Act, which introduced reforms in the administration of seven ancient foundations. Also in 1864 the Schools Enquiry Commission, under Lord Taunton, began a more general enquiry into the state of the other endowed schools (not already surveyed). This was where the Perse came under consideration.

The Taunton Commission drew attention to the deplorable state of affairs throughout the ancient foundations, showing that in nearly every case bequests of pious benefactors had been grossly abused. Not only were most of the schools corrupt and unethical in their administration, but they were inefficient and inadequate in their methods, failing to give the service for which the bequests were made, and which

50

the public had a right to expect. Their very existence now operated against the establishment of more efficient schools under state control.

Many schools, throughout the eighteenth century and the first half of the nineteenth, had so far reduced their numbers, often deliberately, as to constitute a scandal. Sedbergh, one of the worst examples, had only 13 pupils in 1868, although the Headmaster's house was a mansion able to accommodate 45 boarders, and the ten senior boys were frankly making a nominal attendance in order to qualify for valuable leaving Exhibitions. It has been observed that six schools in the West Riding who came under scrutiny at this time had a total of 195 pupils between them, and yet employed 15 masters, an average of 13 boys to each of them. Clearly, George Eliot had not exaggerated in her picture. The Perse had at least kept its numbers up, in recent years.

The problems of curriculum reform were highlighted by a law-suit in 1806 concerning Leeds Grammar School, at which Lord Eldon delivered what became the legal definition of a grammar school, namely, one established 'for teaching grammatically the learned languages, according to Dr. Johnson's definition'. It was only by means of a special Act of Parliament that the Leeds trustees were able to modify their curriculum to provide commercial education, and few other schools could do likewise until the Taunton Commission had reported. The Commission found, not only that such reforms in ancient schools were required, but also that in at least two-thirds of the towns in England there was no education above elementary level.

Before the Commission visited Cambridge, the Town Council held its own investigation, appointing *ad hoc* a Perse Grammar School Committee. The Committee, however, met once only, having, the members reported, found 'great difficulty in getting another meeting'. Alderman H. Smith reported to the full Council, on 5 June, 1862, submitting a written statement listing 'defects of management' in the school, but conceding that 'you have some time past had under your consideration measures for improving efficiency in the school'. The statement, rather surprisingly, commended the continuing emphasis on classical teaching, but argued that an 'English' alternative was needed. At the meeting when this was discussed, apparently inconclusively, Councillor Wetenhall reported a case of unduly harsh discipline in the school, a boy of fifteen having received twelve severe cuts on the hand because he smiled while reading 'a ludicrous passage' in Shakespeare. The Usher, James McDowall, already mentioned as a man of violent temper, 'says he is amenable only to Chancery'. It was stated that 'any candid enquirer' should refer to 'a gentleman of Caius College' for information 'on the above subject'.

The Commissioners' Report, while implying criticism of Mason, found much to praise, for by 1866, when they visited the Perse, his successor, Frederick Heppenstall, had been in charge for two years, and had already introduced many reforms on the lines generally approved. The school must have appeared to its inquisitors at least rather better than the national average, having made a quick recovery from a condition rather below it.

The Commissioners found that salary and pension arrangements were satisfactory. Mason was receiving £220 — 'but of that sum £120 has to be supplied from the general funds, there being no accumulations in the superannuation account with which to pay more than £100 a year thereby provided for. In this matter the Trustees appear to have dealt liberally with the school'.

The Commissioners were obviously well aware of the criticisms made against the school in the recent past, both at the Guildhall meeting and as current hearsay. Their Report stated that 'there have been in times past various complaints urged by the inhabitants against the constitution and management of the school, which, though regarded as an institution purely for the benefit of the town, is entirely under the control of trustees who are independent of municipal influences. But there can be no doubt that the existing body of trustees is well qualified to deal with all educational questions arising in connection with the school, and, being on the spot, their advice and assistance is readily obtainable'.

Earlier the Report had reviewed the achievements of the school, lamenting that they had in recent times been 'almost exclusively in mathematical studies' but anticipating that the balance would be improved since the new Headmaster was a good classical scholar while the Usher was 'equally distinguished in Mathematics'. In reviewing the work seen in the classical forms they had found the boys showing 'a want of taste and elegance and their manner was somewhat listless'; the present master had 'endeavoured to assimilate the classwork as far as can be to that of a public school . . . The result in so short a time was encouraging'. It should be remembered that the Taunton Commission had noted a general decline in classical teaching, precisely the area which most founders had intended to be the basis of the work; even the teaching of elementary Latin was often ludicrously weak. At the same time it was apparent that, as the Inspectors were to find, very little had been done in most areas to bring the instruction more into harmony with the material needs of the age. They accordingly recommended that classically-based schools should cater equally for the scientific and technological subjects which were becoming vital to national progress, and should also introduce commercial or 'English' studies for the less academic. The Commission recognised three grades of school: the first with a classical curriculum, preparing boys for the universities, the second for boys up to seventeen years old who intended to enter professional or managerial careers, and the third giving an elementary education up to the age of fifteen. The Commission were very much aware of the class-distinctions which entered into education even at this period; but they properly insisted that Grammar Schools were intended to help clever boys of any class. About a hundred schools in the country, including the Perse, were classified as First Grade.

The Commission did not wholly condemn the control of the Perse hitherto exercised by Caius, but it did regret that the constitution 'did not foster that feeling of common interest which should bind a town to its principal place of education'. The Scheme which was proposed, and presently approved, introduced fundamental changes in the Trust, but retained three Caius representatives on the Board, the others being appointed by the Council of the University Senate (3) and the Town Council (6). Thus the demand for municipal involvement was at last met. At Newport the powers previously vested in the Master of Caius were transferred to the Charity Commissioners.

After 1870 School Boards were constituted in many towns, and the Commission proposed that two of the Town Council seats on the Perse board should in due course represent the local School Board. The idea of such a Board was not, however, popular in the town, and none was ever established. This may have been because Cambridge promoted Higher Grade Schools, being one of the first authorities to do so. The Cambridge schools were not typical.[31] The Perse governing body was also allowed three co-opted members; one of the first of these was Mr. William Eaden Lilley, principal of the well-known local firm, who represented the Liberal interest, and was to play an important part in subsequent events in the story of the Perse.

Another important change had followed the report of the University Commission of 1860. The Perse Scholarships and Fellowships were then abolished and merged in the college scholarship fund. Thereafter Perse boys had no preferential treatment at Caius — but the school received no compensation for the loss of what had been a deliberate provision of the founder. However, some technical amends were made when in 1933-4 the College reintroduced the Perse Fellowship title.

The Scheme approved on 23 April, 1873, and a Revised (or 'Altered') Scheme sealed on 13 March, 1891, refer to the school as 'the school of the Perse Trust, hitherto known as Dr. Perse's School'. The Trust as newly constituted then became a Board of Governors, Mr. Heppenstall being 'deemed to be the first Headmaster under this scheme' and the former Usher and Assistant Usher 'deemed to be assistant masters of the Perse School for Boys'. There are details of salaries and of permitted arrangements for boarders 'either in the house of any master, or on the hostel system, or in both ways'. With regard to the change in style of the Master's position, it should be observed that Bailey had always referred to himself as Headmaster.

The curriculum prescribed by the scheme was in effect the one already adopted; but it went further in making the 'Classical' and 'English' sides so distinct that the school became virtually a dual organisation, with different conditions of entry and different courses of instruction; the official Scheme gives full details, adding that both sides will 'work under the control of the Headmaster'.

The 'English' School as thus established was at first reasonably successful, but it presently became a target for criticism and indeed for bitter argument. The dual organisation continued until the situation changed when the County Education committee established the County School (afterwards the Cambridgeshire High School) where courses in technical and commercial subjects were freely available. However, there were obvious objections to the dual arrangement, and by 1887 the union of the two parts of the school was being proposed.

In 1869 the Endowed Schools Act appointed a special commission, united in 1874 with the Charity Commission, which had very wide powers of reorganisation over ancient endowments, and had been given a special directive to urge the extension of available endowments to provide girls' schools. One of its most important achievements was the introduction of the modern system of registration, inspection and examination of all schools. In 1895 it was reported (by the Bryce Royal Commission) that new Schemes under the reforming Acts had been needed for 902 endowments out of 1448.

Much further legislation followed, tending to reform the curriculum. The Royal Commission on Technical Education of 1884 led in 1889 to the Technical Instruction Act, extended by the Act of 1891, which empowered the Councils to levy a rate for the promotion of technical education, and permitted county councils to provide scholarships.

There was, however, an instruction in this Act that other studies were not to be neglected. Indeed, the curricular pendulum was now swinging the other way, the Bryce Commission complaining that the work in a number of schools had come to be dominated by science, literary subjects being neglected. Most important of all in the series of political developments was the Board of Education Act, 1899, which was followed by the Balfour Act of 1902. All this means that soon after the dawn of the twentieth century the threefold division of education into elementary, secondary and technical, controlled by local education committees, had been achieved.

By this time the Perse had been catering for the new requirements for twenty-five years and more. It had, necessarily, to accept a measure of Local Authority control, but the struggle to maintain its essential independence entered a new and sterner phase. The school was very fortunate in that at this time of change, reorganisation and threat it had such an excellent Headmaster as the Rev. Frederick Heppenstall, who had, as has been mentioned, anticipated many of the reforms and suggestions then current, and shown himself to be in line with the most advanced educational thinking of the time.

Heppenstall[32] certainly ranks as one of the truly great Perse headmasters, for he saved the school at this time of unprecedented crisis. His appointment opened a new era and seemed to mark the end of the sad period of decline in Perse affairs. This was recognised at the time by all thoughtful people in Cambridge, and one of his pupils later spoke of the relief which was generally felt when 'one of the dearest and best of men was appointed Head'. His achievement must be judged all the more notable when it is appreciated that throughout his time at the school he was a very sick man, fighting an incurable disease, which killed him four years after he left, when he was only 44 years old. An obituary notice, after asserting that he had raised the Perse 'to a more prosperous condition than it had before attained, speaks of his 'indefatigable exertion and over-anxiety'. These words appear to sum up his character, for he was 'abnormally sensitive' and yet a perfectionist, and a very strong personality, a born leader who worked himself hard and expected the same hard work from everybody under his command.

Heppenstall introduced the discipline so obviously called for in the school,[30] ruling with firmness, as a benevolent dictator rather than as a martinet, although his relations with the staff were sometimes strained. Such was his personality that not only did disorder quickly become a thing of the past, but there grew up a healthy *esprit de corps* which has remained typical of the Perse. His standards and his philosophy are well shown in the question he would put to boys likely to do well: 'Are you working up to your strength?' He was himself a fine scholar, who had weakened his health by hard study. He had been ninth Classic, a Senior Optime, and had taken also Honours in Theology. He would have gained a Fellowship at his old college, St. John's, if he had not married on graduating. He raised the Perse to a high position in Classical studies, his special interest, and for several years more classical scholarships were gained at Cambridge by his pupils than by 'almost any of the big public schools'. In his teaching he insisted on rigid accuracy, tracing every detail 'with the exactitude of astronomy' and developing the linguistic rather than the human side of the texts.

At first there were only two assistant teachers, and all the classes used 'Big School', the great Jacobean hall. When the Junior school developed, it used the extension, built in 1842.

The Usher at this time was the Rev. John Wisken, who had a fine record of service, holding office from 1865 until 1891, and continuing under the next two Headmasters. An Old Persean, he graduated from Caius as 8th Wrangler and became a Fellow. He then became Master of Newport Grammar School, providing another link between the two schools. His Usher at Newport was yet another Old Persean, Samuel Peacock, and both were involved in a quarrel with their Trustees when they asked for increases in salary over the £150 and £70 being paid. They pointed out that in most endowed schools 'commodious dwelling-houses, rent free, are provided for the Master and Usher, who could thus accommodate remunerative boarders', and suggested that if this arrangement was not possible a capitation fee might be charged on each scholar. When the Trustees refused this request Wisken moved to the Perse. Peacock, however, stayed on at Newport until 1876. He was acting Master in 1865-6, after which the school closed for a short period. His tenure ended in unfortunate circumstances when, after the Endowed School Act was passed, Counsel declared that he had a vested interest in the school and should be required to resign, with compensation. His old pupils then organised 'a Testimonial to show their respect and esteem for him, and to express their deep regard at his leaving'.

Wisken must have been a man of fine character, playing the exacting role of Second Master, when the staff increased, with great tact, not only under Heppenstall, but under his difficult successor, Allen. He was a first rate teacher, and it is due to him that in this period mathematical studies also bloomed at the Perse, with excellent results in the Mathematical Tripos. He also gave, outside school hours, some lectures on elementary Science. The third master at the beginning of Heppenstall's time was the Rev. Asplen, nicknamed 'Pronk', who had not taken an Honours degree, and taught English subjects. He none the less liked to wear his M.A. gown at all times, and used to walk to school from his house in Panton Street in gown and top-hat. He had, incidentally, to collect his salary of £100 by personal, half-yearly collections from the 'free' boys.

The staff came to be considerably increased under Heppenstall. In 1867 a French master and a drawing-master were engaged to assist in the enlarged curriculum, and in 1873 a master, Mr. R. M. Lewis, was specifically appointed to teach Science, although he was given no equipment. He was the first Science master ever employed at the Perse. Before he left, Heppenstall had seven assistants, and could claim to have achieved a re-orientation of the curriculum, which had, of course, in some measure been anticipated by Davy, Bailey and Mason.

A great weakness of the 'forties and 'fifties, as has been mentioned, was that games and other out-of-school activities were almost totally lacking. It was Heppenstall who, following a national trend, began to introduce a number of interests and developing the idea, just beginning to gain favour, of *mens sana in corpore sano* and *esprit de corps*. Like every good schoolmaster, he was deeply interested in boys as persons. He made games, for the first time, an accepted and popular part of school life, taking part himself, for all his physical weakness. But he did not, as some schools were doing already, make them compulsory. He had, of course, no private playing-field available, but unusually good facilities were available at Parker's Piece, within a reasonable distance of Free School Lane.

The hours of class-teaching were from 9 to midday and from 2 to 5; in winter the school ended at 4 o'clock, as there was no artificial light. (An extra hour's tuition was arranged for promising boys, science classes and scholarship candidates). The holidays were much shorter than they are to-day.

This meant, of course, that the time available for any kind of games was limited, and in winter there was virtually no time. In consequence, the main game played was cricket, in which some satisfactory results were scored, Heppenstall himself taking a prominent part. The first sporting success scored by a Persean was, however, in football; in 1872 A. T. B. Dunn gained a Cambridge (Association) Football Blue; this was a credit to the Perse in only a small way, as Dunn had gone on to Eton, but he certainly gained his first liking for the game under the inspiration of Heppenstall. He went on to gain international honours also, and the Dunn cup bears his name.

There are several other spheres, outside the class-room, in which this great Headmaster's hand seems to show. In particular, anxious to encourage the team-spirit, and again following a national trend, he appears to have devised the school colours and the House system. The colours were originally red, black and white. Later the red was changed to violet; it was Rouse who later substituted the classical purple, truly 'fishing the murex up'. Swann-Mason, of Barnes-Lawrence's staff, later received credit for having introduced the House system, but there is reason to think that he adapted and enlarged on the work of Heppenstall, and Allen also, in this matter. The Houses had at first colours for names, but were later named North, South, East, West.

A very important event of Heppenstall's last year was the appearance of a school magazine in embryo, a forerunner of the *Pelican*, though not yet printed. It took the form of a presentation album prepared for the Headmaster's pleasure by the Sixth Form, consisting of stories and poems beautifully written out and illustrated by hand. Entitled *Christmas Annual for 1874*, one number is preserved in the school archives. The Editor of this *Annual* was Allison J. O. Pain, a brother of Barry Pain, the popular novelist, who went on to Sedbergh with Heppenstall. A third brother, Herbert, was also concerned, and it would appear that Allison and Herbert were joint Editors; this is implied in a personal letter from Barry to Dr. Rouse, dated 3 February, 1913, which is in the archives and speaks of the Editors as 'the Siamese twins'. Certainly Barry Pain's first known writing appeared in this little book, though Allison's work, sometimes signed with a partial anagram of his name, Aspinella Godillan, takes up most space. Allison became a Scholar of Christ's and took a First-class degree in Classics; he later emigrated to Australia, where he became a successful journalist.

It is interesting to observe that a great-uncle of the Pain brothers founded the firm of opticians still practising in Cambridge (though not now owned by the family) and that their descendants include three recent generations of Perse boys.[33] A later editor of the *Annual* was F. R. O. Flack, afterwards Archdeacon of Port Elizabeth. The 1874 issue is a joy to behold. It is bound in pale blue covers, with the school crest, and every page bears evidence of loving care. The best individual item is a parody of Macaulay's *Horatius*, describing a match against Bishop's Stortford College.

Heppenstall's last annual Report on the school is also preserved, dated 1875. It asserts that 'the school has now settled down into its new form (i.e., with a 'Junior' section) . . . I believe that the effects of the change are in every way beneficial'. Certainly the Report shows how much he had achieved as Headmaster, both academically and in improving the character and 'tone' of the school. Above all, he had fostered a distinctive Persean spirit, which has persisted. During the ten difficult years of his reign he met a good deal of opposition and often ill-informed criticism in the town, but he stuck to his task, wearing himself out in the process. His great year of achievement was 1871, when the Master of Caius, Dr. Guest, awarded the school an extra week's holiday to mark the record number of university successes gained. It was observed that '£1000 yearly was now paid to former Perse boys who at the present time hold Fellowships, scholarships or exhibitions'.

In 1873, at the beginning of his last year, Heppenstall 'put the Perse on the educational map' — then newly drawn by Thring of Uppingham and his friends — in being accepted as a member of the Headmasters' Conference. Membership of the Conference is by invitation offered to Headmasters, not schools, but the Perse has since this date ranked as 'an H.M.C. school'. The first Conference had been held in 1869, and it was in 1873 that the scope of membership was widened.

When Heppenstall announced his appointment as Headmaster of Sedbergh, reaction locally showed that he had come to be greatly admired in the town, and that his reforming work had been welcomed by all except a few hardened opponents of 'the system'. The Mayor called a meeting to organise a presentation and testimonial, and we read in the *Chronicle* that 'the attendance was numerous'. A dinner was also given to him at Sidney Sussex College, which was attended by many former pupils.

VI

VICTORIAN EDUCATION: ALLEN AND THE
MAXWELL SCANDAL

Three very important movements were beginning at this time in the world of education, which were to change the pattern for the future and, in some degree, to affect the Perse. The first was the institution of public examinations, the second the development of adult education, the third the extension of secondary education to girls.

The rise of the examination system has been neatly assessed: 'If I were asked what, in my opinion, was an essential article of the Victorian faith, I should say it was, *I believe in examinations*'.[34] The eighteen-fifties saw rapid growth in the work of the various bodies established to provide external examining facilities. All the grammar schools were quickly drawn into the system, success in examinations having become essential for the claiming of grants from public funds.

The Cambridge Local Examinations Syndicate was one of the first in the field, being established in 1858. It was commissioned to examine the Perse boys in Heppenstall's time, and in his last year a Persean named G. W. Johnson scored a notable success: he was placed equal first among the whole of the Syndicate's 2333 candidates, achieved the distinction mark in Classics, English, French, Mathematics, Mechanics and Applied Mathematics, and won a half-share of the £12 prize given by the University for the first boy. St. John's College made a special award, for a number of years, of two Sizarships, one in Classics and the other in Mathematics, each tenable for two years; Johnson secured the Classical one and was placed second in the competition for Mathematics. In this same year a leading local private school, Bateman House school (afterwards acquired as the Perse Preparatory) had five successful candidates.

At first parents had to pay for entry to the examinations, but in 1899 the Governors resolved to pay half the fees of boys entering for the 'Local' papers on the Headmaster's recommendation, and the whole fee of any pupil who gained a First Class certificate. Public examinations have remained with us ever since — with the notable exception, to be considered later, that Dr. Rouse's peculiar philosophy led him to oppose the system with vehemence, so that in his time it was rare for a Perse boy to sit any outside examination other than the 'Littlego' and the college scholarship papers.

The second movement was the initiation of what would now be called further or adult education. This had began in the establishment of clubs for working men which offered educational as well as sporting facilities and were often centred on a library. One of the earliest of these was the Cambridgeshire Mechanics' Institute, established in 1835 with rooms in Sidney Street, which developed into the Cambridge Working Men's College, set up in 1855 in Market Hill. It was hoped that this would help to improve Town and Gown relations; but in fact demonstrations against the University reached a new height at this period, a particularly ugly incident occurring in 1846 when the windows of Christ's were smashed by a mob.

Most important of all was the conception of making higher education available to the commercial classes by building a new college affiliated to the university. This was achieved with the inauguration of Cavendish College, founded in 1873 by the County College Association Ltd. It took its name from the Duke of Devonshire, then Chancellor of the University and one of the main promoters. Boys were admitted at 16, and a particular welcome was given to the sons of business-men and to intending teachers. However, out of 281 students admitted between 1873 and 1885 only 64 were sons of business men, and, despite the excellent buildings, afterwards occupied by Homerton College, the 'novel experiment' did not succeed. In 1887, when a new attempt was made to put the college on its feet, the Appeal issued admitted that 'many causes contributed to depress the College'. This might almost have been written about the Perse at this time.

There are, incidentally, several points in the story of Cavendish which connect with the Perse. When the college was first opened in temporary premises at Norwich House, the first Warden was the Rev. T. J. Lawrence, an Old Persean. Among the first Directors of the 1887 Company were Prof. J. P. Postgate of Trinity, founder of a Persean family, Robert Sayle, E. B. Foster, the banker (one of the principal subscribers, who gave £5030 to the building fund to match, and surpass, the £5000 given by the Duke), and W. L. Mollison, Tutor of Clare, who lived at Pendeen House.[35] Heppenstall subscribed £5 to the fund as 'late Headmaster of the Perse', but his successor, Allen, apparently took no interest. Sayle subscribed £25.

Lawrence in his first Report as Warden administered what looks like a gratuitous snub to his old school, and one wonders if there is an interesting story behind his behaviour. He wrote that Cavendish as a new school did not threaten others, as 'one good school more at Cambridge should not injure a good school at Ely or anywhere else'.

No Old Perseans appear to have joined the college as students, but the Perse must have watched the venture with great interest. The idea of the County College for boys of 16 might be thought to have foreshadowed the modern idea of the Sixth Form College, and it is perhaps a pity that the Hills Road College which grew out of the County Boys' School did not, as was suggested, take the name of Cavendish in commemoration.

Another important development saw the beginning of the state secondary school. Local authorities had up to this point been responsible only for elementary education, but a number of authorities, including Cambridge, established so-called Higher Grade Schools, which offered some advanced studies. Before long it was apparent that the new schools in Cambridge would threaten the Perse, because they would provide a good education at a much lower cost than the Governors could offer and might mean the end of any help from the town and county councils.

The other important movement which was now gathering momentum was the campaign for secondary education for girls. Elementary education had for many years been available on the same terms for both sexes, but until this period the only more advanced schooling for girls was in the spheres supposed to be essentially feminine. The avowed purpose of such schools was either to impart a veneer of suitable 'accomplishments' or to equip pupils to be governesses, a genteel career open to women; we may look to the adventures of Anne Brontë and her sisters as illustrating this phase in educational history.

The earliest known school which offered a serious academic education for girls was the Princess Helena College, founded in 1820 in premises near Regent's Park and afterwards transferred to Preston, near Hitchin. A number of other schools of the same type followed, notably those associated with the almost legendary Miss Beale and Miss Buss and the Girls' Public Day School Trust, the last-named specifically formed to provide for girls 'the best education possible corresponding with the education given to boys in the great public schools'. The cause of female emancipation in education was greatly helped by the establishment of the Higher Local examinations in 1869, enabling girls to compete at an advanced academic level with boys, and by the foundation of Girton College in 1869[36] and Newnham in 1871.

Cambridge — characteristically, one might perhaps assert — had been backward in recognising this need, in spite of the developments in the University. Elsewhere a number of old-established grammar schools had long since recognised that their activities might well be extended to girls; in Greenwich, for example, the Chairman of the Governors of the Roan Foundation drew attention to the need as early as 1814, when he pointed out that the founder, in this case, had spoken of 'children', not 'boys', and action followed.[37] In the case of the Perse, although the school had been specifically founded for boys, it was in due course accepted that some of the funds could be diverted.

The Endowed Schools' Commission had supported the call for the establishment of girls' schools. Accordingly, the 1873 Scheme for the Perse allowed for the appointment of Managers for a Girls' School, and for the allocation of a quarter of the sum held by the Trust for its provision, the fund so formed being retained 'unless and until the school shall be provided'. The curriculum, as printed in the Scheme, would allow for German, but not for Greek, and would add Domestic Economy, the Laws of Health and Needlework. 'Unless and until the school be provided' Exhibitions and prizes could be given for meritorious scholars 'attending girls' schools not being elementary schools', or, if they thought fit, the Managers might accumulate the funds for the purpose of providing a site and building for the girls' school. The drain imposed by these provisions, even before the new school was established, was one of several difficulties which Heppenstall's successor had to accept, and the scheme made for continued financial embarrassment for many years to come.

The new headmaster was John Barrow Allen, who served from 1875 until 1883. As the following pages will show, it is not easy to pass judgment on this man's achievement. He was certainly a good scholar, and was hard-working and anxious to maintain a high standard of work. He was not afraid to criticise where criticism seemed due, but did not always face his problems in a straight-forward way. Moreover, he soon acquired the reputation of being a martinet, 'subject to somewhat unnecessary and unjustified outbursts of anger'. Thanks to his predecessor's work, he took over a school with a growing reputation, whose numbers had just increased from 119 to 175. However, his autocratic behaviour quickly lost him the goodwill with which his headmastership started, and the school achieved a degree of national disrepute, being mentioned in Parliament and in a highly critical leading article in *The Times*.

He came into the news because of incredibly inept behaviour when he decided to dismiss one of his senior masters, to whom he had taken a dislike, two terms after he took office. The master, Mr. Frederick Maxwell, had had a bad report from the Inspectors, but, instead of using this as justification for the dismissal, Allen wrote to Maxwell telling him that, since he was a Methodist, he was unacceptable to the school. 'A Churchman myself,' he wrote, 'I object to a Nonconformist colleague'. He went on to assert that the other masters did not care 'to work with a master with whom they do not care to associate out of school'.

This approach was a highly dangerous one, at a time when feeling ran high in Cambridge, not only between 'Town and Gown' but also between Church and Nonconformity; the leaders of the Town party were generally Liberal and Nonconformist, and had begun the movement, which has since persisted, of opposition to the University and to the Perse as a home of what they consider privilege.

In the tremendous row that followed, the London *Evening Standard* remarked acidly that 'if the precedent which Mr. Allen seeks to establish were generally acted upon, the educational progress of our grammar schools would be arrested every time the Headmaster was changed'. In Parliament, when the matter was raised, the minister concerned merely declared that he had no jurisdiction over the grammar schools.

Having become notorious as a religious bigot, Allen now chose to shift his ground and declare his original reason for wishing to dismiss Maxwell; he quoted the Inspector's report, implying that he had hoped to spare the master's professional pride by wounding his religious feelings instead. Upon this, Maxwell wrote to *The Times* to point out that he had had a great record of examination successes and had never before come under criticism. At the same time the Cambridge Council of Methodist Churches passed a resolution at a mass meeting condemning the 'intolerance of the recently-appointed Headmaster' and expressing sympathy with Maxwell 'in his persecution'. The Governors' point of view was given in a letter to the local press asserting that the dismissal would never have been allowed 'if the objections made against Mr. Maxwell could have been reduced to the single charge of Nonconformity'.

Heppenstall became involved in the argument. He wrote to the *Chronicle* to point out that criticism of the way the Junior School was run in his time was a criticism of himself, and complaining that the Inspector had seen only one class taken by Maxwell and then made an unfair generalisation which should have been refuted. The school staff, led by Wisken as Usher, also wrote to the press, extolling Allen and asserting that under him 'the school bids fair to rival some of our best Public Schools'. They felt that 'when Mr. Allen becomes better known many of the hard names that have been applied to him by newspaper correspondents will not only be discontinued, but their use deeply regretted.'

Feeling ran so high that the Governors were challenged to take action against the Headmaster. Mr. W. Eaden Lilley, of the well-known local firm, a Governor and a Nonconformist, wrote to say that Mr. Allen's contradictory assertions 'produce a painful impression' and demanded an extraordinary Governors' meeting. His letter went on to say that 'we do not think that a gentleman unable or unwilling to work with others of differing religious creeds, or to tolerate on his staff any against whom he chooses to allege an inferiority of social position with the majority of his staff, is qualified for the Headmastership under the scheme of this school, intended to supply the educational wants of the sons of tradesmen and others in Cambridge'.

In due course the emergency Governors' meeting was held, and the motion was actually proposed that Allen be given six months' notice. This was, however, overruled by an amendment censuring him and allowing the sentence on Maxwell to stand, though his tenure was extended for a further term; he did not avail himself of this, preferring to open a private school of his own, first in Bateman Street and afterwards in a London suburb. The Governors promised those who had sent in a 'memorial' that 'they will view with the utmost displeasure anything in the future administration of the school which may be calculated to give offence to the Nonconformist bodies'.

Lilley did not allow this to be final, but wrote a further letter to the *Chronicle* in which he enclosed a letter received from a former Cambridge magistrate who had moved away, and who now proposed a fund to finance an appeal against the dismissal and action against 'an unchristian act of intolerance'. But nothing seems to have come of this, and the school and the town settled down to 'business as usual'. Allen appeared to have 'lived down' the unhappy reputation he had acquired. However, he never quite recovered from the bad odour which the affair generated. The antagonism was made worse by the failure of the 'junior school' or commercial section — the department of which Maxwell had been in charge.

Whether or not Maxwell's dismissal had been justified, the junior school went from bad to worse under his successor, so that the official report on the department in 1882 was described as 'execrable' by the leader of the anti-Perse party in the town, a Liberal councillor named Nichols, who afterwards declared himself a socialist, and was presumably also a Nonconformist.

The Governors were gravely concerned, and took the unusual step of themselves giving notice of dismissal to all the masters in the junior school; they then, to quote Mr. Nichols, 'appointed, or caused Mr Allen to appoint, a gentleman from one of the high schools, who was supposed to be a very clever man, to take the headmastership of the junior school'; they gave him a staff of 'masters already educated in the theory and practice of teaching in one of the training colleges'.

At the Speech Day, in July, 1883, the Chairman reported all this and declared that the junior school was now beginning to make some progress, but 'had to compete under great disadvantages with the higher-grade schools in the town, which offered a good education at a very small cost, as they were enabled to do so by a Government grant' Allen spoke quite frankly of how 'the whole of that portion of the staff which had been engaged by himself' (for the junior school) had been replaced. However, both Allen and the Chairman spoke in glowing terms of the work of the senior school — 'any school of whatever eminence might be proud of the reports received from the examiners — but did not mention that the principal awards were all in mathematics. They also both commended 'the satisfactory discipline maintained in the school during the past year'.

Feeling in the town began to run high, and the 'Town versus Gown' situation was exacerbated, since it appeared that the towns-people were being cheated and their boys victimized. Critical letters appeared in the press. In particular, one gentleman signing himself 'Old Persian' wrote to the *Chronicle* about 'the deterioration which seems to be taking place in the Perse School'. If, he asked, the work of the junior school was execrable, 'what are the senior boys doing?'

A reply, written by 'Another Old Persean' (this time using the accepted spelling) sought to justify the situation, emphasising the special difficulties which obtained, not of Allen's making.

The criticisms had a more public airing when, on August 9th, they were discussed, at length and with some acrimony, by the Town Council. The main speaker, apart from Mr. Nichols, was Dr. Cooper another Liberal, whose extreme views led his party later in the year to disown him and withdraw their support. He directed his attack against Allen, on personal grounds and because under him 'the chief efforts . . of the school was (sic) to train a number of sons of persons of superior social position in the town for the University curriculum' while neglecting 'townspeople whose sons did not look forward to a University career and for whom another kind of training was more essential'. This neglect was, he asserted, a great scandal.

Mr. Nichols commented that 'he felt bound to say that there was no public school in the kingdom where there were such bad reports. He did not attribute the fault so much to the junior masters as to the senior masters, and in particular the Headmaster. It was all very well to blazon in the press the creditable achievements of the boys, past and present, who had gone to the University, but they wanted to train their youths to be good tradesmen, good citizens, as well as to go into the various professions'.

This was grossly exaggerated and unfair, despite the admitted weakness of the commercial department, but worse was to follow, when Mr. Nichols made a personal attack on the Head: 'a painful contrast,' he said, 'was in his mind between the school as it was now and as it was under that good man Mr. Heppenstall, and he certainly would express one opinion he held if no other, namely, that until the present Headmaster were removed the school would never prosper'. At this there were cries of 'Hear, hear!' Details were then given of the fall in numbers and the financial failure of the school.

Two Governors tried to present the other side of the question. One pointed out that 'the falling-off in numbers was attributable rather to the working-up of the higher-grade system than to the decadence of the Perse School'. The other said frankly that 'the public had a strong prejudice against the school, and although he, as a Governor, did not know, he had a strong suspicion that it rested with one individual'. The debate ended inconclusively, the matter being referred, rather oddly, to the Parliamentary Committee.

On 25 August the *Chronicle* published a leading article attacking the school, giving a detailed statement of the provisions of Stephen Perse's will and asserting that the discussion at the Town Council meeting 'calls for enquiry how far the will and intentions of Dr. Perse is (sic) carried out with respect to his benefactions to such natives of Cambridge, Barnwell, Chesterton and Trumpington as need help and assistance in their education. It appears desirable that those, and those only, should enjoy Dr. Perse's benefaction for whom his will designed them'. The point of this attack must have been that a number of non-Cambridge boys, presumably boarders, were in the senior school; there was, of course, also the now familiar contention that the junior school was failing in its duty.

How far the scandal led to Allen's resignation it is now hard to say, but he stayed only one further term. If his enemies drove him out, his friends gave him a fair send-off, for, at the end of the Christmas term, the masters and present and past pupils presented him with 'a testimonial consisting of a very handsome clock and candelabra.' John Wisken, as Second Master, in making the presentation 'alluded to Mr. Allen's kindness to the boys under his care and his encouragement of their sports and games: also to the pleasant relations existing between him and his colleagues'.

Maxwell, in setting up a private school of his own, added to the number already established in Cambridge, including one which revived the grand title of The Grammar School. This was kept by a Mr. Lowe at 6 Trumpington Street, and a contemporary advertisement claimed that he had then 26 former pupils at the University, 21 of whom had obtained scholarship awards.

Despite the bad odour caused by the Maxwell affair, Allen might claim a number of solid achievements during his brief tenure of office University results were throughout excellent. Social life in the school flourished, and dramatic, musical and sporting activities were vigorous. In games, new ground was broken by the development of Athletics. Allen was an innovator also in that the Old Persean Society had its origins in the sporting activities, centred on Parker's Piece and on the sporting associations of the 'Prince Regent', which he fostered. In short, he continued and developed the pioneering work of Heppenstall, and in doing this has earned the respect of the generations that have followed.

The most distinguished Persean of this period was H. F. Baker, who began an important career by winning, in 1883, the St. John's sizarship given on the results of the Local Examinations in which he gained first place in mathematics of all candidates. That sizarship had been won twice before by Perse boys, but Baker excelled in that he was 'only a few months over sixteen years of age' at the time and had consequently to decline the award.

The following year Baker was elected to the top Foundation scholar ship and went on to become a Fellow and a highly distinguished scholar; he was bracketed with three others as Senior Wrangler, won Smith's Prize and became the first Lowndean Professor of Astronomy and Geometry who was essentially a geometrician, in which sphere he established a school 'famous in and beyond the British Isles'. He wrote a number of books, one important one when he was in his eighties.

Baker retained a keen interest in the Perse, and proved himself a

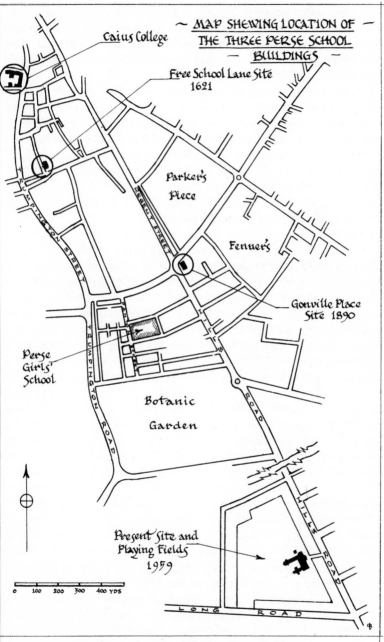

Map showing location of the three Perse Buildings

man of the widest interests. In particular, he loved the classical Greeks of whom he had been taught at school, being 'fascinated by their eager curiosity in all things natural and supernatural, their subtlety and their love of beauty, and he believed that a study of their world was as good a stimulus to a scientific life as any'.

Barnes-Lawrence's prospectus of 1895 pays tribute to both Heppenstall and Allen (whose prospectuses are largely copied) in reporting that in the fifteen years preceding his appointment in 1884 the Honours obtained at the Universities included 50 scholarships, 24 sizarships, 8 exhibitions, 5 Fellowships, 1 University scholarship, and 2 Goldsmiths' Exhibitions. Of Tripos results he reports that there were 6 Wranglers, 5 Senior Optimes and 2 Junior Optimes; while in Classics and other subjects there were 8 'Firsts' (including the senior in the Law Tripos and the senior in a Moral Sciences Tripos), 16 'Seconds' and 13 'Thirds'.

At Junior School level, it is hard to say either whether the dismal criticisms at the time of the scandal were at all justified, or whether there was, as Allen asserted, an improvement in later years. Having disposed of Maxwell, he thought the work done by 'the little boys' quite satisfactory. In 1877 his Report shows that he found everything as he would wish except for the standard of writing in the lowest form, but he said he would 'take steps to remedy this at the commencement of the ensuing term'. In 1879 the outside examiners spoke of the 'general excellence of the work of all boys' which 'bears testimony to the interest and care bestowed so equally by Mr. Allen and his staff upon the younger as well as the more advanced boys'. In 1880 Allen asserted that 'there is no reason to suppose that the teaching of the department has deteriorated in quality, and no dissatisfaction on the part of parents has been communicated to me'. He attributed the continuing fall in numbers to 'the prevailing depression in trade'. That year the staff was again reduced. Whether the work did or did not improve, materially the junior school was certainly a failure in this epoch.

The *Cambridge Chronicle*, in the last year of its life, 1934, published a series of 'Pictures of the Past' which included groups of Perseans of 1883, 1889 and 1897. In the 1883 group Allen appears as a formidable figure with heavy moustaches. A football team wears vests of horizontal stripes of white and (presumably) violet. A group of the 'upper forms' numbers 24. Most interesting is a group of 'Pelicans' — Old Perseans at Cambridge colleges — numbering eighteen and including four well-known personalities: F. E. E. Harvey, F. Heffer, P. J. Spalding and G. A. Wootten.

VII

BARNES-LAWRENCE: THE GONVILLE PLACE SCHOOL

Herbert Cecil Barnes-Lawrence (Headmaster, 1884-1901) proved to be one of the greatest of Perse Headmasters.[38] Educated at King's School, Canterbury, Durham School, and Lincoln College, Oxford, he had taught at Manchester Grammar School and Giggleswick. When he was appointed he found the Perse ranking high among schools of its class and acknowledged to be outstanding in its academic record. Yet there were many unsatisfactory features, which must have made his task a challenging one. The Free School Lane buildings had long been hopelessly inadequate; there were no facilities for games; the provision of the girls' school, though obviously necessary, was an acute financial embarrassment; equipment and facilities in both schools were below the standard that parents and staff had a right to expect. Feeling in the town sometimes ran high against the school, and recent events had increased the animosity. Altogether the very existence of the school might be in question.

The new Head tackled his problems urgently and energetically. In March, 1887, he felt ready to make a bid to save the situation. He began by issuing a strongly-worded Appeal, in the name of the Governors, setting out the desperate need to augment the endowment. He distinguished three main objectives, which he set out in the following terms:

(i) To make provision for the maintenance of the standard of education now required by the Scheme of Management;

(ii) To make provision for securing the permanent maintenance and union of the Grammar school and the Commercial school;

(iii) To make possible the early removal of the school to a more suitable position and the erection of New Buildings adequate to its increasing wants.

This Appeal, which opened the 'Queen Victoria Fund', a distinct endowment fund, was issued in March, 1887.[39] In acknowledgement

of the title, subscriptions were invited to be paid annually on 20 June,
the anniversary of the Queen's Accession. A copy of the Appeal is
preserved in the City Library.

The document begins by setting out the urgent financial difficulties
in which the school now found itself:

'We, the Governors of the Perse Schools, desire to lay before the
Town, County and University of Cambridge the financial condition of
the Perse School for Boys. It will be a surprise to many to be told that
since the original bequest of Dr. Stephen Perse in 1615 the School
endowment has not been augmented by any benefactions public or
private. The income of the school is derived from (a) school fees; (b)
interest on certain moneys in the Funds; (c) the rent of a farm in
Essex. This rent has been lately reduced through the depression in
agriculture.'

The statement goes on to give details of expenditure, which included
the requirement of the official Scheme of Management to provide free
education for the foundationers and to make provision for the girls'
school. The total annual expenditure amounted to £1,840, while the
total income was £1,526. 'The deficit is entirely accounted for by the
falling-off in the rent of the farm and by the contribution to the Perse
School for Girls. There is little hope of improvement in the rental of
the farm, and the contribution to the Girls' School, which has
conferred a great benefit to the Town of Cambridge, is an essential part
of the Scheme'. Moreover, the Girls' School then existing was itself in
debt through its recent removal, in April 1883, from its original
premises in Trumpington Street, close to St. Catharine's'[40] to Panton
House, which was a leasehold property with five years still to run. It is
described as having 'the peculiar advantage of a large and secluded
garden for exercise and recreation'.

Apart from the deficit and the need for new buildings, the appeal
points out, there are 'further deficiences and drawbacks. There are no
Open Scholarships to help deserving boys or retain clever ones; the
two school-rooms, many of the class-rooms, and the furniture are alike
inconvenient, antiquated and in bad condition'. Yet, in spite of all,
'Under the present Headmaster and his Staff the School is in a very
satisfactory condition in point of numbers, discipline and success. The
numbers have increased from 91 in 1884 to 175 at the present time'.

The Appeal succeeded to a sufficient extent, to allow the building of a
new school. This had been in the Governors' minds for many years,
and there was a clause in the 1873 scheme stating that they might at
any time remove the school to 'some other convenient site and provide

*The Gonville Place School: exterior showing the 1890 Hall
and (beyond) the 1934 addition; the Fives Courts on the left*

thereon convenient buildings with a place for cricket and other games';
for this purpose they might 'expend such capital sums as may from
time to time be sanctioned by the Charity Commissioners'.

It was now possible to provide the buildings, but not the playing-
fields; it is interesting that the latter were specified in the 1873
scheme as of equal importance. The site now chosen was, of course,
that in Hills Road, close to Gonville Place, and we shall refer to it as
'Gonville Place' to avoid confusion with the later school. It was
opposite the Roman Catholic Church which was at that time under
construction. The architect for the school was W. M. Fawcett, and the
cost of the work was £14,500. The formal Opening Ceremony was
performed by the Rt. Hon. H. C. Raikes, then Postmaster-General, on
4 December 1890. The *Pelican* reports that there were many speeches
on a variety of subjects, but 'the toast of the School . . . was relegated
to the tail of the procession and did not come on till almost 5.30, when

the audience was rapidly thinning and everybody was beginning to feel that he had had about enough of it. The company did not disperse until nearly 6.30'. The Headmaster held an At Home in the evening.

Like the old school in Free School Lane, the new one was mainly notable for its fine hall — known, like the old one, as the 'Big (or sometimes Large) Room' — which had a fine queen-post timber roof, worthy to succeed the beautiful Jacobean hall of the original building. Both inside and out this hall was attractive. From the road it was virtually all there was to see of the school, and it was surmounted by a central cupola carrying a pelican weather-vane; a central door-way, added in the 1930's, on the whole enhanced the effect, as did the Virginia creeper that was allowed to grow to soften the red-brick.[41] Two porches, one leading to the hall and the other to the Masters' room, flanked this central feature. A brick niche over the hall-porch was never filled, as had no doubt been intended, with the founder's effigy. Inside the walls were unplastered, relieved in a memorable way by the roof, by the wooden balcony on the east side, and by the painted honours-boards, naming former Head-boys and those who became Fellows of Colleges. (How many schools, one may ask, can speak of a 'Fellowship-board' as a familiar feature?). There were also shields, detailing individually the academic distinctions of old boys. The provision of these was an idea of 'B.L.' himself; they were first installed at Free School Lane, and the *Pelican* said slyly that 'we may remark they are not wholly unconnected with the desk-lids in the old Big School'. Barnes-Lawrence's Report for 1884 records that 'nearly thirty memorial shields, including one to the late Professor Palmer, have been placed on our walls, following an appeal to old boys to subscribe to the fund. The balcony led to three upper classrooms, and was the traditional perch of Old Perseans at functions. The balcony stairs were out of bounds during school hours to all except those going to the centre classroom. High up at the northeast and south-east angles were two rather curious features, semi-circular convex shapes, panelled in wood and supported by something suggesting a Gothic fan-vault, the whole a little like a pulpit with no opening at the top. These usually intrigued newcomers, who wondered what their function could be, until they discovered, by going upstairs, that they provided access to the end classrooms of the upper floor.

The furniture in the hall consisted of a series of long wooden desks, as for a lecture-room, which continued in use until 1930. Three masters' desks stood either at the far end or under the balcony. Lighting, until the 'thirties, was by gas, at first a series of fish-tail

The Gonville Place Hall 1953. Showing the Fellowship Board and Honours Shields and (high on right) the 'pulpit' leading to upstairs classrooms. A Headmaster's period is in progress

burners radiating like spokes, and later a sophisticated type of lamp, with wall-switches to actuate a bye-pass. There was no permanent stage; and when, later on, plays and concerts took place here, a temporary platform on trestles had to be arranged, blocking the way to the Head's room and the masters' room.[42]

The remainder of the building fell much below the architectural achievement of the hall. There were twelve classrooms, a Headmaster's room and staff-room, an ample cloakroom, and a small library, which was later used as a prefects' room, and subsequently as the Bursar's office. Toilets and washing-facilities were very limited, and there was no provision for serving meals. Modifications and improvements were made when funds permitted. The two most serious omissions were science laboratories and gymnasium; the first need was later supplied, but no satisfactory gymnasium was ever built on the site.

The Fives Courts in front of the school, added in 1893, served to compensate in some measure for the lack of games facilities. The gravelled playground was used also as a parade-ground for Corps and Scouts; it had obvious disadvantages in being close to a busy road.

It must have been apparent, even within a few years of the move to Gonville Place, that it was a dreadfully restricted site.

A pleasant feature, common to schools of the era, but lacking in modern buildings, was the school bell, rung by the porter from a rope just inside the cloakroom, which signalled the beginning of each session to boys in the playground and to residents in the surrounding area. Not so pleasant were the bells of the Catholic church, whose clock chimed every quarter-hour. Since lessons were of 45 minutes and there were no clocks in the class-rooms, the chimes were of some use. Occasionally, too, hymn-tunes were played on the carillon, creating a great nuisance to classes. Masters often had to stop their lessons during the performance, especially at eleven and around twelve o'clock (when the Sanctus bell rang). The Governors made representations to the church authorities on several occasions, but these had little effect, except that the chimes were usually switched off during concerts and other special functions.

An interesting event of the period was the transfer of the choirboys of Trinity College to the Perse. The college had had a private school for its choristers at various times, but no records survive to show when one was first established. It appears that about 1840 the school was run jointly with St. John's and that in the sixties it was similarly held jointly with King's (a minute in the record-book at Trinity records that on 12 November 1870 a committee was appointed to discuss with

King's the 'question of the separation of the choristers of King's and Trinity').

In 1896 Trinity finally decided to close its school, and the Perse Governors were asked whether the choir-boys could be taken at Gonville Place. Barnes-Lawrence replied, giving full details and enclosing a prospectus. The Junior Dean made an agreement with the Governors, at first insisting that the fees paid should be at the under 13 rate, irrespective of age, a concession which was later withdrawn. Apparently, the Trinity boys wore the College gown at school, at least on occasion, for Rouse, when he instituted the weekly school singing, observed that 'there must be many boys in the school possessed of some vocal talent besides the select few who sport the Trinity gown'.

The Perse owes a great deal to Trinity College. In 1884 when some almshouses attached to the college were closed, the endowments were diverted to found scholarships for boys leaving the school, and Trinity Leaving Scholarships as such were established in 1909. Among the many Trinity personalities who did much for the school should be mentioned Sir J. J. Thomson, his son, the O.P. Sir G. P. Thomson, and Sir James and Lady Frazer (of 'Golden Bough' fame) who concerned themselves especially with the French teaching initiated by de Glehn and Chouville. Trinity have for many years had a representative on the Board of Governors. Further, it is on Trinity land that the playing-fields and the new school came to be established.

Barnes-Lawrence earned universal respect. He was a tall dignified, kindly man, with impressive features and a commanding presence, an urbane manner and gentle speech. A fine scholar, he had excellent taste and a sense of style something of which was transmitted to his pupils. He was a good disciplinarian, as T. F. Teversham and H. P. Cooke, both of whom have written reminiscences of him, aver. 'Barney had a long cane' and maintained a high tone in the school. He was tactful, but could be severe when the occasion so required; beneath his friendly manner 'one sensed that no nonsense would be tolerated'. He set a standard, and insisted on its maintenance, of thoroughness and accuracy in work and above all in speech. 'It was impossible even for a schoolboy without a due sense of shame to murder the English tongue in his presence . . . All that was vulgar or childish or mean shrivelled and died in his presence. If he seemed above all of a scholarly temper, he was also a man of the world in the best sense of that term'.[43] In the little volume of essays he wrote, entitled *The Days of our Youth*, Cooke summed up his memories of the Perse in these words: 'There are many, both masters and boys, I recall with delight and advantage . . . One figure abides above all, great as gentleman, master and scholar. I mean Herbert Cecil Barnes-Lawrence, most courtly and tactful of Heads'.

The Rev. A. W. Smith has provided a description of his first encounter with 'Barney' on his first day at the Perse in 1899: 'I was one of the many country boys who journeyed daily on the Haverhill line; country boys did not have the same status as town boys. On arrival at the school there I stood, a lonely little boy by the fives-courts. Then B.L. called to the bigger boys to give me a little practice at the courts. Immediately I felt welcome'.

Wisken continued in office as Second Master until 1891, when he retired; he died in 1914. The next Second Master was an equally notable figure, Robert Russ Conway, who served with Barnes-Lawrence until they both left for Weymouth College. At Weymouth Conway was Second Master and Bursar until 'Barney's' retirement, when he in turn became Headmaster. The College is now defunct. Conway, an Old Haileyburian, was a distinguished athlete, having run for Cambridge in the mile and cross-country and became President of the C.U. Hare and Hounds — which office he held throughout his career at the Perse (1888-1902). He was also a good cricketer and, devoted to all games, was known to have subsidised the Perse Games Fund from his own pocket. He was a fine teacher, who understood boys and had a sense of humour. Incidentally, he, like Caldwell Cook and de Glehn after him, liked to wear knickerbockers, which custom earned him the nickname of 'Bockers'. The last years of his life were marred by arthritis, and he was eventually bed-ridden. He died in 1950.

The 1895 Prospectus lists twelve assistant masters, with a Miss Adam (in charge) and a further master in the Preparatory department. The division into the Classical and Commercial sides was still accepted. We have an account of life in the Commercial side from Mr. Teversham, who was at school from 1894 to 1899. He records that the staff there were largely undergraduates, 'many of them ignorant' — though he remembers that at one time it included Rushmore, subsequently a master at the Higher Grade and Second Master at the Perse. The Master in Charge of the Department was W. R. Gurley, a choral scholar of King's, who was, not surprisingly, an excellent musician, but struck Teversham as 'an awful snob, whose ignorance was really appalling'. On the other hand, R. S. Swann-Mason earned general admiration, especially because he was 'a splendid cricketer'.

Three staff of the period became notable in the University. Rushmore became Master of St. Catharine's, while J. H. Widdicombe (1892-

1895) became Fellow and Tutor of Downing (he was also at one time captain of the county cricket team) and G. H. A. Wilson (1896) became Master of Clare and a University M.P.[44] W. E. Phillip (1895-6) had been a Fellow of Clare. T. H. Easterfield (1895) subsequently became Professor of Chemistry at Wellington, New Zealand.

Another notable member of staff, in the period before the Prospectus just described, was George Edward Jackson, who was headmaster of the Junior School from 1876 to 1881, and, with his sister, managed a boarding-house. He was a mathematician from Magdalen, and had taught at Liverpool College before coming to the Perse. When he left he became Headmaster of Odiham Grammar School, Hants., a school with Cambridge connections, advertising regularly in the local press. Jackson earned a reputation for thorough teaching, friendliness and deadly bowling on the cricket-field.

Among distinguished O.P.'s of the time was C. E. Ayerst, who, as Assistant Commissary-General, was assassinated at Poona in 1897.

The school flourished academically under Barnes-Lawrence, more than ever before. At a time when standards were steadily rising, his staff achieved a remarkable number of scholarships and Tripos successes at the Universities, a number going to his own Oxford. In 1900, when Harold Cooke won his scholarship at University College, the question was asked, 'What other public school in the United Kingdom can exult in an average of four scholarships a year on every fifty boys (the number in the Classical school)?' In 1896 there were forty Old Perseans at Cambridge, a truly remarkable record for so small a school.

Financially, however, there continued to be problems, aggravated by the costs of establishing the new school and maintaining the girls' school. By now the public had long become used to appeals for help from the foundation, as a poem in one of the early *Pelican*s, that for July 1891, shows. It is entitled 'An appeal from the Perse School to the Townsmen of Cambridge' and runs thus:

> Will there never come a season
> Which shall rid us of the curse
> Of Appeals, unmet, unanswered,
> For an impecunious Perse;[45]
> When our Townsmen cease to wonder
> That we thrive not as of yore
> Now our income is diminished
> By two-thirds or even more?

Various committees 'considered the financial condition of the school' and in 1893 the Charity Commissioners were asked to inspect the affairs of the Trust. The Frating property had now become a positive liability. While the school itself was 'carried on without a loss' in most years, the cost of repairs on the farm was so heavy that by 1894 there was an overdraft of £1,174 at the bank. Throughout the 'nineties there was an annual deficit 'contracted mainly by expenditure at Frating'. In the consequent economy drive the staff were the worst sufferers, and it was stated frankly that their salaries were 'deplorably low'. The outcome was a further public Appeal, dated 10 June 1893, the wording of which shows how very grave the situation had become:

The Governors can only suggest one of two alternatives. Either the working expenses must be reduced or the income must be increased. The Governors see no immediate prospect of an improvement in the income derived from the farm, and the only way of immediately diminishing expenditure would be to turn the school into a second-grade school which would cease to prepare boys for the University. They think such a change in the character of the school would be a serious misfortune for the inhabitants of the town of Cambridge.

The Appeal drew attention to two continuing needs; (i) the establishment of scholarships or bursaries for deserving boys attending or leaving the school; and (ii) the provision of a playground, i.e., a playing-field, which was especially needed for the younger boys. Again a landmark in the Queen's reign was used in an attempt to attract funds. It was proposed, when a meeting was called at the Guildhall to make plans for celebrations, that 'assistance to the Perse Schools . . . is a proper manner of commemorating the Queen's (Diamond) Jubilee'. However, nothing came of this, though the occasion was honoured in extending the boys' summer holiday for 'one additional week'.

Despite all the financial worries, the reputation of the Perse continued to rise, helped by the new buildings. Science, in response to popular demand, now began to take a real place in the curriculum. Previously, although the provision of science teaching had been often urged, only very elementary work, such as could be done in an ordinary class-room, had been possible. Wisken, as has been mentioned, used to give lectures, after school hours, on botany and chemistry, and Lewis, styled science master from 1873 until 1882, tried to cover a vast subject without any proper facilities. Barnes-Lawrence, in arguing the case, wrote in his Report for 1890 that, 'Although Classics and Mathematics will, I trust, long continue to be the staple of instruction here . . . it is precisely because I see the waste of time and energy in some cases over uncongenial studies that I venture to support the growing and just demand for science teaching'.

The Perse was distinctly behind the national trend in introducing
scientific and technical education. Rugby, under Dr. Temple, had
introduced science classes on a voluntary basis from 1859 and compulsorily in 1864. Uppingham had opened woodwork shops in 1862
and a new 'scientific workshop' in 1882; metalwork was added in
1884. The first science laboratories in Cambridge University were
erected in 1863. In the field of examinations, the Cambridge Local
Examinations Syndicate had first offered science papers in 1878.

The first Perse laboratory was a separate building, tacked on to the
school, as Arthur Hawkins observed, 'by the simple expedient of
filling in the space between the back of the school and the boundary
wall. Since these were not parallel a peculiarly-shaped room was
produced, with only two parallel walls'. It was, however, quite large,
and was well equipped for its time. There was a separate store-room,
and a balance-room and a room for fume-chambers were also provided
— the latter with vents near to the Headmaster's room! 'In those days,
white paint without lead was unknown; so that by the end of each
term the walls had turned dark brown. They were brightened by
washing with hydrogen peroxide.'[46]

The adjoining class-room, room 1, the windows of which had
become 'borrowed lights' into the new laboratory, was put into use as
a science lecture-room, the master's desk being replaced by a long
demonstration bench. At a later date two further class-rooms, rooms 2
and 3, were fitted out as additional laboratories; before they were
equipped they were regarded as science-rooms rather than labs. By the
'twenties room 2 had been equipped as a reasonably adequate physics
laboratory, and the annexe building became exclusively a chemistry
laboratory. In the late 'twenties room 3 (under the balcony) was made
into a biology laboratory — of a very makeshift character, with trestle
tables on stilts instead of benches and with no supply of water or gas; a
connecting door was made allowing use to be made of the facilities in
room 2.

Science teaching received a great stimulus from the setting up of the
Science and Art Department at South Kensington. The Department
had grown out of the Great Exhibition of 1851 and was at first under
the aegis of the Board of Trade, its purpose being to 'foster the competi-
tive position of British industry' through the sciences and arts. It came to
play a vital part in education through the payment of grants to
secondary and higher-grade schools, and it also helped to finance the
technical colleges, polytechnics and civic universities which were being
developed at the time. However, it imposed strict conditions and close

supervision which often made the grants unacceptable, as the Perse was to find.

In November 1894, the Governors decided to apply to the Depart ment for its sanction in the formation of an 'organised science school' as part of the Commercial side of the Perse. In the following June (1895) the Governors resolved that the Headmaster 'be authorised to take the preliminary steps necessary for the institution of organised science classes in the school' and 'to make the necessary alterations in the laboratory required by the Science and Art Department'. The Governors constituted themselves, 'in our corporate capacity, a Committee for the superintendence of a Science class to be held'. Funds to operate the new class were applied for from the Department and from the local Technical Education Committee. It was, however, the Borough Council who, by giving a grant, made the building of the Science (Chemistry) Laboratory possible.

The support now forthcoming was insufficient, and the conditions imposed by the Science and Art Department were not easy for an impoverished foundation to discharge; moreover, an Inspection led, in 1899, to criticisms (received in March 1900) of the 'final arrange ments of the school as a school of science' which, however, the Inspectors afterwards withdrew. In June 1900 the comment was made, by the Governors, that 'the Headmaster, who under our Scheme of Management is supposed to have full control of the internal organisation of the school, finds his authority circumscribed in matters relating to the Organised Science School and the Commercial department generally'. Consequently, in June 1901, it was 'resolved that the Headmaster be authorised to make arrangements for dropping the Organised Science School after mid-summer next, so far as the changes which cannot be conveniently postponed are concerned'.

In charge of science teaching during this vital but frustrating period was J. H. Widdicombe, whose organisation and teaching resulted in the Perse gaining five Scholarships and Exhibitions to the University in three years.

Barnes-Lawrence was no narrow academic. Like Heppenstall and Allen, he recognised the importance of games, and continued their work in this sphere with great energy. It was he who having long campaigned for a school 'playground' arranged with Caius to rent a private ground, rather than depending on Parker's Piece. The ground, which was first used at mid-summer 1888, two years before the move to Gonville Place, adjoined Fenner's and was later used for the tennis-courts which are still in use. What became the University cricket ground, originally the private ground of a Mr. Fenner, was first let as such in 1848. A number of Old Perseans[47] have written about games on this field, which was rough, having, not many years previously, been 'a flourishing wheat-field'. The boys were asked to pay a subscription towards the rent, but were slow to do so. In consequence the tenancy was given up in 1883, but the College, aware that it would be sold the following year, allowed a further year at a generously reduced rate. Barnes-Lawrence then searched energetically for a new field, writing to the Master of Trinity in particular to ask his help, and forming a 'Playground Committee' which continued under Dr. Rouse, when a permanent solution to the problem was found.

To allow a programme of school games to continue, Barnes-Lawrence made temporary arrangements, including the use of college grounds out of university term. In 1900 a field at Newnham, not suitable for cricket, was in use. In 1902 there were negotiations with St. John's for a field in Madingley Road, and later a field in Cherryhinton Road was considered. It was only in 1905 that Trinity leased the ground in Luard Road which was eventually to become the site of the rebuilt school; this did not become Perse property until 1908.

The non-sporting societies of the time included a very successful Orchestral Society and a Chess Club. Years before the idea became fashionable, there was an annual Hobbies' Exhibition, forming part of the Prize-giving proceedings. It is known that Barnes-Lawrence took a special interest in the encouragement of out-of-school pursuits of all kinds, being thus years ahead in his thinking. There was also a cycling club; on one outing 'every machine ran away with its rider'.

Certainly Barnes-Lawrence started the school Debating Society, which was to grow into the Union Society, and the *Pelican* magazine, which developed from Allen's 'Christmas Annual'. In his last year he firmly established the Old Persean Society — which, as has been shown, really began in 1883. The *Pelican* was advertised for sale 'to those interested in the Perse School' at 1s. 6d. annually, post free, Vol. 1 covering the years 1889 and 1890. The Perse thus owes a tremendous amount to Barnes-Lawrence, who instituted a number of important activities which have survived.

Many of the rules and conditions which obtained at this time continued into Rouse's time and beyond. In particular, the hours worked included half-holidays on Tuesdays, Thursdays and Saturdays, and the lesson times were from 9 to 12 and from 2 to 4, but 9 to 12.45 on the half-days. Holidays were much as they are today; the prospectus states that 'the midsummer holidays last approximately seven weeks'.

Perhaps Barnes-Lawrence's most engaging quality was that he positively enjoyed the task he undertook at the Perse of building up an institution which had, after an erratic history, reached a time of crisis when its survival was in question. In this, of course, he repeated what his predecessors had done, for all of them, and especially Heppenstall, had had to work very hard to 'keep the ship afloat'. Heppenstall had declared that he looked upon himself as a 'restorer of decayed schools' and he went on to rescue Sedbergh from an even grimmer situation. Barnes-Lawrence is recorded as saying, 'I seem to have followed in his steps with Perse and Weymouth' — and certainly he, more than all his predecessors, could claim that when he left for Weymouth College the Perse was at last in a reasonably strong position.

In his letter of resignation, Barnes-Lawrence spoke of his time in Cambridge as 'years of continual struggle against the adverse fates which have pressed so heavily upon the school'. He continued to suggest to the Governors that 'though I have never despaired of its future it may well be that a younger man should now grapple with the difficulties'.

Those words did not overstate the problem facing the next Headmaster; and the Governors may well have despaired of finding a young man of the necessary calibre to take over the direction of the school. But they found Dr. Rouse — chosen from 52 applicants (all the Governors but one, who abstained, voted for him) — who proved to be undoubtedly the greatest Perse Head of all.

VIII

DOCTOR ROUSE

William Henry Denham Rouse (1863-1950) came to the Perse when he had already made his name. He had had a brilliant career at Cambridge, being a Scholar and then a Fellow of Christ's; the College, later in his life (1933) further recognised his worth by making him an Honorary Fellow. He could have commanded a high position in the academic world, and did hold the post of University Teacher of Sanskrit (under the Special Board of Indian Studies) from 1903 to 1939, for, born in Calcutta, he had studied the ancient Indian languages as well as the Classics.

He was, as he recalled in a little brochure he wrote after his retirement, entitled *To Young Teachers*, 'forced into schoolmastering by circumstances . . . I was driven or guided into school work against by own ambitions, and I am thankful it was so; I can tell young people that there is no more satisfying or more delightful work for life than the care of boys and girls'.

His first teaching posts were at Bedford (1886-88), Cheltenham (1890-95) and Rugby (1896-1901). While at Rugby he wrote the school history, published in the 'English Public Schools' series by Duckworth and Co. in 1898.

He seems to have made a somewhat shaky start and to have had at first some difficulty with 'class management' — which made him patient with the one or two poor disciplinarians who later served on his staff. At the Perse, though he was not a headmaster that boys feared, he maintained always an excellent 'tone' in the school.

He had come to feel that a teacher in a great public school was circumscribed by tradition, and is said to have contemplated abandoning teaching and becoming a barrister. He was looking for a post where he would be free to develop his very individual ideas, and the Perse offered exactly that. Like Heppenstall and Barnes-Lawrence before him, he felt that it was for him good fortune to find a school which was in low

William Henry Denham Rouse, Litt.D. Headmaster, 1902-1928

water, 'and which nobody cared about; consequently, they did leave us alone without meddling'.

The breadth of his interests is shown by his having become F.R.G.S., M.R.A.S., and President of the Folklore Society. He had travelled very extensively as an award-winning student in his youth, and in later life he would go abroad whenever he could, whether to the countless summer-schools and conferences he attended, or to his beloved Greek islands, where he often went by himself and sometimes as a popular lecturer for the Hellenic Travellers' Club.

He was an amazing worker, full of energy and vitality, for, in addition to his school responsibilities, he earned his Doctorate of Letters, awarded in February, 1903, by writing and editing countless texts in the classics and in English; in particular, he was Editor of the Loeb Classical Library and of Blackie's 'Highways and Byways of English Literature' and was joint Editor of the *Classical Review* from 1907 to 1920. His career as a writer had begun when he edited the Christ's College magazine — which, later on, in welcoming his return to Cambridge, mentioned his long connection with its management and editing: 'His initials appear below an article in the first number, issued in 1886, and have been familiar to our readers ever since'. A frequent correspondent of the *Times*, his letters to that organ, though usually on educational topics, covered also such subjects as Italian trains and the design of postage stamps.

He was not at first sight an impressive figure.[48] He was short of stature and portly of build. He walked with short, shuffling steps, hardly lifting his feet, which were clad always in half-Wellingtons, yet with a peculiar majesty; and he rode his bicycle with an equally strange and individual dignity, perhaps because he was also a good horseman, out riding at six on most mornings. His cycling technique was due in part to there being an enormous bag slung within the frame of the machine, stuffed with books and papers, so that he could ride only with his legs wide apart. When he walked his cycle across the playground, holding only the near-side handlebar, he seemed to be leading it, as if it were indeed a horse.

He could look impressive, and was especially so on Speech Days, when, resplendent in his scarlet gown, he seemed to outshine the distinguished speakers he had invited down for the occasion.

In walking he habitually stuck both hands into his jacket pockets, with the thumbs outside. He always wore a neat beard, and it was often said that he looked more like a farmer or a sea-captain than a headmaster. The fascination he exerted over everyone he met lay most in his eyes, which sparkled continuously with wit, pleasure, mischief and, if need be, anger. He could sigh with singular eloquence. Altogether, small though he was, he had an unmistakable 'presence' and commanded respect wherever he went. Perhaps his personality came out most at the morning and evening assemblies in the school hall, which he frequently took by himself. No hymns were sung, nor was there usually a Lesson. He read always the same well-loved prayers, taken from the Book of Common Prayer and the Rugby Prayer Book; but he read them so well that the listener never tired of them. A great source of his charm, shown then, was his beautiful voice, enhanced by great skill in reading and interpreting. On the front of his classroom desk was the little couplet (written out fine by one of his favourite pupils) giving advice which he always followed:

> Learn to read slow: all other graces
> Will follow in their proper places.

He spoke, as Louis de Glehn put it, 'in a gentle and occasionally incisive tone, as one having inward authority'.

In short, he achieved the difficult position of being at once dignified and genial. Even the most insensitive of the boys recognised that they had a great man in their midst. To the school as a whole he was 'The Old Man' or often 'The Old Boy', a name which fittingly emphasised his youthful outlook. The lower school looked on him with affectionate awe, but to the Sixth Form, who knew him best, he was truly 'Guide, philosopher and friend'. He liked his old pupils to call him Orbilius — a name which neatly suggested the English 'Billy' as well as the schoolmaster of the poet Horace.

Always gentle and considerate, he was generally anxious to respect another's point of view; but on certain matters he was intolerant, as when he spoke of the activities of politicians and administrators whom he despised and classed as 'stupid people' (pronouncing the 'u' as a disdainful short syllable).

One matter on which he did assert himself was smoking. He insisted that, since boys would not be allowed to smoke, staff should not do so at school; consequently, break-time normally saw several masters, including Caldwell Cook, promenading in Harvey Road to enjoy a cigarette. He himself smoked on occasion, but never in the school or in the company of boys.

Rouse had many unusual ideas, and his enemies might call him a crank — and did so freely. Some of his ideas were old-fashioned and some many years ahead of his time. He disliked many modern inventions, including motor cars and especially motor bicycles; he always used the full names, with a long second 'o' to the 'motor' — speaking with a delicately-implied nausea. He would speak of car drivers and motor cyclists as having 'made friends with the mammon of unrighteousness'. He disliked equally the cinema — above all when it abused the word 'epic' — wireless, when it came in, and, most of all, the telephone, which he called 'the greatest modern curse'. There was never a telephone at the school in his time, nor was there (except, one recalls, for the use of the O.T.C.) a typewriter. The Secretary, 'Daddy' Broome, did all the correspondence in long-hand.

Indeed, the good Doctor had an almost Erewhonian horror of machinery, or at least of machines more complicated than watches and pedal-cycles, and was convinced that they would eventually enslave mankind. In the nineteen-seventies, with such things as television, computers, the Concorde air liner, an expensively mechanised post-office and juggernaut lorries as an every-day part of life, we may well feel that in this matter, as in much else, he was greatly in advance of his age. His feelings are enshrined in one of his most polished pieces of writing, a pamphlet designed to introduce the Loeb series entitled *Machines or Mind?* In this he deplores mankind's growing dependence on machines and points out that 'Civilisation lies in the mind and soul, not in machines'. The pamphlet goes on, as one would expect, to offer readers the classical literatures 'to employ your leisure. They will not earn you one shilling of money, or build one motor car; but they will fill your mind with wisdom and beauty'.

He became reconciled to the gramophone and to wireless, because he came to appreciate that both helped to spread an appreciation of good music. It was, however, only in his retirement that a wireless-set (they were not then called radios) came into his house, when he provided one for his staff at Histon Manor. Then, as Eric Warmington recalls, after hearing the sound of a Bach cantata coming from the kitchen quarters, he tried thereafter never to miss a Bach programme when performed. He loved Bach and Beethoven above other composers, and had all the Beethoven string-quartets, cloth-bound in a fine series, in his bookcase.

In the educational world there were two matters which Rouse disliked intensely. One was the public examination system; the other the bureaucratic control of education by 'huge parasitic bodies, County and City Education Offices, with Directors, Inspectors and hordes of clerks, besides the Board of Education (as it then was) at the top'. The comment is taken from an article in the London *Evening News* of

30/31 January in 1928, in which he gave full reign to his feelings on
both topics.

Examinations, he argued, are 'quite misleading as a guide to
comparative merit' and had been designed in the first place for children
who would not be going to universities and therefore might require a
paper qualification at a lower level. Some headmasters, at Leeds
Grammar School, for example, had welcomed public examinations to
test the efficiency of school staffs, and at the Perse John Barrow Allen
had taken the same view.

On a more political note — and this is by no means unimportant in
the context — Harvey Goodwin had said of examinations that 'We
want something which shall endear us to the middle classes'. Rouse
assumed that his boys would either go to the universities or be
employed locally, and that in the latter case his word ought to suffice;
thus the system seemed irrelevant to his work.

It is perhaps ironical that the buildings where he worked are now the
offices of the Cambridge Examinations Board (or Local Examinations
Syndicate). No boy at the Perse in Rouse's time took a School
Certificate examination unless his parents absolutely insisted. The only
examinations he approved were the University and College Entrance
and Scholarship papers — and these, he maintained, could be taken in
a boy's stride. There was, however, a very well organised internal
examination system, which certainly tested the work done in the
Perse. Outside examiners, usually Cambridge dons and sometimes Old
Perseans, set and marked the papers, and their Reports were printed,
bound in volumes and preserved. This was another of Heppenstall's
ideas, and common practice in the public schools of the time, and
Rouse, like Barnes-Lawrence, was happy to continue it. The set of
Reports preserved today in the archives goes back to 1870 (the system
lapsed in 1928). Occasionally, too, a 'holiday task' book was given out
to be read in preparation for a test at the beginning of term; it would
always be a classic, such as Erasmus' *Praise of Folly* or Prescott's
Conquest of Peru. Those studying the Classics and Modern Languages
would also be set specialised holiday reading. Occasionally a General
Knowledge Test was given to the whole school. This would be prepared
by the Doctor himself and printed, and a copy has been preserved of a
rather clever one used in September 1924.

Rouse's attitude to bureaucracy is illustrated in the story of how,
when asked how he managed as Headmaster to cope with the required
paper-work and carry on his full programme of teaching, he said
simply, 'I realised from the beginning that any letter from the Board

which had not answered itself within three months was not worth answering.'

In a paper read at the conference on new ideals in education, held in Bristol in 1932, he expressed the opinion that the policy of the Board of Education had been mischievous for many years because they interfered in the minutest details, and the time of Inspectors, he said, was largely taken up with work which an uneducated clerk could do.

Outside teaching and the world of scholarship, his main interest, as has been mentioned, was in travel and outdoor life. He also greatly enjoyed food and drink, and, of course, old books. Presents to his friends took the form of books or bottles of brandy or sherry. The specially favoured were privileged to enjoy Waterloo sherry, Napoleon brandy or that prince of sweet white wine, Château d'Yquem. He liked his beer — though he would lament that, as with so many other things, it was not what it had been before 1914. He enjoyed excellent health, and continued to do so after his retirement, when he spent twenty golden years at Histon Manor. Many of his old pupils will remember a visit to the Manor with special delight; it was an experience not easily forgotten. He would usually be discovered in his library, surrounded by his treasures, and possibly literally hidden by them, or at the top of a ladder among them. Visitors were most graciously received and hospitably entertained. He used to invite the sixth form — successors to those he had taught — to read Greek with him, and regular parties of Girton students. An invitation to tea on a Sunday often included the cryptic warning 'Nymphs expected' which was a promise of Girton company.

His love of old books, and especially of those beautifully bound, was communicated to his friends. When about to leave Histon, he had to disperse his library, which he did by dividing it mainly between his school and his college, with generous gifts elsewhere. Each received around 3,000 volumes. 'There was no wholesale throwing-out, no haste to be through with a distasteful business, but each book was looked at and commented upon, almost as a living thing, and his cheerfulness and at times almost hilarity during this painful parting was something that can never be forgotten.'[,9] As an expert on old books, Rouse was often to be found at the market stall in Cambridge of the famous 'David'; he introduced many of his pupils to him, and when the old bookseller died the Doctor wrote a special little book as a tribute to him. David's son was a boy at the school.

Despite an amazing memory, the Doctor was occasionally absent-minded. A story often told records how during the First World War, when he was an officer in the Officers' Training Corps, he one morning rode to school dressed completely in khaki except for a bowler hat! F. A. Rayner (afterwards Classics Master at the Judd School) was a witness of this and recalls that all the boys crowded to the gates to see the wonderful sight, and a tremendous cheer went up. The Doctor/ Lieutenant, however, was not amused; he fumed at anyone daring to raise a smile and the atmosphere in his classes was tense all day. This was the one story about him which he never retailed against himself. The porter (a stand-in, not the great Medland, who had returned to the Navy) was sent back to Glebe Road to fetch the missing military head-gear, and the return journey was made in full uniform.

Such was the Doctor. The outstanding quality of the man, which explains his great merits and his apparent inconsistencies, was his directness — suited to his reputation as the pioneer of the Direct Method of teaching. This was admirably expounded in the memorial article published in the *Cambridge Review*. Directness, it pointed out, was 'the essence of all that was great in him; and what of him, except his physical stature, was not great?' His other great quality was vivacity, and the two summed up his character and were 'the source of his power'.

The article goes on to speak of the apparent inconsistency of the mixture of conservatism and daring innovation in Rouse's philosophy: 'But there was no real inconsistency. Where the old ways were simple and direct and answered their purpose, he was satisfied with them. A horse was a straightforward animal, easily managed and understood, a beautiful creature and a pleasant mode of conveyance; a motor car was a complicated monster, difficult to control and not always to be relied upon to serve its purpose. But Rouse's interst in the past was never that of a mere antiquarian; and if the old methods were unserviceable he had no compunction about replacing them by new ones. If a method of classical teaching presented as dull and deadly what was really living and warm and human, that method must go, and it did.'[49]

Like Caldwell Cook, Rouse insisted on the correct and precise use of words in English speech and writing. He hated neologisms and hybrid words. One wonders what he might have said of some of the misuses current today. In contrast to the unambiguous directness of the classical languages, he complained, in *Machines or Mind?* that:

'Modern English is full of roundabouts, of metaphors without meaning, verbiage, shams. One talks of a one-sided 'point of view': how many sides has a point? Another says that 'the line of demarcation here assumes shadowy dimensions': what are the dimensions of a line?'

I look at my *Times* leader and read: 'The value of such a statement . . . lies largely in the effect which it produces': what other value can it have than the effect it produces?'

His fine feeling for words was very well illustrated in the various translations of classical works he published; best of all in the *The Story of Odysseus* and *The Story of Achilles* — translations of Homer into 'plain English'. The *Odysseus* begins 'This is the story of a man, one who was never at a loss . . .' and the foreword runs, 'This is the best story ever written . . . Until lately it has been in the mind of every educated man; it is a thousand pities that the new world should grow up without it.'

Certainly the Doctor had no time for 'translator's English' or for jargon of any kind, and boys who offered him work in that vein were sharply rebuked.

Everything he wrote was polished in style and illuminated by neat touches of wit. His school text-book *A Greek boy at home* was referred to in *The Times* obituary as 'an original story in classical Greek, which is quite a work of genius'. Neatest and wittiest of all, probably, was *The Latin Struwwelpeter* — a version of the German children's classic which he often quoted. And it should not be forgotten that once he used his classical skill in an advertisement for Guinness, headed 'Lines suggested to a classical scholar by an advertisement' — that containing the then famous Toucan.

His writing had its critics. One reviewer grumbled that his translation of Plato's *Dialogues* was 'unelevated'. The colloquial style of his *Odyssey* aroused hostile comment. Most interesting of all, Ezra Pound pointed out that:

'Kind sir, will you be angry?' seems to me fairy-tale. 'Pardon me, sir, but I hope you won't be offended' is suggested instead. And 'a man with a mind like that comes near to godhead' should be 'When a man's got a mind like that even the gods respect him'.

Pound, however, greatly respected Rouse, and once, writing to a third person, said that, looking for a good writer, he was 'trying W. H. D. Rouse, Ogden, etc. In fact, want all the live minds'. His final letter to Rouse urged him to write his memoirs, since publishers would welcome some reminiscences *if* you put 'em in current language . . . After all, you have lived thru one of the stinkingest periods of world history on into a dawn of sorts'. Readers will agree that it is a pity there were no Rouse memoirs, though they will hardly agree that there was 'a dawn of sorts' three and a half years before the Second World War.

The mainspring of his interests was a love of people and the way they live. His early years in India — where his parents worked as Wesleyan missionaries — had given him a strong interest in folklore, and he developed this through his extensive travels in the Aegean and elsewhere, as well as in the realms of gold of literature. He had a very deep appreciation of English life, in all its facets, especially country life, simple humour, song and dance. All this quickened his writing and his teaching.

'A deliberate and insular patriot',[49] he insisted on the vital role that England and the Empire must play to preserve civilisation, if necessary by military might. He was a great admirer and supporter of the Royal Navy, as the ultimate force in British power, and from 1907 onwards maintained a school branch of the Navy League. He urged parents to support the O.T.C., not only for the training it afforded, but because it might enable them to play a part in defending civilisation . . . He deplored the way politicians had conducted foreign policy in his time; the rot in international affairs, he would say, was already setting in, and he largely blamed Lloyd George, one of his personal *bêtes-noires*. When the Armistice was declared in 1918 he did not immediately grant a holiday in celebration. He, alone perhaps among headmasters, refused to treat the occasion as one for rejoicing, and harangued the school to the effect that the Allies should have pressed on into Germany and given the enemy a taste of his own medicine.[50]

Another slightly eccentric belief he held concerned the value of country life. A man, he thought, can achieve a true balance in his life only when in close contact with animals and the soil. He believed that every school should have its own farm, and he himself for many years ran Glebe Farm, adjacent to his home, probably losing a good deal of money in furtherance of his ideal.

He was essentially an open-air man; yet he never took any deliberate exercise other than horse-riding, cycling and skating when a frost allowed this. His keenness on skating led him sometimes to give an extra half-holiday to allow the boys to go skating; he was very anxious that every boy should learn to swim and skate — and ride, too, if possible. In one year (probably 1919) he is known to have granted five extra 'halves' in a fortnight to allow for skating — and there might have been a sixth but for a thaw.

Although critical of science generally, he respected medical opinion and insisted that all boys coming into the school must be vaccinated. Twice, in 1903 and 1908, he was threatened with legal proceedings because he refused to accept boys who had not been vaccinated; the

Governors upheld his view. He was also in trouble because his cosmopolitan outlook led him to accept a number of boys from overseas; and in 1911 he was criticized by the Town Clerk, who on enquiring how many 'Jews and members of coloured races' were at the Perse was told firmly to mind his own business. Yet another row followed his insistence that boys must attend their classes regularly; this was in 1912, when a long and acrimonious argument, which led to questions in Parliament, arose because he had expelled a boy whose attendance was unsatisfactory. Four other public schools — Bedford, Bradford, Cheltenham and St. Paul's — were then asked to state their 'method of dealing with breaches by parents of the school regulations relating to attendance at schools' — and all agreed with Rouse's view.[51]

The Doctor was very 'tough' by nature, and was practically never known to wear an overcoat or gloves (except, indeed, as military uniform) however severe the weather. On one occasion, after his retirement, he walked most of the way from Christ's to Histon, having missed the last 'bus. In retirement, incidentally, he usually wore a delightful moleskin coat, and, on occasion, a little skull-cap.

IX

FAME AND FRUSTRATION

The appointment of Dr. Rouse heralded the greatest age of the Perse, in which it became internationally famous. But at the same time the foundation hovered on the verge of bankruptcy, and was threatened by the attitude of its opponents, and especially the intransigence of the local authorities, given new powers under the 1902 Education Act. The paradox of concurrent fame and failure seemed to run almost like a scientific law of inverse proportions: the greater the success, the greater the threat.

In Cambridge, as we have seen, the situation was exacerbated by the old Town-and-Gown conflict, the University still being viewed as a preserve of privilege and the Perse counting as a Gown institution. Some ill-feeling remained also from Allen's time. The reorganisation of the school into classical and commercial sections had partly met the objections raised, as had the institution of Town Governors in the 1873 Scheme. But the demand for full local control was increasing, and became feasible through the new Act, which was hailed as sounding the death-knell for schools like the Perse, unless the Governors agreed to its integration into the new 'state' system. Cambridge had now created two excellent single-sex Higher Grade schools, which were later (1913) housed in good new buildings. They attracted some very good staff, including one or two who became Perse masters, who worked for degrees while teaching. Among the boys who attended the Melbourne Place school (now Parkside Community College) were some who came on to the Perse and afterwards had distinguished careers, thereby disproving the assertion that the Perse was a home of privilege. Under the Act, the local Councils could either take over the old, and sometimes discredited, grammar schools, or create new schools. Only a few chose to promote the Higher Grade schools, which continued to operate at a rather lower level. Having failed in preliminary overtures to the Perse Governors, the Cambridgeshire authorities began forthwith to plan their first 'provided' schools, the County (later High) Schools for Boys and Girls, which opened in 1900. These offered the traditional grammar school courses, together with the instruction in practical and commercial subjects which public opinion was demanding. The Boys' school operated an 'approved' curriculum which could be associated with an 'Organised School of Science' as proposed by the Board of Education, but at first it was argued, in spite of the difficulties encountered around the turn of the century, that the Perse ought to become a School of Science.

While the Act was in preparation the Cambridgeshire Education Committee made it clear that it was anxious to take over the control of the Perse, but the Governors steadfastly opposed any diminution of their authority, and urged that the Foundation, so far from being integrated into any new scheme, should receive financial compensation, since the new school, which would charge fees 'less than half of the lowest fee charged at the Perse', would virtually halve its intake of boys. The Board of Education called a public enquiry, held at the Guildhall on 26 October, 1900, at which the Perse delegates suggested a subsidy of not less than £500 a year to cover their loss and asked that 'the question of whether the Perse School should be a School of Science should be left open'. The County Technical Education Committee replied that a pecuniary grant would be illegal unless accompanied by a condition that the school should become a School of Science. The delegates contested this and insisted that the Governors alone could direct the Foundation's affairs. The Governors, quite properly, resented the implied 'suggestion of mismanagement' in the County Committee's claim. They were obliged to agree that 'the school, notwithstanding large grants received from the Government and the Technical Education Fund, had been in a struggling condition for some time' — especially since the Frating farm, the main endowment, had proved a liability. They pointed out, however, that 'by reason of considerable sacrifice on the part of the Headmaster, but also partly in consequence of the increase of fees and partly by the exercise of an enforced parsimony in the working of the school, which the Governors would gladly have avoided, the accounts for the past year show a balance on the right side for the first time for many years'. The school therefore had a definite future if allowed to continue with 'aided' status.

The argument that the Perse should receive compensation because of the competition offered by the County school was continued with some heat. Copies of the Representations made were sent to all County and Borough Councillors and Committee-members. A circular was sent, a little later, to all parents, explaining the situation and including, in justification of the claims for special treatment, 'a select list of Honours gained by old pupils from 1896 to 1901'.

The Act allowed the local councils, because of the 'aided' status implied, to nominate representatives to the Perse Board of Governors; but that body naturally opposed any fundamental change in its constitution such as would give the councils a controlling interest, and urged that neither council should have more than five representative members.

Embodied in the Act was a system of grants applicable to both 'provided' and 'aided' schools. This allowed for additional grants for special courses, and the reputation of the Perse for language teaching, especially in the classics, was already so high that it was immediately allowed a grant. Moreover, since the award implied special praise from the Board of Education itself, the case of the Perse against the local authorities was thereby strengthened. The grant was increased in 1907, as the fame of Rouse's methods grew. In this grant we may see the beginnings of the Direct Grant system.

The Perse managed to preserve its independence, with no change in its character, despite the competition offered by the new County school. But it could operate only by continuing the policy of 'enforced parsimony'. The number of boys had for some years fluctuated, but with a general trend to a decline: in 1884 there had been fewer than a hundred, in 1898 there were 195, in 1900 there were 213 — the highest figure for some time — but in 1902 the number fell to 106 'with a prospect of further diminution' and at one point it dropped to 72.

The years from 1901 to 1908 occasioned financial worry, as is clear from the Governors' Minutes, which contain frequent references to the Bank overdraft and to the constant expense entailed by the Frating property. Frating brought in nothing, involved heavy expenditure, and when offered for sale, as it was several times, did not attract a buyer. Dr. Rouse was, all the while, making appeals for the many improvements which were urgently needed: increased salaries, a proper playing-field, Leaving Scholarships, boarding-houses, a new Preparatory school, improvements to the main school buildings. There were many areas in which money could usefully be spent, and the Doctor was not short of ideas. Eventually, nearly all the desirable essentials for which he rightly clamoured were secured, but the financial struggle, over many years, was intense.

In fact, Rouse came to feel that he was usually left to solve these recurring problems himself — which to a great extent suited him. He wrote that 'At the Perse they even left me to find the money somehow; so I worried the Governors till we got some from public funds. I got myself the help of one incomparable champion at the Board of Education' (Sir Robert Morant). Yet just at this point the Doctor nearly abandoned his work in Cambridge, being short-listed for the post of High Master of St. Paul's. The first improvement was in salaries, which were increased in 1903, but this was done only by rescinding a decision to appoint an additional master. Fees were increased in 1906 and in 1910; in 1906 the Board of Education considered that 'the fee for boys under 13 is still low'.

Academically, however, Rouse's methods were now beginning to make their mark. The Report of a General Inspection held between October, 1905, and June, 1906, commended the work of the school and spoke of the language teaching as 'specially noteworthy. Not only is it doing work of exceptional merit in French and German, but it is showing that new methods can be adopted in the teaching of the Classics with great advantage'. Grants from the local Councils were, largely as a result of the report, increased, and at the end of 1906 the Mayor was able to speak of how during his year of office 'that great school had been put on something like a reasonable footing as regarded finance, thanks to grants from the County and Borough Councils'. A further Inspection — such visitations were more frequent in those days — produced the comment: 'The work of the school maintains its high standard of previous years. The school is thoroughly deserving of strong support from the Local Authorities, and the fluctuating amount of the grant from the County Council from year to year has not tended to make the task of the Governors in managing the finances an easy one'.

Closing the Commercial side in 1901 was a gamble, since just before the change the Classical side had represented only a third of the pupils; but obviously the Commercial side could not stand up to the competition of the new, and better equipped, school. A further threat developed since feeling began to grow against the granting of public funds to a 'private' school. In March 1909, a speaker at the Borough Council meeting said that he 'had a most decided objection towards voting £400 of the town's money for secondary education at a school composed of middle-class children whose parents were well able to pay for their education'. This sort of ill-informed objection had been heard before, and was to be heard often in the future. On this occasion the Mayor, W. P. Spalding, himself an Old Persean, rejoined that elementary school-boys in the town had preference over others at the Perse and that the school 'had not been treated in the way it should have been treated'. He pointed out that comparison with the County school was unfair as 'the two cases were not parallel'.

The attitude, at the time, of the Board of Education was a mixture of helpfulness and the kind of bureaucratic interference that often aroused Rouse's anger. Whitehall by its special grant recognised the brilliance of the language teaching. This grant was first paid in 1907, and in the same year the Free Place regulations gave a grant from public funds on condition that 25% of the school places should be given to boys from elementary schools. However, in 1913 the Board was requiring the appointment of an additional language master, without offering any assistance to pay his salary. Another important requisite was achieved in 1909, when Trinity College provided three Leaving Scholarships for Perse boys. In 1910 a new Scheme of Government was approved; with amendments, this still applies.

On two occasions, in 1906 and again in 1910, the Old Persean Society 'came boldly into the field to champion the cause of the Perse' by calling a public meeting at the Guildhall. At the 1906 meeting a Resolution 'heartily recognised the great value of the pioneer work at the Perse School in all branches of higher education' and resolved 'to support that work to the best of its power, both morally and materially'. In 1910 a fund entitled the Perse School Donation Fund was opened and Harold Cooke published an *Illustrated Pamphlet on the Perse School*.[52] The Chairman of the County Council, in accepting a copy, wrote that 'With the Perse School filling up in numbers and increasing in reputation, one can regard with unalloyed complacency the general progress'. Such complacency, however, did not pay the bills.

The school was now becoming well-known in the educational world, not only because of its teaching methods, but also because of the excellent academic results achieved. In his Report for 1911 the Doctor pointed out that an analysis of the Tripos results for that year showed that Dulwich and Harrow had each scored six First Classes, the Perse, along with Rugby, Marlborough, Bradford and the City of London each scored five, while Westminster, Cheltenham, St. Paul's, Tonbridge and Oundle each scored four, and Eton only claimed one. By August 1913, Rouse was able to write in his Report that 'In the past year public attention has been directed upon the school, and I hope that our work may prove useful in improving the conditions of education in England. The Governors will be glad to see that the purpose we originally had in view, which no doubt then seemed too ambitious, is not unlikely to be realised'.

The need for a proper playing-field, as well as for improvements to the buildings, had always been in Rouse's mind, and he started working to achieve these aims as soon as he felt the financial position would allow. By 1911 it began to appear a possibility, and it was then that he began to press for action. A Governors' Minute of July 1911 quotes figures which gave hope: 'On December 31, 1905, the adverse balance at the Bank was £1,635; at the end of 1906 it was £1,321; in 1907, £1,130; in 1908, £792'. In the strength of this apparently consistent reduction in overdraft the Governors were allowed to buy the first part of the Luard Road playing-field. What is most important is that they then recorded the opinion that 'the financial position will right itself if the number at present in the school can be maintained or increased'. However, on this occasion the Chairman, Alderman Tillyard, pointed out that the payments to the Building Society to repay the loan now arranged would amount to £300 per annum, and 'he was afraid they would entirely swallow up the amount which they had year by year succeeded in setting aside to reduce the overdraft'.

Rouse campaigned next for the provision of proper boarding-houses. When the school moved to Hills Road houses were no longer provided for the Headmaster and Second Master, but they, and other masters, remained entitled to take in boys as boarders if they could find premises of their own. Among others, Swann-Mason, Green and Amyes had small boarding establishments of their own. In earlier times many masters, including Maxwell (of the Allen scandal) had taken boarders, and Barnes-Lawrence had taken in a few boarders himself. When he was first appointed, Rouse took a smallish terraced house in Brookside and ran this as a boarding-house. He began immediately to press for an official establishment, but the Governors made it clear that they had no funds to build a school house as such. At the same time, I. H. Hersch began to organise his important scheme for providing a specialised education for Jewish boys. Luckily, both he and Rouse had some private means, and they decided on a joint venture, consisting of two houses side by side on a site which was available in Glebe Road, and was conveniently near to the newly-acquired playing-fields. A new era in the history began when these two specially-designed buildings were opened in 1911.

During the 'twenties, from 1920 to 1928, a third boarding-house was operated by the Milsted family. Mr. W. P. Milsted, a retired Indian Civil servant, who established it, died shortly afterwards, but his widow, for whom the Doctor had a special sympathy and regard, continued his work. Mrs. Milsted had four sons who attended the Perse; and the boys who passed through her hands included some notable ones. The house was the end part of Scroope Terrace, opposite the Leys School, and now forms part of the Royal Cambridge Hotel.

Because all three houses attracted a number of boys from abroad, a very important social effect followed their establishment. Rouse, having been born in India and being a member of Christ's College, the first of the Cambridge colleges to open its doors to overseas students (1864) and non-members of the Church of England, was highly sympathetic to bringing in foreign boys, and Hersch was Jewish. Few among the great public schools had provided specialised facilities for boys of the faith.

Boys came to Hillel House, as Hersch's house was named, from all over England, and a few from abroad — especially during the wars, when the numbers were increased by refugees. A number came to be well known in adult life. Hersch was a keen and practising member of the Jewish faith and set a high standard and moral tone. The House had its own individual personality, and for many years there was an Old Hillelians' Society. It was a great loss when the House in its special form disappeared, as later pages will show.

The difficulty raised by the existence of Saturday morning school was compensated for by the use of House Tutors, and members of the house do not appear to have suffered greatly from the loss of certain lessons each week. The remainder of the school took the situation as a matter of course — though an occasional half-envious glance might come from the playground on a Saturday morning, when the Jewish boys passed along Hills Road on their way to the synagogue.

The presence in the school of such young people could not but emphasise the spirit of tolerance and breadth of outlook which was part of the Perse regime, and of great value to all. Indeed, there was never any feeling of anti-Semitism in the school, and an Indian in a turban was treated as just another boy. 'We were subconsciously educated to perceive the evils of tyranny and intolerance from the start; to behave properly towards our fellow house-boarders, whatever their colour or creed, was as natural to us as raising our caps to a master or a schoolfellow accompanied by a woman'.[53]

It is said that in the 'twenties, when officials of the Colonial Office were asked, as no doubt they often were, to advise on the best schools for boys from overseas, the order of preference quoted was usually: Eton, Harrow, Rugby, Perse.

The provision of a preparatory school, separately housed, but linked closely to the main school, was another facility which Rouse thought urgently needed. Although a bachelor, he was fond of young children, and it was typical that he interested himself in the very youngest as well as in those of the usual age-range of seven to eleven. The former group was catered for in an unusual way by the inception of a school which he ran privately, the latter by the establishment of the official Perse Preparatory School in Bateman Street in 1910. In the foundation of this important section of the Perse, which has continued to play a vital role in subsequent history, the Doctor also made use of his own not inconsiderable private means, for he personally laid out the purchase-price of the house (which had previously been a private school) and only asked the Governors to reimburse him in respect of the rooms actually used for teaching.

Despite limitations imposed by the building — originally a villa, but with a useful hall built on at the rear — and by the absence of adequate playing-space, the Preparatory School proved a highly successful venture. Much is owing to its redoubtable headmistress, Miss Catherine Burrows, who ruled there for twenty-four years, retiring only in 1934. Her philosophy of education was summed up in her standard piece of advice to parents, that they 'should not manage their boys but understand them'. She was serious but not fierce, kind and tolerant, able to release the reserve from a shy boy and get the best out of the slow and reluctant. She would often help those who sought her further assistance after school hours.

The 'Prep. for the Prep.' which the Doctor established as a personal venture was the Chesterton Preparatory School, a very remarkable institution which was in existence from 1911 until as recently as 1972. Its connection with the Perse was declared by its use of the same colours for the caps and jerseys worn by its pupils, but with the stripes running vertically on the caps.

This school was in de Freville Avenue. Miss Katherine Wilson was Headmistress until she died in 1931, when her work was continued by Miss Hodder, who had been one of the school's first pupils. Miss Wilson's principal assistant was Mrs. Amyes, wife of Charles Amyes, of Rouse's own staff. Rouse took a great personal interest in the school. It was said to be 'under his direction' but it was later stated that 'he owns the goodwill and lets the premises on a quarterly tenancy to Miss Wilson and her brother, who take the fees'. The Doctor referred affectionately to the pupils as 'his babies' and in December 1911, a concert held at the main school delighted him by representing 'babies,

children and boys' from Chesterton, the official Prep. and the main
school. He spoke of Miss Wilson as a 'pioneer of the spirit which is
changing   the shape of education in England — where it is not
interfered with by officials . . . She had a spark of the divine fire . . . a
real genius for teaching young children'. A full appreciation of Miss
Wilson's work was published by her colleague Mary Flack under the
apt title *A Stroke of Genius*.

The prospectus of the school, a beautifully-illustrated booklet
published in 1913, states explicitly that it was 'primarily intended for
boys who will eventually pass on to the Perse School' and adds that
there is accommodation for fifty children, including some little girls,
aged from 4 to 8 years. The prospectus goes on to describe the
pioneering work of the main Perse itself. There are interesting illustrations of classrooms and of the geography garden.

The conception of the Chesterton school was years ahead of the
time, the basic idea being that the children 'could practise anything
which kept body and mind in action without outside interference' and
that 'in all subjects the children's natural activity and love of doing is
encouraged'. They thus 'acquire knowledge in each subject through
the medium of *all* the senses'. All this reflected the philosophy of
Caldwell Cook's 'Play-way'[54] which began to develop at the same
time. The children did not sit at desks watching a blackboard all the
time. The classrooms, in the form of large huts, were well equipped for
the time, but many lessons were held out of doors — there were four
acres of grounds — and largely took the form of hand-work, model-
making, gardening, basket-work, weaving, sewing and painting.
Physical exercises included dancing, 'drilling' and the performance of
'old English singing-games'.

Another important principle was the synthesis of so-called 'subjects'
into what the modern jargon calls 'integrated studies'. An example,
illustrated in the prospectus, was the creation by the children of a little
garden model, showing a desert area in miniature, teaching history,
geography, nature-study and English literature at one time. The
geography lesson lay in showing what is meant by deserts, mountain
ranges, caves and oases; history and literature lessons on the crusades
and on Scott's *Talisman* were vividly illustrated; nature-study
concerned itself with camels and palm trees; and there was a practical
application in the making and erection of miniature tents and encamp-
ments.

Miss Wilson ran a boarding-house, catering especially for children
whose parents were abroad and available also for upper school children

in the holidays.

The Doctor's personal part in the Chesterton school came to an abrupt end in November 1923, when the Governors questioned whether he ought to be operating a private school while serving as their Headmaster, and formed a special sub-committee to investigate. The committee acknowledged that the intention had always been to provide a 'feeder' for the main school and reported that Rouse intended 'ultimately handing it over to the Governors as a free gift, clear of all debts'. In spite of this, however, the Governors chose to ask him to dispose of his interest in the school, which he did. Although no longer financially concerned, he remained deeply attached to it for the rest of his life.

A pressing need which could not long be left unsatisfied was the improvement of the school premises. The Gonville Place buildings were only twelve years old when Rouse took them over, but they were already inadequate, being on a cramped site, with no gymnasium, no office accommodation and only one poor laboratory. The new Headmaster was soon campaigning for improvements, and once the new playing-fields were acquired he was advocating as the ultimate aim a new building adjoining the fields.

Accepting that facilities for the Corps were more urgently needed even than a gymnasium, he, at Parker-Smith's suggestion, soon (1908) arranged for the erection of a small armoury at the rear of the school. This perforce did duty also as a makeshift 'gym', but it was very small — so small that today the floor of the now demolished building provides barely adequate parking-space for four cars of the Examinations Syndicate. It was sometimes facetiously called the 'Garmoury'. The addition of a further class room by building an upper storey on this diminutive structure was proposed in 1909, but the estimate of £195 for the work 'so far exceeded the suggested cost' that the Chairman gave orders that 'the classroom should not be proceeded with and the new Armoury should be completed'.

The Headmaster's room, in Rouse's time, was not only his study, but also his classroom-cum-classical library; his philosophy was to spend the minimum time in 'being a headmaster' and the maximum in teaching, which was what really interested him. He left as much as he could of the administrative work to his secretary, who had to use a corner of the masters' common-room as his office.

The idea of extending the site by the purchase of the adjacent properties had been held, if not canvassed, from the first. On the Harvey Road side was Pendeen House (often mis-spelt as Pendene),[35] one of a line of early Victorian villas which then extended to St. Paul's Church. On the other side, Gonville House was a large detached building of some pretension. The Doctor argued with reason that the site would prove unsuitable unless the adjoining plots could be added. A newspaper report quoted how 'he would be extremely grateful if the owner (of Gonville House) would make a present of that plot of land, with the house on it. Further, it would be a graceful act if Caius would make a present of the plot of land on the other side (Pendeen House). Caius was a very public-spirited college, and made its gifts with great munificence to the University. Perhaps their own school had been overlooked by accident'. He had obviously had his eye on the two adjacent properties ever since his appointment.

Rouse could now claim that he had proved that, given a modicum of public support, a school like the Perse could exist alongside the new 'State' system, filling a different and essential role. He resisted the claim that his school should become essentially a School of Science — but, as will be shown, he did not neglect the claims of science altogether — and proved beyond doubt that the classical curriculum to which he was strongly committed could be reformed in such a way as to give a realistic training for contemporary life, and could produce men of note in both of those great fields in what we may call the Estates of Culture. At the same time he felt — and this is of the greatest importance — that he could continue to cater for all classes and all creeds, and that the fees ought to be kept low and scholarships be available to as many poor boys as possible. A remarkable series of boys from the poorer parts of Cambridge, passing through his hands, went on to make their names in the outside world.

A further financial crisis, in spite of all the efforts made to avert it, occurred in 1914, just before the outbreak of the first Great War. Dr. Rouse himself must have provided some help in containing this, for in July 1914, it was resolved at a Governors' meeting 'That a Vote of Thanks be given to the Headmaster for his generosity in offering financial and other assistance to the school, and for his devotion to the interests of the school in other ways'.

In the meantime preparations had begun for celebrating the Tercentenary of the foundation, due in 1915, and the Old Persean Donation Fund received new impetus from this, while at the same time a further Fund was launched to provide fitting, and of course concrete, celebration of the great anniversary. The two Funds were later merged and used to secure the playing-fields; a grant had already been made to help with the establishment of the boarding-houses, and

Pendeen House was purchased in 1914.

However, any ideas that were in the minds of the Headmaster, the Governors or the Society were frustrated, or postponed, by the outbreak of war. When the Society's appeal was renewed it had to be entitled the Tercentenary and War Memorial Fund. The money then raised was intended for the rounding-off of the school site by the purchase of Gonville House, which was done in 1919, Caius contributing £250. During Rouse's time no attempt was made to develop this additional area, which it was left to Wootton to employ in his major scheme of the nineteen-thirties. Pendeen House, however, filled an urgent need for extra class-room space, and in particular gave Caldwell Cook, after the war, the opportunity he needed of providing a theatre-room, the Mummery, about which a good deal will need to be said in a later chapter.

The war of 1914-1918 inevitably hindered the work of the school and brought sadness and deprivation. Nearly everyone was involved in national service of some kind, and the Corps and Scouts particularly so. An important and significant effect of the war was the reception into the school of a number of refugee boys, mainly from Belgium and Serbia. Those who were boys at the time remember these vividly enough, and felt that all made a good contribution to school life, emphasising the spirit of the Perse, that class, race and creed are of minimal importance. There were thirty or so of these boys at the school, throughout the war period, and no fees were paid for them. The cost of operating the school, however, rose, and in 1916 staff salaries were cut. It was immediately announced that 'a sufficient sum to make up the deductions from the Assistant Masters' salaries had been provided from a private source' — perhaps, one may guess, from the Headmaster's own pocket.

After the war ended, some extra accommodation was provided by the erection of two wooden, ex-Army huts in what had been the garden of Pendeen House. One of these for long bore the stencilled mark 'Lot 14'. As so often happens, these 'temporary' rooms continued in use for nearly forty years, one being used as a workshop, the other for Parker-Smith's geography classes. The *O.P. Chronicle* proudly asserted that 'Geography can now boast of a room, complete with museum and a lantern-room'. In 1922, an adjustment to the Old Persean Fund, originally intended for the purchase of Gonville House, diverted it to provide the extension to the playing-field which became known as the Tercentenary Field and incorporated the Bowden cricket pitch, named in acknowledgement of a generous donation made by the

Nottingham industrialist, Sir Harold Bowden.

The achievements of Old Perseans in the war, for which a Memorial was now being sadly prepared, were worthy of its history, and bear comparison with those of other schools. Altogether over 530 old boys were on military service, many leaving school prematurely. Decorations won included seven D.S.O.'s, one D.S.C., four M.C.'s and bar twenty-nine M.C.'s, seventeen O.B.E.'s and a number of colonial and foreign decorations. Dr. Rouse declared that 'although the V.C. had not been awarded there was reason to think that it had been earned'. In all, eighty-six were killed on active service.

The Tercentenary celebrations were necessarily postponed until after the Armistice. A service was held in Caius Chapel, at which the Bishop of Woolwich, an O.P., preached. Later there was a Dinner at St Catharine's. Speech Day took on a special significance, and the prizes were distributed by H. A. L. Fisher, President of the Board of Education in the Lloyd George government. The Union Society held a special Visitors' Debate, when a principal speaker was the editor of the *Morning Post*.

Demobilisation after the war was rapid enough to allow a further celebration dinner, on a much bigger scale, held in the School Hall on 7 November 1919. To allow a hot meal to be served, since no catering facilities existed in the building, Mr. Appleton's classroom was turned into a temporary servery. The Dinner was attended by Prince Albert, later King George VI, and Prince Henry, later Duke of Gloucester, both first-year undergraduates at Trinity at the time, who, as guests of honour, were fulfilling their first public engagement. The Bishop of Woolwich, President of the Old Persean Society, was in the chair, and another guest was the Marquis of Crewe, who had presented the prizes at Speech Day, which preceded the Dinner.

The War Memorial was unveiled in 1921 by General Lord Horne. It took the form of a carved oak panel, surmounted by the pelican standing out bravely, an emblem which had become newly apt. The beautiful carving was by an Old Persean, Cyrus Johnson.

From 1919 the word 'Grammar' was dropped from the official title of the school, as is evidenced from the covers of the *Pelican* and the annual Reports.

In 1920 a further crisis in the affairs of the Foundation led the Chairman of Governors, Ald. A. I. Tillyard, to utter a sharp warning about its future. He was speaking at Speech Day, when the Headmaster, in spite of the problems, was 'in optimistic mood'. Emphasising the paradox of success in failure, Ald. Tillyard recalled that during the twenty-one years in which he had been a Governor he had seen the fortunes of the school at their lowest ebb in recent times, and also at their height. The low ebb was just after the County Boys' School opened, when there was a total of only 59 boys at the Perse, 13 in the preparatory department. The current number of boys was 346, of whom 74 were in the preparatory school. Yet the foundation was in desperate financial straits, being threatened with a deficit on that year's workings of some £1,700, which even the recently agreed increase in fees would not nearly wipe out. The increase in numbers meant that accommodation was severely strained, but there seemed no prospect of new buildings or playing-fields. The salaries paid to the staff, while comparable with those paid elsewhere, were such that 'most of the assistant masters, unless they had private means, were condemned to celibacy'.

Without wishing to spoil the vision some of his friends had, of a fine new school, Mr. Tillyard said he had to point out that the school at the time could barely continue at the existing level. 'The greatest care would be needed lest the school lost its independent position and had to depend for its support on the County Council'.

The place of the school in the County scheme of education was once again discussed at length, about this time, by the Cambridgeshire Education Authority. It was, of course, a critical period, when so much public money had to be spent on restoring public life after the war and on implementing the many reforms which had perforce been postponed. The Council received a report from the Higher Education Sub-Committee which set out the circumstances which made two types of local secondary school, the Perse and the County, a desirable pattern. The choice put by the Sub-Committee was between two possible recommendations, 'either (a) that the Perse School should receive adequate financial support from the County Council; or (b) that the County Council take over the management of the school.' There was a long discussion in the Council, much turning on the meaning of 'adequate' in the first choice. It was, at first, agreed (the voting being 11-2) that recommendation (a) be accepted, two decisive reasons being that it would cost the County a great deal more if they took the school over, and that no action of the sort could be taken unless the Governors asked for it. After further discussion, however, it was decided to refer the whole matter back to the Higher Education Sub-Committee with a view to their arranging a conference on the future of the school, to be attended by representatives of the Governors, the Borough Council and the County.

The position of the Perse was thus resolved for the remainder of the reign of Dr. Rouse. Further problems of its position in the national scheme of education, along with other schools of similar character, were to arise in the 'thirties and afterwards, and were to lead to the school's inclusion in the list of Direct Grant Schools under the 1944 Education Act, and to its attaining independent status after the repudiation of this system by the Wilson government of 1975.

However, the work of the school between 1920 and 1928 was allowed to proceed on a relatively calm course, and the ideas begun on the Doctor's appointment in 1902 continued to be developed by the dedicated staff he had gathered round him.

Much could be written about the methods of discipline obtaining in the Perse since the time of Barnes-Lawrence, who introduced 'public school methods', implying a strong cadre of prefects, corporal punishment, and a lively house system, with games, the Corps — and later the Scouts — and societies of many kinds providing an essential background influence, at once stiffening and sweetening the social life. Wherever possible, the boys themselves took responsibility in managing societies and maintaining the *esprit de corps*.

The prefects' authority was enlarged by Rouse, who brought many Rugby ideas with him. Both at school and in the boarding-houses they had authority to cane, or 'swish', but were required to keep a record of punishments; the books for 1916-25 survive, although damaged in the fire of 1941. The masters, except for the Second Master, did not use canes. The main sanction available to them was detention, a rigorous system involving a note signed by the parent. Masters like Appleton would sentence an offender after the manner of a 'hanging judge'.[55]

The wearing of caps was enforced, so far as practicable, though even in 1908 there was a 'hatless brigade' and Rouse then laid down that a tie or some other school badge must always be worn. Blazers were then acceptable in school only as part of a complete sports outfit.

Rouse's own comments on discipline in *To Young Teachers* show his belief that indiscipline mainly arises from boredom, and therefore if the boys' interest is captured they will not need dragooning. He believed in 'freedom with self-restraint'. But on occasion he would conduct what today would be called a 'purge', as in 1912, when a notice to masters, which had been preserved in the *Headmaster's Book*, and is headed 'Punctilio', complains of slackness of demeanour and untidiness in the school.

The next few chapters, forming, not surprisingly, the largest section of this volume, will try to analyse the achievements of Rouse and his staff during this tremendous period.

X

DIRECT METHOD CLASSICS

We come now to consider the teaching of the Classics which Dr. Rouse initiated. The *Concise Dictionary of National Biography* says, with admirable conciseness, that Rouse's distinction was that he 'taught Classics by (the) direct method of speaking only Greek or Latin' and this is, of course, the bare bones of the thing. The idea attracted the attention of educationalists[56] all over the world, within a short time of its inception on Rouse's appointment to the Perse in 1902. By 1908 'the popular Headmaster of the Perse School' was giving an interview on his methods to the *Cambridge Chronicle*, and by 1910 the Board of Education had begun a special grant to meet staffing expenses — a distinction shared with only four other secondary schools. Also in 1910 the Board published a special pamphlet entitled *The Teaching of Latin at the Perse School*, which was followed by a similar pamphlet on the teaching of Greek, which appeared in 1913.

In 1910 Rouse founded the Association for the Reform of Latin Teaching, which is still active, and has several Old Perseans among its members, who call themselves the 'Arelates'.[57] The Association holds an annual conference, at which demonstration lessons are a feature. The 1913 Conference was held in Cambridge, attended by over 200 teachers, and reported at some length in the local and national press.

Dr. Rouse gave a particularly fine inaugural address at this conference, in the course of which he explained his method in memorable terms, as follows:

"The Direct Method is to associate an act or a thing, and later a thought, with its expression in a foreign language, without the interference of an English word. For example, we do not say, 'The Latin for *I walk* is *ambulo*, 'but the teacher actually does walk and, doing so, says, Ambulo'. When a certain number of words are thus learnt these are used to explain others, and Latin is learnt very much as we learned English".

111

The newspaper correspondents present at the conference were impressed with the illustrative lessons which were a feature, and particularly so when they saw 'the boy supplanting the teacher' — a method which was characteristically Persean.

After another fifteen years' experience Rouse and his principal lieutenant, R. B. Appleton, published a very full account of their work in *Latin on the Direct Method* (University of London Press, 1925). This book is, in effect, a complete teacher's guide, with full illustrations, including Latin dialogue taken from actual lessons. The introductory chapter, written by the Doctor, sets out the main argument.

Rouse goes on to point out that to use Latin in speech, as a living language, was the traditional English method. The uninspiring alternative, which he calls 'the current method', was in fact peculiar to the nineteenth century and was 'the offspring of German scholarship, which seeks to learn everything about something rather than the thing itself'.

It was fundamental to the method that the work of learning would be enjoyed. One of the neatest of the epigrams which Rouse coined to explain his philosophy appears in this book, when he points out that 'No less work is done in a Morris dance than on a treadmill, but it has a different effect on the human spirit'. Equally fundamental was the idea that the object of learning the languages was to enjoy the literature to which it provided a key: 'To him the antiquity of the classical authors was an accident; his love of them was due not to their age but their living qualities and universal appeal'.[49]

The Doctor publicised his methods through his teaching, through his books, through the A.R.L.T. and in any other way that presented itself. Making use of one of the machines he affected to despise, he even recorded a Latin course on gramophone records. This provided a set of ten lessons by the Direct Method, in which, to quote the Linguaphone Company's notice, 'you can hear him actually taking a class of schoolboys from the Perse School' and 'will know exactly how the words sound when spoken by an acknowledged authority on Latin pronunciation'. The Course was supplied 'together with its amusingly illustrated text-book' — to show 'what the master should draw on the blackboard'. There are, to emphasise the enjoyable nature of the lessons, 'some little songs in it'. The Linguaphone Company also issued two Greek records prepared by the Doctor, one 'The Sounds of Ancient Greek' together with the alphabet and 'specimen words and sentences'; the other 'Passages from the Greek Classics', taken from Demosthenes, Homer, Pindar and Sophocles.

Latin as taught in the Lower School will be considered in our appreciation of Appleton's work. We speak first of the Doctor's own sphere, the classes of the Sixth Form, taken in the room that was at once his teaching-base and his Headmaster's office.[58] For he was a teacher rather than an administrator. No other headmaster can ever have had as full a time-table as his — eighteen periods a week with the Sixth Form alone — and yet the general conduct of the school did not suffer. Enjoying excellent health, he was absent from his classroom only on the days, or usually half-days, when he went up to London to transact editorial business and visit the Athenaeum Club, where he was a popular member. There were others who met him only on these visits who came to know and respect him; Eric Warmington has described one visit, made in his company, when an old flower-seller asked him who the 'lovely gentleman' was, who always gave her something.

Visitors from all over the world came to watch Rouse's Sixth Form lessons. A register was kept, which makes impressive reading. The visitors were allowed to sit at the side and observe but were ignored so far as the lesson was concerned.

The method was to read the classical authors as extensively as time allowed, with the minimum of grammatical and textual comment, but always with the comprehension questions in Greek or Latin, and always with an oral summary at the beginning of each lesson, again in the appropriate language. This might perhaps have appeared to the casual visitor to be somewhat haphazard and unmethodical. The procedure has been described by A. W. Eagling, who was subsequently Headmaster of the Cambridgeshire High School:

All the Sixth Form, including the historians, were lumped together for the reading periods and the pace was that of the fastest; the others had to hold on and pick up what they could. I remember that when I first went into the sixth form I was confronted with the *Agamemnon* of Aeschylus — my first introduction to Greek poetry. The gentlemen in the Upper Sixth, who were preparing for their College scholarships, romped happily through the complicated choruses, while I trailed behind — far behind. Yet, somehow, something of the meaning and something of the majestic grandeur of the poetry seeped through and that first taste of the sixth form was a thrilling if somewhat frightening experience. We had, in fact, been well drilled on the language side and Rouse's main interest was in the literature. And we read widely. Before I went to Cambridge I had read in class the whole of the *Aeneid* and of the *Iliad*, to give but two examples. I don't claim that I could have translated it

all, but I understood most of it at the time. I had also read several
plays by Plautus — a great favourite with Rouse, but merely a name
to many undergraduates. We always read from the Oxford Classical
Texts and would plunge briskly in after the Doctor had given us a
brief note on the author. The method was largely question and
answer work, with *aliter Latine*, and translation was the last resort.

Apt topical allusion would be made; one remembers frequent
references to Lloyd George, Chamberlain, Churchill and Coué, and the
biting criticisms made of 'Lizzie Scott' when the Shakespeare Memorial
Theatre was built. Any public figure, any event, local or international,
would be brought into a lesson, and anyone thought stupid would be
pilloried in the style of Juvenal or Aristophanes. A great deal of
general knowledge came into all the lessons.

It was in the composition periods, when English poems and passages
had to be rendered into Greek or Latin verse or prose, that Rouse's wit
and elegant taste came out most memorably, especially when it
sharpened the brains of such pupils as Arthur Peck, Humphrey
Jennings, Kenneth Thompson and D. A. W. Philipps, some of whose
contributions are recorded in *Scenes from Sixth Form Life* (Blackwell
1935), a little book compiled from jottings the Doctor had made
over the years. The first two periods on Saturday mornings
were given over to extempore versions of limericks or notices from the
'Agony' columns of *The Times*. Those who could provide a good
version or who answered well in class were rewarded with a 'donum' —
a gift of a Greek postcard, of which there was a store in the Old Man's
desk. The greatest honour of all was to copy out one's work, whether
done in class or at home, in the Album, the great volume of fair copies
started by Barnes-Lawrence and continued in this epoch.

In this context the rule that no English should be used in class was
relaxed — so long as the outcome was witty. The Doctor himself
would recite English poems which seemed apposite. He had by heart a
great stock of little poems, and was especially fond of 'Ruthless
Rhymes' and 'Struwwelpeter'. Two of his favourite quotations must be
noted; first, the neat little poem which sums up the mysteries of
philosophy:

> The cheese-mites discussed how the cheese got there,
> And stoutly they argued the matter;
> The orthodox said that it came from the air,
> The heretics said, From the platter.
> They argued it hot and they argued it strong —
> Perhaps they are arguing now —

But of all the philosophers in that great throng
Not one ever thought of the cow.

Secondly, he liked a delightful little poem which playfully defends plagiarism:

When 'Omer smote 'is bloomin' lyre
'E'd 'eard men speak by land and sea,
And what 'e thought 'e might require
'E went and took — the same as me!

After reciting one of these little gems, the Doctor would chuckle in an infectious way, almost as if he had just, for the first time, seen the point of the joke.

In the same spirit some outrageous puns and limericks were perpetrated in the Old Man's class, occasionally in English, more usually in Latin, and sometimes as a bilingual joke, such as is contained in:

A Greek and a Roman went into a shop
Refreshment to seek for the body:
The Roman said briskly, *Habebimus hoc*,
But the Grecian said, *Hexomen toddy*.

A number of spontaneous classroom examples, which gave him particular pleasure, are recorded in *Latin on the Direct Method* and in *Scenes from Sixth Form Life*, one of his last books, incorporating his own Obiter Dicta as well as samples of sixth form wit.

A touch which his pupils will remember was his occasional neat use of the blackboard. He would draw a Greek vase with beautiful symmetry by holding a piece of chalk in each hand, and then smile over his spectacles as if to say 'That was clever!' And there would be other little drawings to illustrate a story being read.

He loved also fanciful etymology. He would demonstrate playfully that the word 'tunic' could be derived from the Greek 'chiton', and would point out that the island of Erin is well named if it be derived from the Greek word for strife. When he retired to Histon, he amused his friends by asserting that the village stood on the River Hys, really a variant of Styx.

Periods devoted to Greek literature were particularly memorable. He loved especially Homer, Pindar, the great dramatists and Aristophanes. Thucydides, often topically apt, was enjoyed, and one recalls the highly appropriate annual reading of Pericles' Funeral Oration, at Armistice-tide. His lightest vein was evident in the reading of Herodotus, that delightfully uncritical historian; he would quote, with a meaningful shake of the head, 'Herodotus, Herodotus, You were a gullible old cuss!' His lessons of Religious Instruction centred on reading the Greek Testament, especially the journeys of St. Paul, which he, who had sailed around all the Greek islands, made especially alive.

In furtherance of the principle that 'the labour we delight in physics pain' (which quotation formed a dedicatory motto) the Doctor wrote a book of *Chanties*, songs in Greek and Latin set to well-known tunes, so cleverly as never to violate the classical 'quantities'. Perhaps the neatest was a Latin version of the Vicar of Bray which taught the history of the early Roman kings. A Greek chanty told the story of the battle of Salamis and brave Themistocles. The tune *Green Grass* was used in two well-liked songs, one a Latin version of The Old Woman Who Lived in a Shoe, the other a singing-game in Greek, in which various animals were chosen as partners for a dance. This made a good spectacle for Speech Day. Perhaps most celebrated of all, and certainly most rousing, was *Caesar's Triumph*, to the tune of *Clementine*:

> Ecce Caesar nunc triumphat, qui subegit Gallias,
>
> Ecce turbam nunc reducit quae refert victoriam:

This was used in one of Appleton's plays; and dear R.B.A. never minded when the verse was sung which introduced lame Scipio:

> Mox videbis Scipionem claudicantem sedulo,
>
> Semper incumbit bacillo, quod regit tardos pedes.

Rouse would sing the songs himself, to introduce them to classes in the middle school, as well as occasionally — often on a Saturday morning — letting the sixth form romp through them. Incidentally, in the second edition — it is notable that the book ran to this, in 1930, after the Doctor had retired — the author lamented that, popular though it had proved in schools, 'it is not mentioned in the *Classical Review* and, if you can believe me, it was not mentioned in *Punch*'. One feels that indeed *Punch* slipped up badly, for if ever writing achieved clever humour this certainly did.

In his classical teaching Rouse was aided by a number of other masters, all good scholars and most of them competent teachers, even though none could approach the Doctor in skill. The two greatest were W. H. S. Jones and R. B. Appleton. Jones was one of the original team, with de Glehn and Turnbull, who joined the staff with Rouse in 1902; he remained until 1921, when he left to become a Fellow, and later President, of St. Catharine's. He published a number of important books, some jointly with Appleton. The best known of these earned him one of his nicknames, 'Malaria Jones'.

Concluding that malaria contributed much to the gradual decline of civilisation in Greece and later in Italy, he produced *Malaria: a neglected factor in the History of Greece and Rome* in 1907 and *Malaria and Greek History* in 1909. He afterwards did further work on ancient medicine, which made him the recognised authority on the subject, and earned him the honour of corresponding membership of the Royal Society of Medicine. His interest in his own physical ailments was a standing joke, and he was said to eat next to nothing. An example of his hypochondria is found in his dedication of his pamphlet *Remember* (written in 1915): 'To the young people whose work will begin when the war comes to an end, by one who does not expect to see it'. He constantly made appointments conditional on his still being alive. Yet he lived to be nearly ninety.

His gaunt figure led to the bestowal of two other affectionate nicknames, both of which were current in the school. One was the rather obvious 'Billy Bones'. The other, 'Corpse', is said to have been given, not because of his moribund appearance or his hypochondria, but because, so it is alleged, he had once posted a notice on behalf of the O.T.C. ordering the 'corpse' to parade. He was, incidentally, a fine shot, and his work in the corps was concerned mainly with shooting.

Among his other books the most important was *The Teaching of Latin*, a defence of the subject against those who maintained it was out of touch with modern life. Two with a special interest to the Perse were *Excerpta Brevia*, written jointly with Parker-Smith, and *Disciplina*, which was concerned with the technique of classroom discipline. This asserts in its first sentence that it is a protest against the modern doctrine of 'do as you please', and to some extent runs against the ideas of Rouse and Caldwell Cook. The fact is that he did not immediately take to the methods of the Perse, though he was, as he said himself, 'gradually converted'.

It would certainly appear that he went a little too far in his disciplinary approach to his school classes, and he did not inspire affection among his pupils. Clearly he found it difficult to get down to the level of small boys, and he was much more at home in his subsequent university work.

A. W. Eagling remembers how Jones took some classes as a part-time teacher about 1923, and recalls particularly how 'the extraordinary facial contortions which were apparently necessary for the pronunciation of Latin soon produced convulsions among our lively group' and did not produce discipline of the standard one would expect. At St. Catharine's, however, Eagling and others learned that there was much kindness and understanding behind that somewhat shy and forbidding manner.

R. B. Appleton was a sad figure. He suffered from disseminated sclerosis, which he fought bravely, continuing to work until he was forced into a short-lived retirement. When he tried to disguise the abrupt whitening of his hair, because of the disease, by dyeing it, the effect quickly wore off, and he thus acquired the affectionate nickname of 'Tabby'. For a time he managed to get about, slowly and painfully, using sticks and swinging one leg from the hip while pivoting on the other. Later, his wife would bring him in her bull-nosed Morris, and Medland, the porter, would propel his wheelchair across the hall and up the ramp on to his classroom dais. In spite of the physical handicap, there were no disciplinary problems in Appleton's periods. He had a very sharp ear and an equally sharp tongue, with a broad Bradford accent. 'When I tap my pencil,' he would say, 'I want to hear a pin drop'; and he could.

Oral work was, of course, the rule in his class. He very rarely used English, and pronounced his Latin slowly and clearly. He had a distinct sense of humour, as is shown in the *Noctuinus* stories he published, but not much of this appeared in the classroom, except in his playful explanations, or in the 'Doric' humour shown when, after a mortal grammatical sin had been committed, he would say, 'Intestina crepitant'. Every boy had a Latin class-name (a good way of teaching the vocative) and there was great competition to answer questions, the first correct reply in Latin gaining the reward of a *punctum* neatly noted in Appleton's mark-book.

An important part of the method was the introduction into lessons of lively topical comment, which when put in the form of conversation between master and class in a classical language was an admirable way of acquiring familiarity with language and culture. Playful explanation and humorous touches came naturally, and the teacher was 'a divine opportunist, who could make capital out of unforeseen situations'.[59]

Appleton did not fail to introduce his classes to the magic of classical literature, and one remembers particularly his enthusiasm for the lyrical poetry of Horace, Catullus, Martial . . . and for Greek tragedy, especially Sophocles. Part of the work was the learning by heart of great chunks of Latin verse, much of which his former pupils still remember. He played his part also in advancing the Perse method of learning 'without tears' through the medium of classroom drama. Best known among the little plays he wrote was one about a Roman triumph, already mentioned. The material of many of his lessons is preserved in the series of books he wrote, *Initium*, *Ludi Persici*, *Puer*

Romanus and *Pons Tironum*.

D. M. Simmonds recalls Tabby's *tour de force* as a disciplinarian, "On the first Armistice Day, 11 November 1918, school took place as usual in the morning and was summoned also for the afternoon, though it was known that the war had ended, and other schools had been given a holiday.

In those days it was the custom for the whole school to assemble by forms in the hall for roll-call, taken by prefects from the Headmaster's desk. On this occasion, contrary to custom and the rules, the boys began to rush into the hall before being summoned by the bell from the belfry. They took their usual places, or were herded into them by the prefects, and then began to stamp and shout. The prefects were powerless.

After a time, first one master and then another came through the door opening into the hall from the Masters' Common Room, tried to subdue the noise, and retired discomfited. Then Rouse himself appeared and rang the hand-bell, but he too retired. Finally, Appleton appeared in the doorway, walked to the desk, rang the bell and stared at the assembled company. For a moment the hubbub seemed to falter; then it died down and was followed by complete silence. In a few words Appleton advised the company to sit quietly and await the good news that was likely to come. In due course a holiday was announced.

It was an impressive performance''.

Appleton became a close personal friend of the Doctor, who acted as Best Man at his wedding.

Other classical teachers towards the end of the period were E. D. Berridge (1925-30) who was also South House tutor and commanded the O.T.C. after Happold left, and R. J. B. Hicks (1921-33). Berridge afterwards joined the staff of Epsom College, while Hicks became Second Master and afterwards Headmaster of Chard School.

Rouse never claimed that the Direct Method was an original idea of his own. Probably the germ of the idea came to him while he was teaching at Rugby, where Dr. Hayman, the Headmaster, had formerly taught at Bradfield College (1868) and had there made some experiments in Direct Method teaching, inspired, at least partly, by suggestions made by Professor J. S. Blackie, of Edinburgh. He owed something also to his friend Professor J. F. Postgate, father of Raymond and Oliver, two distinguished Old Perseans, who was then Professor of Latin at Cambridge.

Some educationists criticised the method on the ground that no ordinary teacher would be capable of employing it. Andrew Lang asserted that 'Dr. Rouse's method is an admirable method, but — only a very clever man, I am afraid, can employ it. The master must be as thoroughly alive as he makes the pupils alive; and this vivacity is not given by nature to all schoolmasters'.

The other common criticism was that the method inevitably meant that, while the best pupils went ahead phenomenally well, the weaker brethren failed to learn enough. This charge Rouse would vehemently deny. He would point out that the essential basis of the method was that 'every boy is expected to ask whenever he does no understand. He is blamed, not for ignorance, but for pretending to knowledge'.

Rouse always maintaind that even the dullest boys followed most of the lesson and took something valuable away; and this is largely true. What is most important is that the majority of the boys could, in a year or two, speak Latin with some fluency and, when Greek was added, could learn to enjoy their Homer and their Greek Testament as well as their Horace and Virgil. An amazingly large number went on to win Open Scholarships and so to distinguished careers; and those whose future lay outside Classical scholarship mostly retained their love for the old authors.

Edward Gibbon put the point neatly, in his Autobiography, when he observed of classical teachers in public schools that 'they deposit in the hands of a disciple the keys of two valuable chests, nor can he complain if they are afterwards lost or neglected by his own fault'. Rouse and Appleton never failed to make clear what was in those chests — but there were some who were not attracted to what was inside.

Harold Cooke expressed the view of those who had reservations when he wrote, in *The Days of Our Youth*:

It is open to question, however, whether more than a few can be 'chosen', no matter what methods are current. The rest understand not, are bored and are left to their own sweet devices.

There were no disciplinary troubles in Rouse's own classes, or in Appleton's, but there were in others, notably in those of R. J. B. Hicks. He was an excellent scholar and a charming man, but he none the less failed sadly in class-management. Since his classroom was directly above Rouse's, the Doctor knew what was going on, and sometimes he would detach a prefect from his own class to deal with trouble above. A wit misquoted a famous line:

Caelo tonantem credidimus Hiccium non regnare.

It would, however, be unfair to dismiss Hicks from our record as merely a bad disciplinarian. He had a Persean quality of mind which commanded the respect of boys in a way that will not be obvious from what has been said. He was interested in every side of school life, including games, though his poor sight (partly, perhaps, the cause of trouble in the classroom) made him an indifferent performer on the field. He helped in Scouting and other activities, and often contributed to the *Pelican*. He could speak and write well, having a gentle but pretty wit. When he left, being eventually dismissed in a reduction of staff during the 1933 crisis, he was given a farewell dinner by some of his old pupils and the senior boys. This, as an expression of popularity, must be unique in the school's history, and unusual for any school.

It is often remarked that many of the accepted educational ideas of today had their origin in schools regarded by contemporaries as wildly experimental. This obviously applies to schools such as Oundle, Rugby, Bedales, Summerhill, Millfield, Gordonstoun. It applies with equal force to the Perse of Rouse's day, as the following pages will show, for his ideas covered not only the Headmaster's beloved Classics, but many other subjects and sides of school life.

The Doctor always said that the real secret of his success was that he 'chose the best staff and let them get on with it'. In fact, he declared that he had never had to look for staff to recruit. 'Good men,' he said, 'came rolling in. I never invited one of them, but they came of their own free will . . . They were men glad to have the opportunity of working out their ideas, and they have made the school renowned'. However, the Doctor's own part was vital, as without his example and inspiration the individuals would not have been a team.

Each of this unique body of men was an enthusiast, dedicated and prepared to work hard in and out of the classroom. All were men of character and originality, and more than a few approached the peak of distinction which would qualify for the name of genius. Indeed, there might be some difference of opinion as to which of them, after Rouse himself, was the greatest. But most of those who were boys at the school during this epoch-making period would agree with the Doctor himself, who said of one colleague that he was 'our one genius, as we all felt'. This especially distinguished master was Henry Caldwell Cook, to whose memory the next chapter is affectionately devoted.

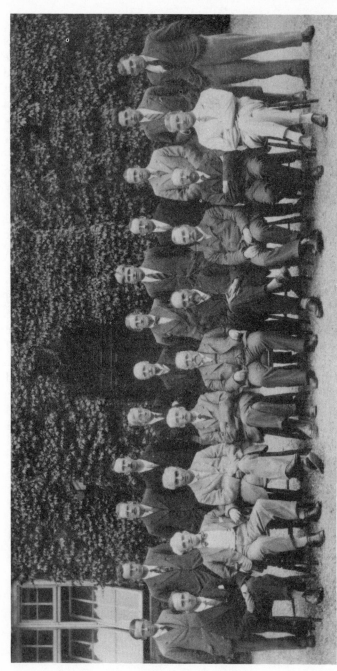

Dr Rouse's Staff: July, 1928. Standing: A. C. Hawkins; R. J. Gladden; R. R. Broome; G. M. Macfarlane-Grieve; C. Amyes; E. Broome; F. C. Happold; E. D. Berridge; R. J. B. Hicks; G. T. Salusbury-Jones, French assistant; T. L. Morris. Seated: W. D. Fraser, R. B. Appleton; I. H. Hersch; R. Parker-Smith; Dr. W. H. D. Rouse; L. de Glehn; V. M. Turnbull; L. Chouville; H. Caldwell Cook. Absent: H. P. Cooke

XI

CALDWELL COOK AND THE PLAY WAY

Henry Caldwell Cook was at once very like Rouse and very unlike him. Both were fine scholars, both were deeply engrossed in their work of teaching boys, and both remained bachelors. Both were deeply concerned with the things of the mind and the imagination; in a word, both were enthusiasts. Both were at once charmingly old-fashioned in some ways and yet incredibly forward-looking, years in advance of the mass of their profession. Both held as their basic principle that teaching is a great art and that education must be a joyful process — 'the labour we delight in physics pain'.

Cook's outlook and philosophy were well summed up in his biography in *Who's Who*, when he gave his recreations as 'folk-dancing, motoring, swimming and teaching English'; all the enthusiasms were equally felt and the order of items is unimportant.

He was a fine figure of a man, very tall, elegant and impressive; he expressed his identity by wearing old-fashioned but beautifully-cut knickerbocker suits, usually of a snuff-brown colour, with a bow instead of a tie, and he always exuded a faint odour of a slightly peaty perfume. His hair was beautifully dressed and he wore rimless spectacles. Altogether he gave an impression of fastidious good taste, and this was conveyed also by his style of speech and manner. He himself liked to use the word 'urbanity' to describe the combination of elegance, courtesy and polish which he made a personal ideal. He carried himself well and walked with an erect grace. He rode a tall bicycle — at one time a Dursley-Pedersen, with a hammock-seat — and this, too, expressed his personality and was in contrast to Rouse's heavy little machine and individual style as a cyclist. A Sixth Form wit once compared the two men with two of Chaucer's pilgrims, putting the Doctor on a rouncy and Cook on a palfrey. In later years Cook used to drive a Lagonda car, an open tourer, which often took a load of boys on a trip into the countryside — for here was a man devoted to the beauty and the subtle lore of the English countryside. Sometimes, too, he would row a party up the Granta for tea at the 'Orchard'; and he often attended the West Runton camps and walked the boys along the seashore to Sheringham. He heartily approved of the Scout movement, with its emphasis on the open-air, rambling, swimming, and its ideal of clean living and social responsibility. He regularly attended the Shakespeare festival at Stratford, often taking boys with him.

The essence of Cook's philosophy of teaching is to be found in *The Play Way*, one of the most important and remarkable books on education ever produced. The influence which his work immediately had may be seen in the Board of Education's Report, *The Teaching of English in England*, published in 1921 and continued, in a sense in *Some Suggestions for the Teaching of English* in 1924.

The difference between the methods of Rouse and Cook is perhaps to be found in their individual view of life; for whereas Rouse was essentially adult Cook gloried in the fact that his teaching was, as the name of his text implies, based on, and aimed at, childhood. It was the younger child that appealed to him and he did not normally take classes in the upper school. He gave his reasons for this in an interview reported in the London *Daily News* on 2 April 1915. 'It's wonderful what boys can teach you — while they're still children. But when they grow up, when they're over 13 or 14, you have to teach them. That's the pity of it! The moment the boy becomes self-conscious teaching methods must change'.

Yet it can be said that he had made his unique contribution, so to speak in advance, to the sixth form boys and the university students, for everyone who came under his guidance was quickly given a sensitivity, a critical feeling, above all an enthusiasm for literature and for clear thought and creative writing which would carry him through his studies and through life. There are many who can never — in spite of all he taught them about expression — adequately express their indebtedness to him.

And yet his child-like view and his Peter-Pan outlook was in some ways a barrier, as well as a source of inspiration. He did not want his boys to grow up, and accordingly called them his 'little men' and his 'play-fellows'; his form library was 'Littleman's Library' and the charmingly precious book he wrote on good manners was entitled *Littleman's Book of Courtesy* (1914). Some of his methods seemed to some embarrassingly and naively directed to the nursery. The supreme example of this lay in his 'stick-wagging' lessons, in which a class recited poetry while beating time with batons, which were cere-

moniously distributed from a wicker basket. Yet this was really a form
of choral verse-speaking. His love of ceremony came into most of his
lessons, especially in 'Speeches', and the boys loved it all — even
when it took the extreme form of a class dismissal ceremony in which a
pin was dropped for all to hear. In short, his classes 'loved the man this
side of idolatry' and were happy on occasion to indulge the whim of
their big playfellow.

Cook's great experiments belong to the 1911-1915 period. His
teaching career was sadly broken by the First World War, which
affected him deeply. 'Afterwards, having lost the first fine careless
rapture with which his teaching career had opened, he abandoned the
more fanciful of his methods'.[60]

Something must be recorded about those 'Speeches'. It is now
commonplace to have 'Oral Composition' lessons in which each of the
class in turn speaks on a subject, of his own choice or dictated to him,
for three minutes. But Cook invented the whole thing, and in his time,
the lesson was a great new idea which students came miles to see. It
was in itself an occasion, and of course a ceremony. Cook himself sat at
the back of the room, and a boy was in charge; a lesser man would
have called him a monitor or a form-captain, but for Cook and his
classes he was an official from a Persean faeryland, known as the
'mister' (accented on the second syllable). To have called him even
Master of Ceremonies or Lord of the Revels would have seemed a
degradation. He wore a richly-coloured robe taken from the tiring-
house (not, be it noted, from the wardrobe). The audience had charge
of what was known as the 'hammer' — a sort of knobkerry which had
to be banged loudly on a bench whenever a mistake was made by a
speaker; if the holder of the hammer missed a mistake it was passed on
to somebody else, providing a further little game that all could enjoy.
At the end of each speech the audience was called on to comment on
the speaker's performance, and then to award marks by voting, as in a
Dutch auction: 'Marks for interest, 10, 9, 8, etc.,' and 'Marks for
style, 10, 9, 8, etc.,' with a show of hands for each mark.

In these lessons and also in written composition, Cook insisted on
clear and simple exposition, without the use of 'smudge language'; the
word 'bit' was not allowed, because 'a bit is something a horse can't
chew', and 'lot' was similarly prohibited — unless one was speaking of
an auction sale. One could only 'lay' eggs, bricks or long odds. 'Nice',
except in its proper sense, was forbidden, and so was 'got'. Needless to
say 'er-um' and similar meaningless gap-fillers, and the meaningless
introductory 'Well', were matters for the hammer. As Spike Hughes

has recorded, 'not one of us who was in Cook's class ever got out of
the habit of using lots of bits of nice easy English when it suited us
afterwards; but while we were there the speaking of correct English
became second nature.'

Spike Hughes, then known as Pat, was one of the several pupils of
this era who afterwards made his name in the outside world. There is
an admirable account of a lesson of 'Speeches' in his *Opening Bars*
(1946).[53] In describing Caldwell Cook's other brilliantly pioneering type
of lesson, the teaching of Shakespeare by acting it instead of merely
reading and dissecting, Hughes first describes the Mummery and the
hammer, and then tells of a typical lesson:

'Our performance, which lasted for three-quarters of an hour at a
time, was in effect like the first read through a play. But the read
through was done with action and 'props'. Bells had to be rung, the
curtain dividing front from back-stage pulled at the right time, and if
the property master let one of the characters go on without his sword
or the letter to be taken from his doublet then the hammer would
strike. The fact that there were no stage instructions to indicate that a
letter was to be taken from the doublet was no excuse. Shakespeare had
mentioned the letter in the text, and it was everybody's job, including
the actor's, to see that the letter was in the doublet . . . In this way we
came to know what Shakespeare was all about. The plays became
something real and alive. We were encouraged in our characterisation
of the parts we played and we were largely cast according to our own
temperaments as assessed by Caldwell Cook.'

During a play, Cook never interrupted to explain a word or a
phrase; the story and the characters were allowed to explain themselves, and the hammer usually took care of any failure to follow the
story or to recognise that a word had to be read as 'followèd'. There
was, however, a class discussion from time to time, usually after each
act, when there would be searching questions and criticisms both of
the play and of the actors who had been trying to interpret it.

Those lessons led to a lasting and sensitive appreciation of Shakespeare, and the drama generally. In addition to Shakespeare, the work
included some of the early Miracle plays, the old 'Mummers' Play',
with Saint George and the Turkish knight, and an occasional Restoration drama, and whenever we could we set about writing and acting
our own play. Shakespeare, it should have been mentioned, was always
in the plain text, usually the Oxford 'Fifteen Plays'. Mime was
another occasional activity.

Many of Cook's lessons, and all the dramatic work, miming and 'stick-wagging', took place in the Mummery, which was his special creation. Again, 'Mummery' may seem a rather precious name; but it was a highly individual room. It was not simply a drama-room, such as state schools have to-day.

In the early days Cook had dreamed of a special building devoted to The Play Way, which would be centred on a replica of the Shakespearean theatre, but would cater also for practical activities and handicrafts associated with the drama.

In 1913 he issued an appeal for 'The Perse Playhouse Building Fund' (a copy of which is in the City Library). It is subtitled: 'A Prospectus for the building of a Playhouse and Workshop for the Boy Players, Playwrights and Craftsmen of the Perse School'. Among the suggested equipment, the scheme proposed the use of 'strong wooden boxes, shaped like enormous bricks and covered with white canvas. These will be used for the building up of the furniture as required, as a child builds with toy bricks'. Such blocks are today, of course, commonplace in all drama rooms.

The Assistant Masters' Association in its bulletin 'A.M.A.' summarised the Appeal and asked enthusiastically, 'Are we on the verge of a revolution in scholastic methods?'

This appeal, however, failed completely to bring in the required money: £2,000 was hoped for, but only £13 was actually achieved in addition to the £200 already subscribed, and Cook had therefore to fall back on the alternative, which became possible when, in 1914, the Governors purchased Pendeen House.

Essentially the Mummery was made out of two rooms in the old villa, with a raised floor in the rear room which extended through the demolished wall to form an apron-stage. There was a proscenium curtain, and doors from the lobby outside opened into the backstage and apron. There was rudimentary lighting — at first gas, which had to be constantly on and 'not lowered for sentimental effect'. Later electric lights of the simplest type (put in at Cook's expense, while the rest of the school retained gas) were controlled from the stage-manager's post beside the rear door. The colour scheme was carefully thought out: the walls were white, the curtains purple, the apron-stage linoleum diagonal black and white squares. The forms and other woodwork were dead black. The mantelpiece shone with copper and brass pots, while bright check runners and vases of flowers provided a pleasing splash of colour. The five principal items of furniture were Jacobean carved oak — a settle, a chest, two throne-like arm-chairs and a pedestal cupboard, used when required as the chairman's desk —

all of which are in use in the 'new Mummery'. On the walls were two pictures, one of the 'Swan' theatre of Shakespeare's Bankside, and one of the Stratford inscription warning posterity not 'to digge the dust enclosed here'. A table at the side held the Perse Players' Library, available only to the Players and to the Sixth Form. This included many of Cook's personal books, often beautifully bound. Besides poems and plays, there were volumes of criticism, much of Shaw, C. E. Montague, 'Trivia' and the short stories of A. E. Coppard. Here also were boards on which one could play that very Elizabethan game, Nine Men's Morris.

The audience sat on wooden forms and often overflowed on to the apron just as an Elizabethan audience would have done; the boys were accordingly 'groundlings' or 'gallants'. Forty, or at a pinch fifty, could be accommodated as audience. The whole room was a fair, if obviously limited, reconstruction of a miniature theatre of Shakespeare's time — though not, of course, a 'wooden O'. The old basement kitchen of the Victorian house was used as the 'tiring house' where a wardrobe of simple costumes and properties was kept. The name was not another piece of Cook preciosity, but was taken from the Bottom rehearsal scene of *The Dream*. The boys made properties and did simple repairs themselves, but mothers helped as required.

Much of the conversion cost of the scheme was met by Cook himself. It should be put on record, too, that, having considerable private means, he worked for his first four years without any salary. He was given an honorarium of £50 when he joined the Forces and a further £20 on his return; after the war, in more straitened circumstances, he drew a part-salary.

Even in a more normal setting the man's personality commanded the attention and inspired the imagination. In the class-room he taught the whole subject of 'English' and the many side-issues which must arise, without cutting it up into sections. Composition, in prose and verse, grew naturally out of literature: he would read an Overbury Character, or a passage from Wordsworth, or a fragment of *Beowulf*, and encourage the class to write something in the same style. Or he would propose 'little adventures' and 'explorations' — frying an egg, climbing a tree, the view from a hill, impressions while lying in bed, and so on — which had to be put into words as vividly and sensitively as possible. Much of this seems commonplace today, but at the time was highly original. Given a project exercise, in which a whole class took part, there would be working-parties after school, sometimes in Cook's rooms, but often privately arranged, with his approval, in the boys' own homes.

With such a teacher questions of discipline never arose, as even the dullest were fascinated. But Cook recognised that no boy should be tortured by sitting upright in a desk for too long, and that if he is his work will suffer. In understanding this he was, as in so much, years ahead of his time. Whenever a form began to show signs of restlessness, he would invite the boys to 'unsit' — to walk about, or to lean easily against something, or just stand; the explanation is quoted from an article on Cook's work which appeared in the London *Evening News*.

When a composition was set there was no formal planning on the blackboard; instead there was an informal discussion, the class being gently guided to suggest the best material and the most effective way of presenting it. When the written work was to be corrected, the method was again brilliantly understanding. Cook never marked work like a printer's proof-reader, but drew attention to the weaknesses, concentrating on one thing at a time. He then went through the script with the writer, 'showing you how to turn dross to gold in such a way that you believed you were doing the job yourself.'[60]

He insisted on precision in the choice of vocabulary, pointing out how incredibly rich the English language is, and how one word is exactly right and better than the possible synonyms. Sometimes he took a whole lesson on the history and use of words, and these were among his most fascinating lessons. Like Rouse, he delighted in fanciful derivations, but took care always to teach the correct derivations. Incidentally, he always called an exclamation mark 'a shriek mark' and something vague a 'thin-gummy-bob'.

His poetry lessons were thrilling: one remembers especially exciting readings of Keats, Shelley and Wordsworth. In the first year the basic poetry was that of Stevenson, de la Mare and the Border Ballads, and these, with Shakespeare's songs, supplied the main material for 'stick-wagging' and were the inspiration of the first efforts at verse-writing.

The boys were encouraged from the first to write their own poetry, finding this within their powers — if they were given the urge and shown a simple model.

The first poems to be written were always in the form of the old Border Ballads, with their simple metres and repetitive phrases. Classes next practised the blank-verse metre, which helped in the study of Shakespeare and Wordsworth and led on to the Sonnet; attempts to intimate the perfection of the sonnet form gave every boy a lasting respect for the key with which 'Shakespeare unlocked his heart'.

Study of simple blank-verse showed how close a correctly written line could be to the language of ordinary speech. The boys were given amusing examples of this, favourites being 'Excuse me, but you're sitting on my hat!' and the notice displayed in the old London trams: 'Prevention of consumption; do not spit!' Both of these are perfect, if not elegant, blank-verse lines. A good play exercise was to rearrange lines which did not quite scan. Rhythm was taught by calling the tune of the verse: 'ti tum, ti tum' — and stick-wagging had helped in this.

The standard reached by the ordinary boy may be seen in the plays and Prologues written for Perse Players' productions, and in the remarkable series of *Perse Playbooks* produced between 1911 and 1923, in the days when production costs were less daunting.

Among the most promising of Cook's pupils was Humphrey Devereux, killed in the 1914-1918 war. In his memory a prize was instituted for an original poem; the high standard expected is shown in that some years it was 'not awarded'. Equally notable was another Humphrey, Jennings, whose work, whether serious or playful, showed great maturity even while he was very young.

A delightful by-product of Cook's class-room teaching was the drawing of maps in the Elizabethan manner — sometimes followed up by whimsical descriptions of what was to be found, where, as the genuine maps often asserted, 'Here be monsters'. The usual design was a fantastic island, known always as an 'ilond' and inevitably containing haunts of pirates, caches of treasure, magic caves and mythical creatures. Homer and Stevenson, as well as *The Tempest* and *A Midsummer Night's Dream*, were sources of inspiration. The seas around were invariably filled with 'Lulla-fish' — dolphins or leviathans 'whose origin was in the stick-wagging interpretation of the Philomel lullaby'.[53]

Cook was passionately fond of dancing and ballet, and especially Morris dancing, which appealed to him all the more because it had its roots in country lore. He introduced country dancing to the school and made it a vital activity. Classes were inaugurated by a visit from the great Cecil Sharp, who came at Cook's invitation to demonstrate the various dances. The idea was taken up with enthusiasm and for a number of years country dancing was a regular feature of Perse life, either in the Mummery or in the hall, or out of doors; although this occasionally gave rise to horseplay, it gave great pleasure to many. The two most notable disciples were Arthur Peck and Arthur Heffer, the former known as Alfred to prevent confusion with his namesake.

Music, with dancing, played an important part in the seasonal festivals he liked to arrange, and the Players always had their Master of the Music — a post long filled by Gavin Macfarlane-Grieve, as man and boy. However, the more sublime music of the great composers did not move Cook or give him the thrill which other aspects of art gave him, and which he was able to communicate so brilliantly to his classes. For his dancing he used what was then an up-to-date machine, an old-fashioned clockwork gramophone in a square oak cabinet, but without a horn. Yet, on his own admission, Cook did not appreciate music to the full, except in its application to dancing and in the settings of the ballads and folk-songs he loved, such as the charming 'I gave my love a cherry' which Sharp had found in Kentucky.

Other members of Cook's staff — he was, of course, head of the English department — became enthusiastic imitators of his methods. The most successful were Happold and Salusbury. Perhaps the most memorable public demonstration of Persean drama came in 1923-24 when several plays were performed, one produced by Cook and others by Happold. Cook's was *The Fight of Finnsburg*, which is spoken of on a later page. Happold, having inspired *The Death of Roland* and *The Duke and the Charcoal Burner*, himself wrote and produced the very successful Christmas play, *The Finding of the King*, which is still in print and occasionally produced in schools.

Two books, of comparatively recent date, give a more detailed assessment of Cook's work than is possible here. Derrick Beacock's *Play Way English for Today* (1943) has a full biographical sketch and classroom details of the method, with specimens of work done in the last few years of the Master's career; it could fairly be called a counterpart, or twin volume, to Rouse and Appleton's *Latin on the Direct Method*. Christopher Parry's *English Through Drama* (1972) is a very sensitive appraisal, connecting with work at the Perse, inspired by Cook, in recent years.[61]

XII

LANGUAGES AND HISTORY UNDER ROUSE

The reputation of the Perse was established by the high quality and originality of its teaching of modern languages, even before Rouse began his great experiments in teaching the Classics. The first grants awarded by the Government were, as has been mentioned, 'in respect of the language teaching'.

Rouse's curriculum envisaged that work in this sphere would begin with French, which would provide the best introduction to the learning of all languages, would accustom boys to the Direct Method and would give them the invaluable trick of thinking in another language. He planned that every boy should learn four or five languages, two of which would normally be classical. He advocated the following programme in language teaching: French at 9; Latin at 12; Greek at 14; German or Italian at 16 — when French could be discontinued. The *Cambridge Chronicle*, in reporting this, made the shrewd comment (probably quoting Rouse's own words) that 'unlike some headmasters, he appears to have learned that the timetable should be the servant and not the master, and has thus been able to accomplish what is found to be impossible in some of our best-equipped and richest public-schools'.

Consequently, as Percy Copping[41] put it, 'though Rouse's sixth-form teaching was the final marvel of the school, the main impact of his method and approach was lower down the school, through Latin certainly, but above all through French and, later, German'. For, in its teaching of all languages, as in much else, the Perse was well ahead of other schools, using methods which have, years later, become familiar — though even now not universal, for French, and Latin, are still made more difficult for the average school-child than need be. Spike Hughes remarks that 'So much time is given up to deciphering a language which is not easy to spell at any time that there is no time left to develop anything approaching a tolerable accent. At the Perse we learned French in the way we had learnt to speak English: by picking it up by ear and then coming to the grammar and spelling'.[53]

It was understood from the first that boys did not dare to speak in a French class-room in any language but French, and a good accent was insisted on, as strictly as a good accent was required in English lessons. Phonetics formed an essential part of the beginners' course — at a time when such activity was found in few other schools. The *Cours français du lycée Perse*, which was the main text, was printed in two parts, bound together in one cover and entitled 'Phonétique' and 'Orthographe usuelle' — and at first every class stuck to Part One, Phonétique. There was constant drill in phonetics, with, at the start of each lesson, a chorused repetition of what the text neatly called the family of sounds, brothers and sisters, together with 'la poupée' — the 'doll or dummy' standing for the closed 'e' which occurs, for example, in *de* and *devoir* and in final syllables (as in *patrie* in *la Marseillaise*).

In those early lessons the details of the sounds were shown, with their phonetic symbols, on a wall-chart. Each class would begin with the call, 'Chantez les sons'. The boys would then sing through the main French open vowels, first long, then short, on the octave scale of eight diatonic notes, from highest to lowest, in a major key, and so back again. Then the master would call for 'Les sons frères et soeurs'; at this the class 'voiced' (hardly sang), on one note only, the whole 'family' of sounds, followed by 'la poupée'. The exercise was rounded off with a revision drill, and with the two gastronomically satisfying phrases, employing all the nasalised sounds: 'Un bon grand pain' and 'Un bon vin blanc'.

The other well-remembered feature of the *Cours français* method was 'La Série' — the series of actions in which a boy moved around the room explaining in French what he was doing and requiring the class to tell him about it; when this was extended to the plural, with two boys in action, it covered the conjugation of all the persons of such verbs as venir, se lever, s'asseoir, ouvrir, sortir, rentrer, including the interrogatives and negatives, and constituted a kind of game which led naturally to classroom dramatics of a kind. In the more advanced stages drama played an increasing part, whether impromptu or based on text-books. There were class-readers from which oral exercises could be developed, the most valued of these being *Emile et Hélène* and other books written by Mrs (later Lady) Frazer.

The great exponent of the method, and the head of the language department, was Louis de Glehn, who, because of his original name, abandoned in 1914, of von Glehn, was always nicknamed 'Vonny'.

He, like Rouse, was acknowledged all over the world as a master of his craft, and published numerous articles on his work, a notable one in *New Teaching*. He had the title of Senior Assistant Master, and, with Appleton, was one of the strongest personalities on the staff. Quite apart from his teaching, he was a very effective schoolmaster; for the Fifth Form (over which he always presided) and for West House he was a model of what a good form and house master should be, making always kindly and helpful reports and showing a deep interest which made each boy want to do his best. Yet he had a fierce exterior manner, and could be positively terrifying. Every boy was in respectful awe of him; discipline in his classes was of the strictest, and there was a general desire not to sit in a front desk, since he was known to enforce a point by banging a finger, wearing a heavy ring, against the head of the nearest pupil, and on occasion even to lift one from the floor by the hair (Leonard Amey[55] remembers suffering this). His exploits never approached the vicious: he would have been terribly upset if he had actually hurt anyone, and underneath he was generous and kind. 'His fierceness was but the fierceness assumed for our good by the determined teacher'.

His methods were vigorous and dynamic; in class he worked hard himself and expected the whole class to play their part with the same vigour.

Yet, for all his vigour, he taught slowly and meticulously, paying great attention to grammar and in fact teaching its formal elements in a way never covered by English or Classics lessons.

'Vonny' was fiercest in demanding prompt and adequate handing-in of written work. On a number of occasions when his enquiry, 'Where is your French homework, ma boy?' — exasperation might make him lapse into English — was met with an excuse, he would order the offender to take it over to his house. At first he lived in Warkworth Street, no great journey, but later he settled in Grantchester; even then the order was always obeyed, the more so as the boy knew that the blow would be softened by the provision of some kind of refreshment at the end of the journey. At Grantchester he at first lived at Byron's Lodge; 'Next to the Green Man, ma boy', he would explain. Later he built a bigger house behind the vicarage. He used to drive to school in a lumbering old Renault, with a crinkly bonnet in front of its radiator. Written work was always corrected in a manner both meticulous and sympathetic, and always promptly returned. The pupil had to correct corrections until, as G. T. Salusbury put it, 'the resultant palimpsest compelled complete re-writing'.

He was an impressive, bearded man, like Caldwell Cook in sartorial eccentricity, but never his equal in elegance; he always wore plus-fours, as against Cook's knickerbockers. He had a deep voice which, though sometimes it boomed when 'Vonny' was enforcing a point, was beautifully modulated, with every consonant carefully sounded. At concerts he often sang bass songs, such as 'Who is Silvia?' and he also took part in the Saturday morning sing-songs.

De Glehn was, as might be expected, a first-class linguist, speaking several languages fluently. He had been brought up, as he used to explain, in a tri-lingual home, his ancestry being a mixture of Alsatian, Polish and Welsh. He had close relations in France, Belgium and Russia, and during the 1914-18 War declared he had kinsmen in all the allied armies, but none on the German side. Among his relations, one was a famous railway engineer and another an artist of repute. His childhood had been spent in England, and he went to school at Eastbourne College; but all his boyhood holidays had been passed in France.

Like Rouse and Caldwell Cook, he had a feeling for linguistic niceties, and the *thèmes* and translations submitted to him had to be precise and, where possible, witty. The standards he expected seemed indicated by the fact that in the fifth form he used printed material headed 'King's College Lecture Room'; he was a supervisor at his old college. In addition he gave lectures to the University and to the Education Department; many of 'Fox's Martyrs' — so called because the principal was the well-known Charles Fox — would do their practical work under his eye, learning much about 'class-management', no doubt. Teaching practice was also available for the young ladies of the Wollaston Road College (now Hughes Hall) — who were supervised by Miss Neroutsos, a lady — known to the boys as 'Auntie' — who impressed classes as a female counterpart of de Glehn, since even on her brief visits she managed to strike a degree of terror into them.

De Glehn was probably the only member of staff, other than the Doctor, who paid regular visits to the Preparatory School. He would burst into a French class in Bateman Street exclaiming 'Bonjour, mes enfants!' and, one thought, hoping to be regarded by the small boys as a breezy old uncle, when in fact he was filling them with awe. Some old boys remember how, one term, after several visits of this kind, he asked in English if the class understood his greeting: after a silence a timid little boy put up his hand and asked, "Is it, 'Sorry I'm late', sir?"

Another good de Glehn story tells how he once appeared before a class with his flies unbuttoned; a boy had the temerity to tell him of it, in English. L. G. characteristically boomed, 'Why didn't you tell me in French?' and then, without a trace of embarrassment, drilled the class: 'Je suis déboutonné; qu'est-ce que je suis?' and made them go through the other persons, 'Tu es . . . ' etc. In this, of course, he showed the same readiness to use an incident to help his teaching that we have noticed in Appleton.

The Play Way had its exponent in the French classroom; 'Vonny' could make a game out of the subtle rule for the agreement of the past participle.

Kenneth Thompson recalls how at one time de Glehn worked an ingenious system whereby all the class played a sort of game based on golf: each was 'given a bogey for the course' and scored according to his performance in the lesson. The best at the time, Ralph Couldrey, was rated at minus 10, while Thompson was plus 20. Thus Couldrey had to score thirty marks to catch Thompson up. When he failed to do so, de Glehn would point at him and say, in tones of monumental despair, 'Eh, mon pauvre Couldrey!' The 'bogey' system, incidentally, extended to individual exercises. De Glehn's comments could be foreseen; thus, given a 'bogey' of 9, a score of 8 would be marked 'épouvantable!', one of 7 'dégoûtant!!' and one of 6 'honteux!!!'

The results achieved by the French department under this direction were very remarkable, nearly every boy leaving the school with a fluent grasp of the language and its idiom, and an accent far more Gallic than most Englishmen ever attain. The record of Marius Goring, though exceptional, was typical of what the best pupils could do. But it must be admitted that the French teaching had the defect quoted as one of Rouse's failings: the weaker brethren too often fell behind and lost interest. The emphasis on good accent aggravated this tendency, since those who could not fathom phonetics, or were too shy to take a full part in oral work, even though their understanding was sound, were relegated to a lower set. If this was taken by Léon Chouville there was no cause for regret, but if it meant being taken by any other teacher the loss was severe.

Any boy passing through the school during this era would be unlucky if he did not at some time learn his French from Chouville, who was another magnetic personality. The two men were in complete contrast, de Glehn with his black beard, bass voice and forbidding presence, Chouville with his drooping blond moustache, light tenor voice and air of courteous humour. Chouville was a Norman, who had taken his degree at Caen, and wrote a charming book about France and the French, with particular reference to Normandy, called *En douce France*, which was occasionally used as a class text-book. Anthony Dunhill has described Chouville as 'the distillation, the essence, of France and the French'. He was another excellent disciplinarian, who drilled his classes like a drill-sergeant, but always with a twinkle behind his myopic pince-nez. Cyril Alliston remembers how 'he could shame you with gentle irony — and with heavy sarcasm, too, if you deserved it'. In contrast to de Glehn's more formal methods, Chouville adopted live conversational teaching. In his class even less English was spoken than in Vonny's. Moreover, the French in use was spoken at a tremendous speed and with very little grammatical explanation. Bernard Coulson has described how 'One was flooded with it, engulfed in it, lived in it and of necessity thought in it; there was no time to think to and fro from French to English'. This gave a training in the language few other schools could offer.

The difference between these two teachers has been well summed up by Eric Warmington[62] : 'It might be said that one learned, in slow motion and laborious accuracy, the pronunciation of individual French sounds from de Glehn; and French fluency from Chouville.'

Like de Glehn, Chouville could be fierce on occasion, but he hardly ever resorted to physical punishment, his verbal castigations being so effective; if he did forget himself and thwack a boy, perhaps with the little pointer he used, his instant contrition would lead to mutual hand-shakes. He had a quick, but evanescent, temper; and when he lost it he would swear comprehensively in French — presumably thinking that no-one would understand him. In later life, however, Perseans travelling in France might find themselves remembering this incidental part of his tuition. In the first War, in particular, those on active service in France discovered that if, when they could not get what they wanted, they swore as they had heard Chouville swear they commanded awestricken respect.

Chouville's great contribution to Perse teaching lay in the enthusiasm which he felt, and transmitted to his classes, for French literature and drama. He would take his classes joyously through Corneille, Racine, and, above all, Molière, much as Caldwell Cook took his through Shakespeare. He was an accomplished actor who had been a member of the Comédie Française, and in consequence class-room dramatics with him tended to be a one-man-show, and an unforgettable experience. If a class had been good, they could readily persuade him to act for their delight the great scene in which l'Avare discovers that he has been robbed. He would lose himself in the part, rolling all over the platform in assumed agony and frothing at the mouth.[6] Off the stage, too, he would consciously or unconsciously often be acting a part. He would be le Professeur français in his more routine elementary lessons, and, walking with his family in the street, le Bon Père bourgeois. Incidentally, a piece of class-room 'business' many will remember was the trick of caressing his moustache with a neatly-folded white handkerchief.'[55]

Both Chouville and de Glehn appeared in plays in French on the Cambridge stage, and especially in performances of the Company of French Actors in Cambridge organised by Lady Frazer. One notable production of May, 1909, led the press to speak of Chouville's portrayal of Harpagon as 'a masterly study, making the old miser a vividly real personality.' Chouville became known to a wider audience when on occasion he deputised for M. Stéphan, whose French lessons on the pre-war radio earned him the reputation of being perhaps the greatest who have employed this medium for their teaching.

Both these great teachers were also employed in the University, having been appointed by the Special Board for Modern Languages as 'listed lecturers' to take classes in French composition and (before 1931) in French Phonetics. This was quite an exceptional arrangement, especially after 1926, when the University began to appoint Lecturers as such. The appointments were from 1924 until 1934.

De Glehn, in particular, became a popular personality of Cambridge life. The student magazine *Granta* affectionately lampooned him in the clerihew

> Mr. de Glehn,
> One of Cambridge's 'he-men',
> Is generally feared
> Because of his beard.

Undergraduates called him 'Edouard Sept' — since his appearance and manner suggested Edward VII. A number of Old Perseans, passing into the University, encountered their old teacher, in what could be embarrassing circumstances. Couldrey, for example, to whom reference has been made, having failed to answer a question in a class at King's, found himself greeted with the familiar, 'Eh, mon pauvre Couldrey!' and found himself 'torn between confusion and amusement'. Among de Glehn's university students was the future headmaster, Stanley Stubbs.

Chouville had a long tenure at the Perse, and stayed on longer than any of his contemporaries, becoming Second Master in 1932. When he retired, as the last of the old 'giants', it was generally felt that the end of the Rouse era had been reached. He had served the school for 35 years, being Second Master for six.

The Old Persean Society entertained M. Chouville at its July supper of that year, 1938, and the occasion was all the more memorable because much of the business, including the principal speeches, was conducted in French, and the evening concluded with the singing of French songs. The whole meeting had the air of a happy party, and the success of the Direct Method was amply shown by the spontaneous and enthusiastic use of what did not appear to be a foreign language. It was appropriate that the President that year was de Glehn, long since retired, and elected to a post usually reserved for Old Perseans and headmasters, as a tribute to his exceptional qualities.

The task of the present writer was happily foretold in the remarks made by Douglas Field-Hyde in proposing the principal toast. No apology is needed for the inevitable repetition of the assessment made in this chapter, nor for transcribing rather than translating what was said:

"Ce sont, said Mr. Field-Hyde, d'ailleurs deux noms qui seront inséparables, l'un de l'autre, quand on écrira l'histoire du Lycée Perse au 20e siècle, tout comme ils seront inséparables, tous deux, de celui de leur chef, le Docteur Rouse".

When he retired, Chouville had the distinction and honour of being appointed Officier d'Académie in recognition of his services in teaching French, and the Governors offered their congratulations. He then returned to his native Caen, where his retirement, though a long one (he died in 1968) included the horrors of the Second World War and the Occupation of France. One of his sons, both of whom were boys at the school, was killed in the war; they had retained dual nationality and served in the French army.

Songs in French were, like Rouse's classical songs, an important class-room activity, long before this came to be an accepted teaching method. Chouville's classes usually opened with songs like 'Quand trois poules'.

German formed part of the curriculum throughout this period; even in the wartime of 1914-18, 'at a time when German is apt to be neglected,' Rouse made it an integral part of the course. Before 1914 it was taught by Herr Rübel, who aroused in his pupils an interest in German poetry, especially Schiller, and in music, especially Wagner. Among the delightful *assistants* of French or German nationality one remembers particularly Herr Georg Bauer, who had a special liking for Grimm's fairy-tales, which, he would assert, provided a model of good colloquial German.

Rouse urged the cultural value of a knowledge of German, and, still more, Italian. Although he disliked the Teutonic approach to classical scholarship, he wanted his boys to understand Goethe and Heine and the other great writers and thinkers. Even more important was an understanding of Dante; accordingly, Italian was taught whenever staffing and the time-table allowed it.

There were successes in Modern Languages at the Universities and elsewhere. In 1909 four Perse boys took part in the all-England examination held by the Allgemeine Deutsche Sprachverein when all passed, three with credit. Among distinguished linguists who passed through the school Sir Herbert Marchant should have special mention.

The third subject which was brilliantly taught in Rouse's time, and helped to make the Perse internationally known, was History. The first History master of a distinguished series was A. J. B. Green, who joined in 1907 and left in 1920.

English and History teaching at the Perse owes much to A. J. B. Green, one of the finest schoolmasters who ever served there. Educated at the Roan School, Greenwich[37] and at Jesus College, Oxford, he was a first-class historian and his teaching produced several notable scholars, including Frank Leavis, who went up to Emmanuel as a History Scholar. Green's influence in the school was remarkable. He really understood boys, and enjoyed their company as much as they did his. Outside the classroom he took an enthusiastic share in every kind of activity, taking part in all games, initiating a scheme for training in athletics which has since become usual practice, and concerning himself also with cycling, debating, the Navy League and in a hundred and one other spheres. He ran a small boarding-house at 89 Hills Road, to which day-boys were always welcome, and often quite large parties assembled for tea after school — not merely for refreshment, but because the boys valued his friendship and advice. Among his boarders were several from abroad.

It was he who introduced Scouting to the Perse, and he was largely responsible for introducing the movement to Cambridge, serving as District Secretary for a number of years. He always personally carried out the enrolment ceremony for recruits; D. M. Simmonds recalls that 'to be welcomed by him into "this great brotherhood of Scouts" was a experience not lightly to be forgotten'.

He was originally appointed to teach English. He quickly made his name; at Speech Day in November, 1908, he was commended in the Headmaster's report as having tackled successfully 'the most urgent of all scholastic questions, the teaching of English'. Evidently his achieve-

ment in this subject paved the way for the subsequent work of Caldwell
Cook. He is said to have 'encouraged precision in the choice of words
and a critical approach to literature'.

On Rouse's retirement Green applied for the Perse Headship, and
the fact that he lost the appointment by a narrow margin — the
Governors were far from unanimous in their decision — may be
reckoned one of the great misfortunes in the school's history, since he,
more than any other perhaps, would have continued the great tradition.
On leaving, he became Headmaster of Guildford Grammar School,
where he stayed until he retired, achieving notable success and earning
general respect.

During the 'twenties, History teaching at the Perse was directed by
Green's successor, another happy eccentric, Frederick Crossfield
Happold. He was a Peterhouse scholar who entered teaching after a
distinguished war career in which he won the D.S.O., and, not
unnaturally, was also put in command of the Perse O.T.C. He was a
smallish man with a large projecting chin and a curious habit of speech
which sometimes made him difficult to follow and caused a light froth
to appear on his lips which could spray his audience. Hence he was
known as 'Shush' and but for his strong personality and power of
arousing interest might have become a figure of fun. As it was, he
came in for a share of good-natured teasing, which he always took in
good spirit.

Although completely unlike Caldwell Cook, he had a good deal in
common with him. He taught some English, adding touches of his
own to the Mummery method and to the Players' productions. Above
all, he provided a valuable liaison between the two departments of
English and History, adapting methods used by Cook for the purpose
of his own subject. In particular, he used 'Speeches' in his lessons,
when they were called 'History Lectures'. However, he did not simply
imitate, for his own very distinctive personality came into everything
he did, and he possessed in full measure the two vital qualities of
enthusiasm and originality which distinguished most of Rouse's staff.

With him, as with Cook and de Glehn, a number of teaching
methods were originated which are now regarded as 'modern' but were
at the time daringly new. His conception of how History could be
made a live subject is well shown in the syllabus he prepared in 1923,
which, after stating that the work in the first two years of the course
should be a general sketch of world history, with only essential detail,
lays down that 'the emphasis is on the picturesque. Models for the
history museum are made out of school. Little plays are used to

illustrate points'. It continues that in the third year 'Boys are encouraged to do as much as possible on their own'. At this stage he made much use of what has since been called the 'Project' method, encouraging research into suitable topics, such as the history of transport, voyages of exploration, great buildings, discoveries and inventions, military campaigns, costume and art. This led boys, usually working in groups of two or three, to produce quite effective pictorial charts. Time-charts and models for the history museum were other practical exercises he encouraged, and homework as often as not took the form of imaginative 'reconstructions', compositions, plays, poems, dialogues and drawings. He was a great exponent of brass-rubbing, at a time when this art was enjoying one of its periodical booms. Cambridgeshire churches offer some of the finest examples of monumental brasses, and the boys were encouraged to make collections, and to learn a good deal about costume and armour from the brasses they studied.

Happold's ideas were embodied in *The Adventure of Man*, a textbook which became popular, and included examples of the work of his Perse pupils. He was himself a prolific writer; his most important original work was the Nativity play of which an account is given on another page, and he also wrote some very effective plays designed to teach history, one of the best of which, showing the ancient civilisations as personified figures, gave Marius Goring an early chance to show his talent, when he appeared as 'Rome'. Other dramatic productions of Happold's were 'reviews' in the modern idiom, in which the musicians and artists joined with the actors and 'rough satyrs danced'.

When he left in 1928 Happold became Headmaster of Bishop Wordsworth's School, Salisbury, where he worked out and developed in his own way some of the 'Rouse and Cook' ideas after they had been temporarily abandoned at the Perse. In particular, in seeking to relate his teaching to the wider interests of the humanities, he pioneered 'integrated studies', treating English, History and Geography as one subject. Here again one of the Perse brotherhood established as a novelty an idea which has since become common-place in the educational world. While at Salisbury, Happold took a doctorate. He also married, later in life, in a fine ceremony in the Cathedral. His son has made a name for himself in journalism.

At the Perse he proved himself a very capable organiser, so capable that he was accused of trying to 'organise the staff'.[46] He certainly made valuable contributions in almost every sphere of school life. One excellent service he gave, in the days when there was no school catering service, was to provide lunches at his house in Bateman Street for train-boys and others who could not go home in the middle of the day; these were prepared by his sister, who also served the Perse Players as Mistress of the Wardrobe and, like many staff wives, was always ready to offer any help to the school.

As Officer Commanding the O.T.C., Happold gave full play to his eccentricity — as is recorded on another page — but he maintained the unit at a high standard, encouraging shooting and using a degree of imagination in organising Displays, Field Days and Inspections. In all this, as in his teaching, he was playing the part of a theatrical producer as much as that of a soldier and scholar.

XIII

MATHEMATICS & SCIENCE; THE SECOND MASTERS

The departments of Mathematics and Science were notable also, both in Barnes-Lawrence's and in Rouse's days. In the Doctor's case, this might be thought to be in spite of his unsympathetic attitude. Indeed, he would speak of the failure of these subjects to 'touch the soul'. With his preoccupation with the humanities, Rouse did not appreciate the austere beauty of the sciences, except perhaps where they formed part of the philosophy of his beloved classical writers, Pythagoras, Hippocrates, Archimedes, Lucretius. In *Machines or Mind?* he calls Lucretius 'the only man who ever made science and poetry meet' and he goes on to invite the reader to 'compare Lucretius with Erasmus Darwin's *Loves of the Plants* and say then whether the ancient or the modern world has the advantage'. Later in the pamphlet he speaks bitterly of 'this world of machines which bows down to the Dragon of Science, falsely so called'. As Goronwy Salusbury puts it, no mathematician could hope to do much with a boy whose education had made him enjoy "only the kind of arithmetic involved in 'A thousand shall fall at thy side and ten thousands at thy right hand' and had reached the conclusion that there was no dignity in Decimals."

In *To Young Teachers* Rouse wrote: 'There is no doubt in my mind that the preponderance of weight in school should be given to the imagination and the mind, that is, to literary subjects, story and poetry and drama, music and singing, gracious utterance of speech, graceful walk and gesture and dance, study of beautiful pictures, buildings, carvings and so forth; balanced by studies of measurement and number, and the use of tools, not machines driven by outside power . . . My ambition was that this system might produce a new type of public-school boy, one who would take delight in his intellectual work and his physical games alike, with equal gusto: not an expert specialist, but an all-round competent'.

After this essay, rather in the style of Morris' *News from Nowhere*,

Rouse went on to lay down that the curriculum of any school must be balanced, and that scientific subjects would, quite naturally, appear in their proper place. Even if he did not show the same personal interest in the science side as in the humanities, he took the trouble to choose the best available teachers of science and mathematics for the Perse, and to give them a free hand. Although, in their public standing, these teachers were inevitably overshadowed by the genius of their colleagues in departments which achieved international fame, the Perse scientists could point to very notable achievements and to pupils who at the Universities won the greatest distinctions.

Rouse's philosophy of education, which has been sketched in earlier pages, argued that the vital thing in the work of a school is, in the words of a favourite prayer of his, to 'make learning a discovery and a joy'. Mathematics and Science, therefore, had their place and it would be wrong to read too much into Rouse's occasional diatribes against narrow-minded scientists.

The masters who taught Mathematics and Science were men of considerable stature and personality. The two principal Mathematicians were V. M. Turnbull and I. H. Hersch. These two were, as it happened, placed equal as Fourteenth Wranglers in the Mathematical Tripos of 1891, but they did not know each other while at college, Turnbull at Trinity and Hersch at Caius. Turnbull was the third of the assistant staff who came to the school with Rouse in 1902, the others being Jones and de Glehn. Hersch joined two years later. Both gave long service to the school, for they stayed throughout the Doctor's reign, Hersch retiring in 1929 and Turnbull in 1930.

Turnbull was a Cumbrian — he once contributed an article to the *Pelican* on John Peel — and spoke with a markedly regional accent; in particular, he always said 'bye' for 'boy' and this gave rise to a nickname by which he was sometimes known. More often, however, he was called 'Twiddle'; this would appear to be an obvious variant on the first syllable of his name, but it has been said to be derived from a habit he had of twiddling his thumbs at such times as when invigilating examinations. He was a good disciplinarian, occasionally fierce, with a habit of imprisoning a defaulter in the space underneath his desk. Without making his subject generally fascinating, he taught it well enough, often covering the whole length of his blackboard with intricate calculations. He got on well with his pupils, in and out of school, though he was not a games man. He was a great gardener, and could often be seen, out of hours, carrying a basket laden with garden produce from his allotment adjoining the Botanic Gardens. Another hobby of his was geology, and he gave his collection of specimens to the school. Like many mathematicians, he also studied astronomy. He lived to the great age of 92, dying in 1961.

Hersch was also a fine mathematician, and, but for a serious illness which struck him when he was about to take the Tripos, would probably have been a Senior Wrangler. After leaving Caius he took a First Class in Experimental Physics at the Royal College of Science, and was at the Woolwich Polytechnic from 1897 until he came to the Perse. He was well known in the world of public examining, serving as a Chief Examiner for both the London and Oxford and Cambridge Boards.

Hersch's left leg was crippled, and he wore a surgical boot, but his progress was never seriously hampered. The boys, rather cruelly, gave him the nickname of 'Pied' (pronounced 'Peed') — but he took this, as he took everything, with unfailing good humour. To move about the town he used a tricycle, with one pedal only. Since Appleton also, while he could manage it, and at one time de Glehn, had tricycles, the school presented an unusual spectacle with the arrival of so many of these machines each morning.

Hersch had been brought up in Manchester, where he saw a great deal of the grinding poverty of the immigrant Jewish community. This gave him a very sensitive social outlook. There is no doubt that he was a man of exceptionally fine character, an admirable person to be in charge of boys, in school and at Hillel House. While a good disciplinarian, and a very thorough teacher who insisted on his pupils' work being equally thorough, he was known for his sympathetic approach to any difficulty and for his understanding treatment of wrong-doers. It was said of him that he was always 'surprised' that people went astray, and still more so that anyone was bored in a world full of interest.

Hersch had two sons, both of whom came to the school. The younger son, Robert, who changed his name to Hurst, became a notable architect, and gave a valuable service to the school in designing the Macfarlane-Grieve Memorial pavilion on the Luard Road ground, and the Memorial Gates at the entrance to the present school, given as a memorial to the Second World War victims.

In their letter to the Board of Education in December, 1901, the Governors pointed out that they had 'just elected a Headmaster whose antecedents prove him to be possessed of the energy and experience and breadth of view which promise that with a reasonably free hand and with the whole-hearted support of the town and county he will succeed in making the Perse School realise the best hopes of the Governors'.

The Doctor certainly tried to fulfil this promise, and to make his curriculum a well-balanced one, giving the scientists fair scope, even though he did not take a close personal interest in their work. Consequently, within a few months of his appointment we find him reporting to the Governors 'on the teaching of Modern Languages and Science' — and asking for additional salaries for the staff, not least the scientists, who are named as deserving increases. He seems to have recognised that Modern Languages, Mathematics and Science were the departments most in need of reform, and soon secured the appointments of de Glehn (April, 1902) and Turnbull (August, 1902). The existing Mathematics and Science Master, Mr. Sandberg, was leaving. The new masters, and W. H. S. Jones (appointed with Turnbull) were all offered yearly salaries of £180 'with a prospect of a rise'.

But the Governors hesitated over the Science appointment, a minute recording that 'Your Committee wish to err on the side of caution, and consider that the engagement of a separate science master should depend on whether arrangements are made to earn grants under the Board of Education. This opinion is fully endorsed by the Headmaster'. However, Mr. B. E. Mitchell, with a London B.Sc. degree as well as a Cambridge B.A., was presently appointed as 'Natural Sciences Master'.[63]

That some quite satisfactory science teaching had been achieved in this period is shown by the minute of 20 November 1901, with reference to the continuing argument about the revised Scheme for the school. The Governors argued that, since the school was one which 'aims at providing a literary education as well as a scientific education of the highest type, they should be given as free a hand as possible. The Governors are most anxious that the high position which the school has attained *in respect of its science teaching* should be maintained and improved.' This seems to imply that under Barnes-Lawrence Science ranked as of equal importance with the Classics. The point was put even more forcefully when, in December, 1901, a letter was sent by the Governors to the Secretary of the Board of Education asking for relaxations in the conditions of the new Scheme. The letter contained the following passage:

'The only chance for the Perse School to hold its own in the face of the serious competition which awaits it is to provide an education of a different type to (sic) that provided by the County School. The Perse School must be a school of the highest and most modern type, offering the choice of a literary or scientific education based upon a sound elementary education of the best type.' There were, it went on to argue, 'peculiar circumstances and exceptional features' which justified special treatment.

In 1906 J. Llewellyn Davies was appointed as Senior Science Master, the first to hold this title. He was a fine teacher, and very popular in the school, being a jolly man, able to poke fun at himself and to make his subject entertaining. Rouse had a particular affection for him, and Eric Warmington[62] has recorded how, when news came of his death — he was one of two members of staff killed in action in the First World War — it was brought to the Headmaster during lesson-time and Rouse was deeply shocked: 'he sat there quite still for a few moments and became pale with emotion'. He had, just before he enlisted, accepted a headship in Cardiff, so that he would, in any case, have left the Perse.

Also in 1906 came G. A. Shrubb, and in 1907 A. M. Smith; both these left to join the staff of the University Botany School. Smith is remembered as a very competent geologist and biologist, who used to give entertaining lessons on the chalk of Cambridgeshire and its component microscopic fossils. From 1909 to 1911 J. Clayton, a man of 'very serious demeanour', taught Physics; he was the first with a qualification in this subject, apart from Davies, who had a double qualification. In 1914 came K. B. Williamson who proved an inspiring teacher of natural history, taking boys out 'bug-hunting' around Trumpington, Grantchester and Cherryhinton; he left after a short stay to give his time to research.

Zoology and Botany were first taught to help a few boys who wanted to pass their 'First M.B.' while at school. The great difficulty was the provision of microscopes. In the 'twenties even a good second-hand instrument cost at least £15, while new German models cost £40. Some boys requiring Zoology joined crammers' classes in the town.

University awards in the science subjects, which had been good in Barnes-Lawrence's time, continued to be so under Rouse. Between 1890 and 1911 there were 17 University Scholarships and Exhibitions in Science, the best years being 1895, when three awards were gained, and 1898 and 1899, each of which provided two awards. Rouse's notable years in this context were 1915 (two awards), 1921 and 1924 (three awards each).

The outstanding scientists produced by the school during this epoch included Sir George Thomson, Sir William Farren, R. R. Mayo and Professor R. G. W. Norrish — a list of which any school might be proud. All became Fellows of the Royal Society and Thomson and

Norrish achieved the outstanding success of winning a Nobel Prize. Only three other schools — Harrow, Westminster and St. Peter's, Adelaide, Australia, — could, up to 1972, claim two Nobel laureates among their old boys.

The greatest Perse science master of all, and the longest survivor of the staff who served in this great epoch — he died in 1975 in his ninetieth year — was Alfred Sidell Mason, who had taught Chemistry at the school from 1913 until 1924, ranking as Senior Science Master during the post-war period. 'ASM' (pronounced 'Azem') as he was affectionately known in the school,[64] was responsible, more than any other man, for establishing Science as a major subject at the Perse. His pupils gained notable successes, rivalling those of the more publicised departments, which Rouse recognised — though, when he wrote to congratulate him on the especially good awards of 1924, he added, with a pardonable touch of jealousy for his own subject, that 'if *we* get one more (we may have another Classic, allow me to inform you; so do not be *too* proud) that will be better still'.

Rouse would sometimes speak scathingly of 'narrow-minded scientists' but such a term could never be applied to Mason, the breadth of whose interests is shown in that, after taking First Class Honours in Science at Reading, he afterwards took a Modern Languages degree at Caius. As a teacher, he became noted for the meticulous care with which he organised his work: every lesson was based on carefully-prepared notes (a set for each class) which he would tick as each point was made. Inevitably, this trait led to good-natured 'raggings' behind his back, but his class-control was above criticism. 'He insisted on great accuracy in written notes and discouraged *talky-talky* verbosity, which for some boys who enjoyed unusual acquaintance with the dictionary was a cruelly helpful discipline'.[65] The same passion for detail, and great energy and enthusiasm, was to be seen in any matter in which he became engaged, and perhaps especially in the organisation of school athletics, in which he took over and perfected the 'All-round badge' system initiated by A. J. B. Green, which became a feature of the Perse.

Mason was a man of fine bearing, 'a tall, upright, spare figure of boundless energy and tenacity of purpose, whose natural pallor was deceptive'. It was a distinct loss when he left the school to become Headmaster of Hampton Grammar School; here he achieved great success and respect. He retained his connections with the Perse, inter-school matches being a regular feature; and when he retired he came to live at Harston, and later in Cambridge, renewing many old contacts. Typically, he did not give up educational work on retirement, but worked for a further thirteen years, full-time, as Director of Education to the Hispanic and Luso-Brazilian Councils.

Rouse appointed as his Second Master Frederick Margetson Rushmore, who had been a master since 1898. He had come to the school after teaching at the Higher Grade school, while studying for his degree at the same time. Rushmore was a military man, generally known as the Colonel, which rank he attained as Commander of the C.U.O.T.C. Infantry battalion. He was one of the original members of the University Rifle Volunteers, enlisting in 1895, and inevitably on coming to the Perse took a prominent part in forming the Corps. He had an intimidating Kaiser moustache and a somewhat metallic voice, but a kind heart beneath. At first he was Master-in-charge of the Commercial school, but subsequently Head of Modern Subjects. He had a good singing voice, having been a Choral exhibitioner; but he was not a ball-game player, rowing and military matters having occupied his student days. He left in 1907 to become a Fellow of St. Catharine's, and in 1927 became its first lay Master, retiring in 1933.

The next Second Master was Robert Parker-Smith, who had been at the school since 1899 and, like Rushmore, had graduated from St. Catharine's while teaching full-time — not a very uncommon thing in those days. Thus the office of Second Master was held in succession by three St. Catharine's men, the first having been Conway.

Only three men, in the long history of the office of Usher or Second Master, had a longer tenure than did Parker-Smith. One was George Barber (1833-61), the second was Wisken, and the third was to follow in the person of Arthur Hawkins (1939-64). Indeed, 'Parker' or 'Arpy' — the two nicknames were indifferently used (the second taken from his initials) — was for an important quarter-century (1907-32) an institution, known to and respected by every boy who passed through the school; and he claimed, with reason, to know every boy. He deserved the name of 'dedicated schoolmaster' and, as was only fitting with the staff he led, was a man of boundless energy and enthusiasm. His chosen subject was Geography, although he had graduated in History; and a feature of his teaching was an attempt to relate his work to the wider interests of the 'humanities'. He, like Happold, with whom he had some rapport, made effective use of the 'project' method, getting his classes to work in groups on a special topic, whether a continent or a small area. In this he was, like not a few of his colleagues, well ahead of his time. A number of his pupils read Geography at the Universities, one or two doing particularly well, and those who read other subjects would acknowledge a debt to him.

As O.T.C. commanding officer he organised Field Days as only a geographer could, and he also conducted most enjoyable outdoor classes in map-reading and field-sketching, usually on Coe Fen — before the Fen Causeway was built. He was a fine shot, a keen cyclist and an excellent photographer. Dr. Whitaker [66] recalls how he would demonstrate his keen marksman's eye by approaching the Geography hut holding its large key as if it were a revolver, and, marching straight at the door, drive the key into the lock without fumbling. He often led parties of boys on expeditions, ranging from cycle-tours on the Continent to day excursions on the river to Ely. He had a fine collection of slides, used both for teaching geography and for demonstrating photographic techniques.

He was prominent on the games-field, where he showed himself a true all-rounder, playing any ball-game with skill and subtlety. Later he was a devoted coach, umpire and referee, in games, as in the classroom, known to be scrupulously fair. It was he who introduced Rugger to the Perse, after a lapse of years.

He was a strong Conservative. When a boy once said in class that the House of Lords ought to be abolished, Parker forgot geography and gave a political oration to show how the Lords save the country from political revolution. His debating skill was on occasion to be seen at Union meetings, and he was a polished after dinner speaker.

When he retired, he went to live at the Manor House, Great Stukeley, near Huntingdon, where some of his old pupils used to visit him. He married late in life, and died in 1964, at the age of 91, having been bed-ridden for the last five years.

Léon Chouville and Arthur Hawkins, his successors as Second Master, are treated on other pages.

XIV

ROUSE'S OTHER COLLEAGUES: THE END OF THE EPOCH

Such great personalities as have been described might seem to make the rest of Rouse's staff appear insignificant, but it would be unfair as well as ungracious not to pay tribute to those who played a supporting role so well.

Five of the most notable were themselves Old Perseans, R. R. Broome, H. P. Cooke, A. C. Hawkins, G. M. Macfarlane-Grieve and G. T. Salusbury (originally Salusbury-Jones). Most distinguished and greatly loved was Arthur Hawkins, who later became Second Master and, for a time, Acting Headmaster; it will be appropriate to speak of him later. Equally well known and respected was Gavin Macfarlane-Grieve, a great friend of the school, who has left his mark in very many ways. He joined the staff, after studying at Durham University and at Magdalene, in 1923, and remained until 1958; he liked to point out that he was successively boy, master and Governor. Quite devoted to the Perse and a tremendous admirer of the Doctor, he used his considerable private means in many acts of generosity to the school and to individual masters and boys. Among his gifts should be mentioned the Pavilion on the playing-field, given in 1931 in memory of his brothers, the Macfarlane-Grieve Shield for musketry (given by the three brothers as lieutenants in 1914), the new fives-courts constructed in 1973 to replace those on the old Gonville Place site, and, above all, the facilities for long enjoyed by the Scouts at West Runton.

'Mac' devoted a great deal of energy to building up the Perse Scout group; a great part of his leisure hours were spent in the company of boys, past and present, from the school, and he entertained very generously at his home, Toft Manor. He never married, and for many years his mother, a gracious lady, kept house for him. At one time he used to give an annual dinner or tea-party to the prefects who were leaving school, and he would on such occasions choose a few words of admirable advice in the little speech he gave. He played a great part in making the Perse the remarkable school it became, not only in his teaching of mathematics and music, but through the wide personal friendships he established with so many boys; this social talent, which he shared with others, especially Caldwell Cook and Happold, and later Brown, McFarlane, Barry and Billinghurst, was an essential part of the Perse education, and in the Rouse age was quite exceptional. The story of the Fifth Cambridge Scouts, which owed so much to him, is separately treated. Gavin died in 1975, at the age of over eighty.[67]

Broome was the son of Edwin Broome, the Drawing Master — his official title — and Headmaster's Secretary, whose service went back to 1897 and who died in 1931, a delightful and gentle soul who made probably a greater contribution to the success of the school than most people appreciated. Bob read Classics and Music at Christ's, taking a Mus. B. degree, and was on the staff from 1905 until 1947. He taught the lower forms music, mainly singing, and is remembered particularly for the part he played in Rouse's time in the weekly 'sing-song' with which Saturday morning school used to end, when everybody assembled in the hall and shanties, folk-songs and carols were roared out by three hundred massed male throats; some voices were cracked, but it did not matter, so long as the songs were enjoyed. The programme always included songs in French, German and Latin, and there was a little printed book of words — no copies of which seem to have survived. Broome conducted, while Macfarlane-Grieve or a senior boy played the piano, and Salusbury or de Glehn, both of whom had beautiful voices, took the solo parts. On occasion de Glehn led the school in a version of *la Marseillaise* which became a mighty roar. When M. Painlevé came to distribute the prizes just after the First War he was delighted to hear the whole school sing the anthem.

Broome's greatest contribution was in training choirs and orchestras for Speech Day and other public functions. Happold's *The Finding of the King*, to which reference is made elsewhere, owed a good deal to Broome's skill in setting the carols, some unusual ones, with which the play was studded. School choirs often provided programmes, singing such works as Stanford's *Songs of the Fleet*. The orchestra naturally varied in standard from year to year, but was usually fully worthy of the school. It was at its best at the very end of Rouse's reign, when some really fine instumental players emerged: we should name Spike Hughes, Harold Fleet — a pianist of a high order and a sensitive accompanist, who graduated Mus.B. — John Wolfe — who became a leading French-horn player and is now a member of the B.B.C. Concert Orchestra — Cyril Peckett, an excellent violinist and viola-player, A.

Schulmann, a fine 'cellist, Stephen Waters, an outstanding clarinettist, and Paul Coles, a flautist. Best known of all, from an earlier generation, is Sir Keith Falkner, the distinguished singer who became Director of the Royal College of Music. There were others, too, who have since made a name as musicians. The contributions all these made at various concerts, and especially at the farewell concert when the Doctor retired, are remembered by many.

Goronwy Salusbury was fond of recalling how, at the very end of the First World War, he was called up to serve in the Army (two brothers of his had been killed) and, after being gazetted 2nd Lieutenant while still in the Sixth Form, returned to the Sixth after the Armistice, went up to St. Catharine's and in due course joined the staff. Salusbury took History, English and Latin. He was a very skilful teacher, and some who had failed to keep up the rapid pace set by Appleton owe their understanding of Latin, and their enthusiasm for things Roman, to the thorough grounding provided in his 'B' set. Similarly, his teaching of his main subjects lacked, perhaps, something of the genius of Cook and Happold, but was as inspiring, and was sound and scholarly; moreover he taught the whole class and not only the best boys.

Salusbury was the great wit of the staff, always ready with a neat comment, an impromptu verse or a two-edged remark. As might be expected, his written reports on boys were both shrewd and witty.

Harold P. Cooke, the fifth of these Old Persean staff members, was perhaps the most remarkable of them all. He was a somewhat gaunt but distinguished-looking man, with finely-chiselled features, who was said always to wear a 'hunted look'. He was a great pipe-smoker, but usually had such trouble in getting the thing to draw that he seemed in effect to be smoking matches.

He suffered from appallingly bad corns — like his teeth, neglected — which gave him a slight limp and caused him to carry a walking stick with him wherever he went. He managed, somehow, to continue to play a limping game of fives, even when his feet were 'killing him'. He is most remembered, perhaps, because of his speech, almost like stage 'Mummerset', particularly in pronouncing 'k' and 's'. Hence he was nick-named 'Goog' or 'Gug' and his creations the O.P.S. and the Union were his 'zezieties'. He was occasionally confused with Cald well Cook — but only by those outside the school.

Certainly he was a potential genius, with a very keen brain, who had been a Scholar of University College, Oxford, and taken a double-First degree, and had afterwards taught at Aberdeen, and as Assistant Professor in Moral Philosophy and in Classics, at Newcastle (then branch of Durham University). He was a classical scholar, a philosopher and a keen student of world affairs, with a flair for neat expression which could have led to a successful career in journalism or politics; indeed, he had been invited to join the staff of one of the great newspapers and had been offered at least one professorial Chair. But he was afflicted with a sad streak of shyness and laziness, which made his approach to most subjects somewhat dilettante, and he was content to live on the slender salary which came to him from part-time teaching, a little University coaching, some examining, the writing of two or three scholarly books, and the composition and solving of acrostics and cross-word puzzles, in which he excelled. He was also a good occasional poet, his work mainly printed in the Sunday papers. Yet he was not a mere book-man; he was a good cricketer and a really excellent fives player and *The Days of Our Youth* shows him as a keen walker and open-air man. After he left the school staff, in 1929, (he had joined in 1917) he became virtually a recluse, but he was always glad to receive visits from his old pupils, some of whom paid him regular calls up to the time of his death in 1956. It was marvellous to find him producing his books on King Charles and on Osiris without undertaking, or asking his friends to undertake, research in the libraries. He had only a slender income in the last few years, though this was augmented by a small pension from the Royal Literary Fund — in itself a recognition of his worth — and by a privately organised fund to which many O.P.'s subscribed.

At the school he soon abandoned normal class-teaching, finding class management beyond him, and took small tutorial groups of sixth formers, specialising in the preparation of scholarship candidates for the 'General Paper', which included questions on philosophy, literary criticism and current affairs, in all of which spheres Cooke was well informed. He was a master of the shrewd Socratic question as much as of the well-informed comment, and thus did valuable work. His classes were held in the room above the Mummery, originally the large bedroom of Pendeen House, which was shared with Broome, who took singing there, and with the Scouts, whose material was stored under the vigilant eye of a large portrait of Baden-Powell. Harold Cooke's shyness and independence is shown in that he was the only absentee when the staff group shown on page 122 was taken.

Outside the class-room his activities centred on two Societies, the Perse Union Society and the Old Persean Society. Barnes-Lawrence said of him that he 'almost created' the latter; but we have shown that its origins lay in the sporting activities of Allen's time. Cooke also did more than any other man to promote the idea of rebuilding the school on the playing-field site which he constantly, and often wittily, urged. He was able to do so most effectively through opportunities offered by the Tercentenary and War Memorial (1919) funds.

Among Rouse's staff there were two who were killed in action in the 1914-18 war. One of these was Major J. Ll. Davies. The other was E. H. H. Woodward, a classical scholar of Hertford College, Oxford, who came to the Perse only in 1913 and was making his name both as a teacher and as a Rugby coach.

Three others who were with Rouse in his early days left to become Headmasters: these were the Rev. W. A.. Parker-Mason (1909-13) who went to Hulme Grammar School, H. L. Watkinson (1915-16) to Mexborough, and D. B. M. Hume (1911-15) who became Headmaster of Chard School. Most of the others not named had quite brief careers in the Perse. Parker-Mason was ordained while at the Perse, and was much teased by boys who told him that he should not now punish them, but forgive all the offences! He was something of a figure of fun, partly because of a ponderous sense of humour which the boys liked to incite. He taught Latin by direct method but in a style of his own. A number of junior masters of this epoch are still remembered with affection. We should name especially F. G. Hambleton (1919-33), who is mentioned in Spike Hughes' book;[53] he was a musician and artist, who, among other subjects, liked to teach heraldry to his classes; at other times he gave interesting courses on ships and lighthouses, which were sketched and studied in some depth. He was absent for a longish period through ill-health and eventually was advised to give up teaching.

C. C. Shinkfield (1919-26) taught woodwork and some science, and was the 'handyman' who constructed the stage for use in the hall, which was dismantled and stored at the back of Pendeen House when out of use, and who rigged up stage lighting as required. He acted as Clerk of the Works to the Governors, reporting at their meetings on any technical matter requiring attention. Shinkfield was fond of telling boys that he was a 'self-made man' — which led to occasional ribaldry, as when, being a lieutenant in the O.T.C., he had to endure a marching-song to the tune of 'John Brown's body' declaring that 'Our second-in-command is a self-made man'. He was also the hero of an occasion when, the Headmaster and all senior staff being late on a foggy morning, he took the Assembly in Hall; opening the Old Man's prayer-book at random, he solemnly read a prayer for rain! He became a Headmaster in Australia.

G. Noel Armfield, who taught from 1919 until 1924, was a personal friend of Rouse's; they had met in 1886 at Bedford School, where Armfield was doing temporary work. He never stayed long in any post, and had at one time been on the stage. Immediately before joining the Perse staff he had been at the County (High) School. A brilliant linguist, he was said to speak fourteen languages fluently, and to be able to make himself understood in another thirty; the obvious parallel was drawn with Edward Palmer. His great skill lay in the study of phonetics, in which he was a nationally acknowledged expert. He had lectured at University College, London and written a number of books and several transcriptions into phonetic script. One book, *English Humour in Phonetic Script*, is in the school archives.

Armfield's sphere was, obviously, in the French department; but he was not in the same class as de Glehn and Chouville and his phonetic skill was no substitute for the genius and enthusiasm of his colleagues.

A very notable old stager was Charles Amyes, who for nineteen years (1911-1930) had charge of Form I, a class midway between the Preparatory School and the Upper School. He was a non-graduate 'general practitioner' who did a valuable job in introducing new boys, with varying educational backgrounds, to the ways of the Perse, and was very well liked. Eccentric in a number of ways, all endearing, he addressed all boys as 'Johnnie' in an incisive tone of voice. His class-control was not good, but was helped by the fact that he had a violent squint and, in consequence, 'always appeared to be looking directly at almost any boy in the class'. He was by training a botanist, and his Nature Study lessons were often memorable; moreover, the little boys soon discovered that an unpopular lesson could be averted if someone produced a bunch of less common flowers and asked what they were. In addition to his work with Form I he took a daily 'Homework class' after school, and at one time ran a small boarding-house, often visited by Appleton and Caldwell Cook, who were his personal friends. At first his class-room was above Rouse's (that afterwards used by Hicks) but when Pendeen House opened he took one of the upper rooms. Amyes' sons, who attended the Perse, found careers in journalism, on the stage, and in television; one, Julian, became a Director of Granada Television.

Other staff deserving of mention include L. R. Missen, W. D. Fraser and T. L. Morris. Missen, an Old Persean and a President of the O.P.S., did a great deal for the Perse Scouts, both during his brief stay on the staff and before and since. He left to go into 'administration' and became Director of Education for East Suffolk. Rouse, who often wrote letters to him, never quite forgave him either for ceasing to be a practising teacher or for joining the ranks of a profession he despised. Among Missen's writings should be mentioned *Quotable Anecdotes* and *Top Table Talk* which have been translated into several languages, and a scholarly book on *East Anglian Archbishops*. Fraser, who was on the staff from 1922 to 1928, made a considerable impact during a rather short stay. He was, like Mason, a liberal scientist, qualified in History and Science and teaching mainly Chemistry. He was a competent cricketer, who had batted for the Yorkshire First XI. He had a fine singing voice, and his performance as the Learned Judge in *Trial by Jury* is still remembered. He left to become Headmaster of the Grammar School at Barrow-in-Furness.

Tom Morris (1925-33) succeeded Noel Armfield as a Modern Language master. He took the English Tripos in his spare time, 'to improve his paper qualifications'. A vigorous teacher, he made his mark on school life in many ways. He was especially effective as a form-master of the Modern Sixth boys. Outside the classroom he played a full part, both in games — he was for a time in charge of cricket — and in the societies. He was forthright in his comments on events in and out of school and well informed on political questions. In the Union Society he is remembered for some incisive speeches. He became Headmaster of Falmouth Grammar School and Mayor of that ancient borough.

Also to be mentioned was R. J. Gladden (1927-32), the first qualified biologist on the staff. He and E. D. Berridge (1925-30) had commissions in the O.T.C. as lieutenants under Happold, and were successively in command.

Mention should be made of the large number of staff who came to act as Housemasters at the three boarding-houses, without teaching at the school. This arrangement was not uncommon in public schools at the time; it was particularly attractive in Cambridge, when research-students and fourth year education students could thereby gain valuable experience. Some of them were interesting and even remarkable; especially so were W. R. Seagrave, a Cross-country Blue, at South House, G. Stokes, at Milsted House, and G. A. Lyward, at South House. The latter did much for Rugby Football in the School, and introduced the striped jersey. He afterwards founded the therapeutic community for adolescent boys at Tenterden, Kent, which he directed for 43 years, in recognition of which he was awarded the O.B.E. He often spoke at educational conferences. At Hillel House the most notable assistant Housemaster was Wellesley Aron, an Old Persean.

At Milsted House Major Bostock and Charles Fox are remembered with affection; the latter also did some teaching.

This is perhaps the best place in which to make reference to Dr. Rouse's sister Alice, who was a charming, rather mouselike, lady, content to give up her life to helping her brother, by keeping house for him and looking after the welfare of the younger boys to the best of her ability. She was, in fact, not very effective in this; completely innocent in worldly matters, she was easily imposed on, and things happened in Glebe Road which would not have happened if a more worldly-minded person had been there in her place. Spike Hughes remembers her as a 'frail, busy little figure, given to talking to herself, whose kindness did much to alleviate the frequent misery of life in a boarding-school'.[53]

She had, as might be expected, a cultivated literary taste, and with her brother jointly edited an anthology of verse for young children, which was used in Amyes' Form I, and was called *A Posy of Pleasant Delights*. She used to read stories to the young boys at the house, which some have recalled with pleasure, but had not the skill in this of her brother, whose readings, especially of Dickens, which he read with intense appreciation — often with tears of laughter in his eyes when he came to the amusing parts — constituted a great experience. She shared his sense of humour in a quieter way. Gavin Macfarlane-Grieve recalls how 'she could tell stories by the hour and her description of boys and parents was wonderful, but I never heard her repeat an unkind tale'.

Miss Rouse was frequently called upon to act as 'The Headmaster's Lady' in presenting prizes and appearing at public functions. She did this with a shy graciousness. The duty was sometimes discharged, especially at Sports Concerts, by mothers of leading boys; one recalls Mrs. Jupp and Mrs. de Candole as having so officiated. Masters' wives also took part in such functions; most memorably, Mrs. Appleton sang Josephine in *H.M.S. Pinafore*.

Of the many parents who made notable contributions to the Perse character during this period we must especially single out Katie Goring, mother of Donald and Marius, who became very much part of the Perse, and gave much of her time to helping to inspire and forward its dramatic and musical life, as well as making her home a cultural centre where members of the school were welcome.

Outside the teaching staff but working as ancillaries there were some memorable personalities. Two ex-petty officers, R.N., filled in succession the post of school porter, named Medland and Milligan. The story is told that when Medland applied for the position the Doctor arranged

to interview him in London at the Athenaeum, on his way back from a
Hellenic Travellers' Cruise. The ship was delayed, so that when the
candidate arrived there was no Dr. Rouse. However, Medland, as a
disciplined sailor, returned the next day, and the next, and waited
patiently. On the third day the Doctor found him at his post and
engaged him on the spot. Medland was a very calm and efficient
person; he had a remarkable hold over the school. Every boy was
addressed as 'mate' and all felt that we were friends of his. Those of
whom Medland did not approve were 'scalliwags' — whether they
were in the Government, the University or the Town. When things
were not going as he thought they should they were 'skewdiwiff'.
Naturally enough, he was not afraid of heights, and used to walk, and
even run, along the beams of the hall, greatly impressing the smaller
boys thereby.

As befitted a sailor, he was a keen swimmer, and was a superb
teacher of swimming, always on voluntary duty at the bathing-sheds
throughout the summer on games afternoons, and often on full days
from 4.15 until six o'clock.

He would also help at O.T.C. field-days and Scout camps, particularly
the latter; at West Runton he naturally took charge of the sailing and
boating. Milligan, his successor, had Irish wit and a touch of
temper, but was equally hard-working and devoted, and equally respected by all. When he retired from the main school, he transferred to the
lighter task of caretaker of the Preparatory school, in Bateman Street.
His sons went through the school, and one became an R.A.F. doctor.

Careful with his speech, Milligan liked to tease boys with an exercise
worthy of Caldwell Cook, asking them to say with appropriate distinctions (as he could) ''Are you sure you saw Mr. Shaw on the shore?''

Another character was Costello, the drill-sergeant, who functioned
in the diminutive building known as the Armoury, which was patently
not big enough for a gymnasium but had to do duty for this purpose
also, when the weather was not fine enough for an outdoor class. The
armoury smelt always of guns and oil. There was no P.E. master, and
gymnasium lessons usually meant exercises of the 'O'Grady says'
type, with a little rope-climbing, since there was little other apparatus.
Costello was a fair performer on the flute, and trained the Corps drum
and fife band. He was the main exponent of fencing and boxing, in
both of which the school excelled at this time.

Anthony Dunhill, now a retired Commander, R.N., offers the
following description of Costello: 'Head and body carved out of
mahogany, ex-Indian army, he was the young officer's ideal N.C.O.

Always immaculate in a white jersey, Costello ran the gymnasium like a parade-ground on the North-west Frontier; he seemed straight out of Kipling. He was, in short, a real professional, and was very good with boys.'

The groundsman in the earlier days was 'Twinkle' Starr, who kept the field very tidy almost single-handed. Another groundsman, popular with the boys, was Still. At the end of the Rouse era the staff at Luard Road included two former professional cricketers, in succession, Jessop and O'Connor. Both were first-class coaches at the nets. O'Connor's son played for Essex and had had a trial for England; he played once in a Test-match, but unluckily made a 'duck' and was never played again — which was something of a tragedy in which his friends shared. O'Connor senior belonged to the distinguished period of the game's history, when Ranjitsinhji was among the great stars with whom he played.

When, in July 1928, Dr. Rouse finally retired, appropriate honours were paid to him. The O.P.S. gave him a Dinner, in the School Hall, and he himself was guest of honour at Speech Day, when it was announced that he had presented to the school much of his library, including some books of great rarity and value. It was an open secret that more would be added in his will. The Chairman, Major Brimley Bowes, announced that the Governors wanted to offer Dr. Rouse a taken of their gratitude, but he had declined anything for himself and asked that any gift should be used to endow a prize for classics, to be awarded 'in perpetuity'. The first Rouse prize was a beautifully bound copy of Charles Doughty's *Travels in Arabia Deserta*, the choice of which showed Rouse's special interest in Arabia and reminded one of Edward Palmer. The winner regards it, in 1976, as among his most valued treasures.

The Doctor is reported in the *Pelican* as having, on this occasion, 'spoken with playful touches of his keen wit' but also with deep emotion. 'Referring to the system that he had established in the school, he said that his only regret was that a greater interest in education was not shown by the present generation and that his frequent invitations to critics, to come and witness the actual working of his methods, was so rarely accepted'.

In the evening the Perse Players gave a special concert — rather, 'a family party, with everything home-made' as R. J. B. Hicks reported. This included two plays written in the school, and original music composed by five Perseans for the occasion; the composers were Bob Broome, Gavin MacFarlane-Grieve (both O.P. staff-members), and (from the boys) Patrick (Spike) Hughes, Harold Fleet and Cyril Peckett.

Last in this programme came an epilogue, written and spoken by Kenneth Thompson, 'to whom', wrote Mr. Hicks, 'our best thanks are due for putting into words, full of feeling and humour, what were our sentiments at that time.' He was surrounded by representatives of all ages and interests, from the Prep. to Old Perseans, who afterwards, joined in 'A Song of the Perse' set to music by Katie Goring, who had, as already recorded, done much for the Perse Players over the years. This was in effect a revue, covering many sides of school life, a typically English entertainment in honour of a great Englishman.

XV

H. A. WOOTTON

At Dr. Rouse's farewell Speech Day, it was announced that the new Headmaster would come to the school 'as a scientist with a deep love and regard for the humanities. He wished to get to know the spirit of the Perse, and to continue the conditions of teaching classical and modern languages, so long as it was possible to get the staff, and to back them in the way they had been taught at the Perse for many years'. A speech by Dr. Hutchinson, then Master of Pembroke, who had been a contemporary of Dr. Rouse's at Christ's and had later taught Mr. Wootton and become a personal friend of his, forecast that the sciences would be given more attention, but the humanities would play their part, 'teaching the scientists to lead rational lives'.

Mr. Wootton's background and experience seemed to fit him very well for his task. He had taught successfully at Westminster School as Chief Science Master, had a distinguished war career, including a mention in dispatches, and had for nine years been Headmaster of Kingswood School, Bath, a great Wesleyan school. He was a man of religious convictions, coming from a prominent Wesleyan family. His brother, John Wesley Wootton, had married Barbara Adam, afterwards known as Baroness Wootton; John, however, had been killed in 1917, within weeks of his marriage.

Certainly the new Headmaster tried to live up to the ideals expressed by Dr. Hutchinson. The curriculum in his time was well-balanced and the academic results well up to the tradition established by his predecessors. But the school suffered sadly because his fine qualities were overshadowed by two faults of character, which were in fact at variance with his essential nature, and probably led to his chronic ill-health. He was an incredibly rude man, and many stories are told of his brusque behaviour, which quickly alienated the brilliant men he found on his staff, whose counsel he ought to have valued, and deeply grieved the Doctor, who in retirement referred to him sadly as 'the roaring savage'. All the 'giants' of the old regime, except only Léon Chouville, left the school before very long because they found they could not work in the new climate.

His other great fault, which seriously affected the running of the school, was that he was loath to delegate his authority, and kept a personal eye on every activity, causing a great deal of needless 'paper work' in the process.[68] His discipline, both in school and in his relations with the staff, was so harsh as to give him the name of martinet. He showed clearly that he thought the discipline of the school needed tightening, and that he, as Headmaster, would be aloof and unapproachable. It may well have seemed to the Governors that in the last few years of Rouse's reign discipline was becoming slack. Few, if any, of those who were boys at the time would agree, but it may well have seemed so. Certainly Rouse had held two principles that must have seemed unsatisfactory to a Governing Body. So far from being an organiser (in the narrow sense of the word) Rouse despised 'paper' organisation and was an outspoken critic of bureaucratic control. As Arthur Peck said in the article he wrote for the *Dictionary of National Biography*, he had "believed in men, not in organisation". He wanted to get on with the job of educating the boys and regarded examinations and administrators as merely hampering his efforts. Secondly, his conception of the curriculum was heavily biased towards the humanities; he had criticised mathematics and sciences as doing nothing for the soul. These essential qualities of his have, we hope, been illustrated in earlier chapters. In discipline he believed in 'freedom with self-restraint', making for a happy school.

The Governors clearly thought that, in appointing Wootton, they were likely to make good those apparent weaknesses in the school. However, in their choice they went to the other extreme, putting the Perse in the charge of a splendid organiser (in the narrow sense) and disciplinarian, but one who lacked the qualities which had, through Barnes-Lawrence and Rouse, come to be thought of as distinctively 'Persean'. The new situation is perhaps most simply described by stating that, whereas Rouse had treated all his staff as colleagues, Wootton treated them, from the first, as subordinates who had to be drilled, and precisely instructed. His attitude came perhaps from the fact that his war service, in 1914-1918, had been as commandant of an Officers' Training Camp and then as Controller in a munitions factory. From the first he brought his ideal of discipline and from both a passion for paper-work.

There were printed forms for all sorts of purposes, and notes from the headmaster to the staff were always typed and formally worded. Detailed reports were required on such matters as attendance on the games field as well as on academic matters, and nothing was ever left to the discretion of the master concerned. The principle of running the school by sending out written instructions became such an obsession that the main contact between Headmaster and staff came to be by notes exchanged between them. The secretarial staff suffered even more, and the point was reached when a small table with 'In' and 'Out' trays was placed just inside the door of the Headmaster's room; the secretary had no need to enter further than the doorway to receive her instructions from the 'Out' tray and put her work in the 'In' tray.

Two of the leading members of staff had left with Rouse, for Headships of their own, namely Fraser and Happold. The departure of these had nothing, of course, to do with Wootton's appointment.

There were to be many other changes in the next few years. Parker-Smith, as Second Master, would shortly be retiring. De Glehn, Hersch, Turnbull and Amyes were all about to reach retiring age, but would certainly have wished to continue had conditions suited them. After one term of the new regimé the last two were firmly told that their appointments could not be extended beyond July 1930. An appeal was lodged on their behalf by the Assistant Masters' Association. Turnbull was, in consequence, allowed a further year, but Amyes' appeal was unsuccessful. The appointments of de Glehn and Miss Burrows were extended. Harold Cooke was given notice to leave in 1930, and Costello, the Drill Sergeant, was retired in May of that year. Appleton's state of health was such that he had, in any event, to give up. Of the remaining staff several began urgently to look for new appointments. Berridge became a Head of Department at Epsom College and Morris, after some uneasy years, Headmaster at Falmouth.

In Hersch's case a new Master was needed for Hillel House, and this, of course, had to be an orthodox Jewish gentleman able to purchase the house and run it independently, but with the approval of the Governors. On this occasion a fine successor was forthcoming almost immediately, in the person of Harry Dagut, who was promised that the House would be recognised, on certain conditions, for fifteen years. When James Buchanan was appointed as Mathematics master, in April 1929, Hersch was free to resign.

The most cruelly affected by the new atmosphere was Caldwell Cook. His independence of mind made him stay on, in spite of increasing pressure, for five years, but he then felt that he could not continue; he spent his last few years, as might be expected, in the loneliness that only a thwarted genius could know. He had lost not merely his occupation but the whole purpose of his life, and he could not hope to find another theatre (this seems the only apt metaphor) for his great talent. He found some solace in drink, but, as Dr. Rouse wrote in a letter to Spike Hughes, 'he did not drink himself to death; he died of a broken heart'. Hughes, in recording this in his *Second Movement* (1951),[53] adds sadly, 'I should have known that'. For many years Cook had had rooms in Appleton's house, 'Hermeion', in Hills Road, and these two fine teachers shared a grave in the Borough Cemetery. Appleton died in 1938; Cook in 1939.

In appearance as well as personality and educational philosophy, Wootton could hardly have been more utterly in contrast with the man he replaced. Rouse was short, bearded, genial and courteous, and one who did not interfere unnecessarily. Wootton was tall, gaunt, austere, unapproachable and unpredictable, and given to dogmatic assertion and crass interference. Rouse was the declared enemy of the narrow examination system; Wootton immediately geared the school to the passing of examinations, so that the Higher School Certificates of the 'O. & C.' Board became at once the proper aim of every pupil.

Wootton appeared to be always about to lose his temper; Salusbury used to remark that, whereas Gloucestershire had its Wooton-under-Edge, Cambridge had a Wootton-*on*-edge. In consequence, he had few friends, and patently never sought one. He was generally disliked by all, inside and outside the school. Parents complained that if they made an enquiry all they received was rudeness, and inevitably the general public in the town heard exaggerated stories of what was going on at the Perse. In consequence the school became unpopular and many parents — even those with long-standing family connections — preferred to send their sons elsewhere. The numbers, though at first they rose, dropped quite seriously, and money for running the organisation, always low in Rouse's time, was shorter than ever. The boys, even the sixth form, were generally afraid of their Head, although they came to know his moods — especially that a request rebuffed on a first approach might be granted on a second application, and that if there was no question affecting official dignity — as when a young student-teacher sought advice — relations could be more cordial. Later, the closer relationships of war-time showed an essential humanity which had been suppressed by the desire to exert authority.

Since the Head struggled to force a ruthlessly systematic way of life on all, mutual antipathy was inevitable. In short, what had been an exceptionally happy school soon became a very unhappy one.

It must, however, be recorded that the Headmaster's insistence on personal control had the effect of softening one area of discipline: since only he normally wielded the cane, the prefects and even the Second Master lost authority in this respect. In the boarding houses, the masters continued to use corporal punishment when appropriate. There had been cases of undue brutality in the prefects' punishments, and this now stopped. It should also be pointed out that Wootton's attitude to ladies was always very correct; when women joined the staff temporarily during the war he harangued the school on courtesy, and asked the prefects to comment.

In planning the curriculum, Wootton, as he said himself, 'brought the school into line with the usual national pattern. His reforms did much to assure the continuing wide range of interests for which the Perse had long been famed. In particular the teaching of Physical Training was reformed, proper lessons in this important area being introduced in 1931, when a qualified instructor, Mr. F. G. Finch, joined the staff, and equipment was provided which allowed the hall to be used as a gymnasium. It was at this point, of course, that the long forms which had been a feature of the 'big room' were removed. In consequence, unless chairs were put out boys usually stood at the morning assemblies, unless required to sit on the floor, and when classes used the hall, as they often did in order to receive special instruction from the headmaster or to listen to a visiting speaker, chairs had to be brought in. Private study periods, which had previously been held in the hall, were transferred to a classroom or to the library when it was established in Room 9.

Morning Assemblies became formal occasions, with a hymn and a lesson. Evening prayers were abolished. Staff were required to wear gowns in the classroom; in Rouse's day this had been a matter for individual choice, though the Doctor had worn his black gown at prayers and his scarlet at Speech Days.

The school certainly flourished academically under Wootton's command — it would not be appropriate to talk about his 'leadership' — and the record of examination successes continued to be immensely above the average for the country; though science, naturally, was especially encouraged, the arts were not neglected. The way in which circumstances over-rule personal prejudice is shown in that two of the three most distinguished of Rouse's pupils were the scientists who became Nobel laureates, while the two most notable of Wootton's were Arts scholars, Douglas Brown and Frank Stubbings. However, the third of Rouse's famous pupils is today quite the best known of all

Perse scholars, the redoubtable Dr. Frank Leavis, who, now over eighty, has been honoured by the Press and the B.B.C. as well as by other scholars throughout the world. *The Times* published a profile of him under the title 'Half a century of arousing academic enmity', while *The Listener* praised his 'well-scrubbed and athletic elegance' and the 'astonishing electric quality' of his mind. As the founder of a school of criticism, and as a brilliant teacher, he cannot fail to become an important figure in literary history.

Wootton himself was a good teacher, though he drove his pupils rather than leading them. He wrote two good text books, one (with M. Hooker) *A Text Book for Chemistry*, the other *Heat for Schools*. Willing to admit that 'a headmaster with a science degree was looked upon with suspicion', Wootton made a genuine effort to secure good teaching in the classics and other subjects; but all the teaching had to accord with his own ideas, and he would not let his masters work on their own, as Rouse had done, but had constantly to supervise and interfere. At his first O.P.S. Dinner he spoke of the resignation of Appleton as 'a great blow to the incoming headmaster' and asserted that he would like 'to follow in the footsteps of their illustrious founder in promoting peace, harmony and good-will'. It was sad indeed that his temperament made the achievement of that aim so difficult. He went on, at that Dinner, to insist that he aimed to continue and enlarge the traditional qualities of the Perse, and to ask his audience, rather pathetically, 'to speak well of the headmaster for the sake of the school'. Looking back to the period, one feels that most Perseans tried to do just that at the time, and since.

The one department with which Wootton did not interfere was the Preparatory School, where Catherine Burrows was allowed to reign exactly as she had always done. Wootton is quoted as saying that she was too well established to suffer change and Miss Burrows said that he 'recognised that a woman liked her own way'; it was, of course, a very good way, as both parties knew.

Wootton was very efficient on the material side, and anxious to follow what he supposed to be approved public school procedure. Consequently, all the details of school organisation which Rouse, with his preoccupation with education, had ignored received prompt attention. Many of the changes made were, of course, long over-due reforms. The telephone — ex-directory — was installed, the lighting was improved, the Ministry forms were promptly completed. A proper office was established. Where Rouse had managed with one part-time clerk, Wootton immediately engaged a full-time secretary, and in May

1931 a further clerical assistant was added 'to enable the Headmaster to devote more time to the general supervision of the school'. The fabric of the building, and such important details as cloakroom facilities, received the urgent attention which was needed.[69]

It seems clear that the personal enmity which developed between Rouse and Wootton influenced the latter in his decision not to move to new buildings on the playing-field site but to keep the school in Gonville Place.

It was obvious that the inadequacy of the existing buildings contributed to the school's unpopularity at this time, and it was common knowledge that the Doctor had wanted to build an entirely new school on the Luard Road site. At his last Speech-day he had said that he hoped to live to see the promised land of which he had dreamed so long. At the dinner given in his honour just before he retired it had been said that the greatest regret the company felt was 'that he will not have in charge the new school he so ardently longed for' and Harold Cooke had wittily pointed out that the Doctor's work had suffered because 'his premises were inadequate to sustain his conclusions'.

It had in fact been generally assumed that a new Head would press for realisation of Rouse's dream and that new buildings on the Luard Road ground would soon be commenced. This is illustrated in that, in April 1929, the Perse badge, along with those of Homerton College, the County High School and the Morley Memorial School, was put up in St. John's Church; the Vicar admitted that in including the Perse he was anticipating events, but pointed out that the site for the expected new school was in his parish, as in any case the boarding-houses had been for years.

The Governors, too, had assumed that the school would move and had for some time been negotiating for the sale of Gonville House, to be available forthwith, with the understanding that the remainder of the site would be offered to the purchaser on its vacation by the school. Records show that in October 1925, the Gonville House site was almost sold to the local 'bus company, the Ortona Motor Co., for £10,000, a condition being made that a 'bus service would then be available to the boys 'at convenient times'. Later, the garage firm of King and Harper started negotiations for purchase, but gave up when they found that a severely restrictive building-line was prescribed.

Wootton was no sooner appointed than he began to argue against the proposed move. The authorities, he maintained, 'could do no good casting envious eyes at other people's premises'. At his first Speech Day he raised the question in his Report, on which the *Cambridge*

Chronicle printed the witty comment: 'At the last Speech Day of the Perse School Dr. Rouse was surveying the promised land of the new school from the top of Pisgah. His successor, unlike Joshua, foretold more years in the wilderness, but he finds the desert air bracing and endeavour more important than bricks and mortar'.

Dismissing the possibility of removal to another site as a mere dream, he turned his attention to the obvious alternative, the improvement of the existing buildings, which had very serious shortcomings, especially in the lack of a proper gymnasium, art-room and up-to-date laboratories. Within a short time, however, he went further, and, whether from genuine conviction or on principle, he argued flatly against moving to Luard Road, and proposed major additions to the Gonville Place site. This inevitably led to debate, public and private, and to a period of vacillation, on the part of the Governors, as to whether they should follow Rouse or Wootton in this important matter. Whereas, as early as 7 December 1928 (in Wootton's first term) it had been agreed that the Governors would not 'at present' advertise the Gonville House site as for sale, some offers to purchase were considered. In particular, the Office of Works negotiated for its acquisition to build a postal sorting-office; they wanted only the back portion of the full frontage and the whole of the Gonville House plot, and were therefore refused. The whole site was then professionally valued at £35,000. In October, 1929, in spite of the decision of the previous December, the sale was still being considered and a notice offering the site was erected. In February 1930, a meeting of Governors and H.M. Inspectors was discussing the size of establishment to be provided when the school moved. The Inspectors then insisted that, failing a move, immediate improvements to the old building were imperative. They pointed out that the cost of the school per head of population was higher than the average for the country and that 'the real trouble was that there were not sufficient boys, and the present number did not form a handy or economic unit according to the Board's standards'.

On 30 June 1930, the Governors held a special meeting to inspect the site proposed for the new school, but no decision was made. Vacillation continued. On 13 February 1931, the committee considered an outline plan for a new building, but left it undecided, so that they might 'make enquiries to ascertain if there is any prospect of raising money towards the building'. It was only on 30 October 1931, that the Governors finally resolved that the old site should be retained, and appointed a committee to prepare plans for the development; only

then was the sale of Gonville House cancelled and the board advertising
it as for sale removed. The Headmaster asserted that, once the future
policy was settled, numbers in the school rose forthwith.

Thus Wootton eventually carried the Governors with him. The plan
for an entirely new school was now positively rejected, despite the fact
that the Luard Road estate had been enlarged by the wise purchase of
an additional field in 1923, as part of the memorial to old boys killed in
the first world war. In February 1933, this field was sold back to
Trinity College as a measure for financing the new buildings at
Gonville Place. In 1931 the estate had been greatly improved by
sweeping away the old, shed-like, pavilion, and substituting an excellent new one, on the Glebe Road side of the main field. This pavilion,
presented by Gavin Macfarlane-Grieve, was designed by Robert
Hersch, an Old Persean and a son of the former master. It was opened
by the Chairman (Mr. A. B. Ramsay) who that year was Vice-Chancellor, as part of the first school fête.

The arguments adduced at this time for retaining the old site now
strike one as incredible. It was not, as had been suggested, inadequate.
On the contrary, the site 'has ample space surrounding it and can
never be inconvenienced by other buildings. The classrooms are large,
well-lighted and airy, and are so arranged that they are protected from
noise or disturbance of any kind'. Much was made at this time of the
sentimental argument that the associations of the old site were enough
to justify its retention. The Chairman said that he felt the school
could be personified as looking back into history wistfully and saying,
'No, I will not go further from home. I will stay where I am, and keep
in touch with all that is most dear to me''.

In June 1931, plans were made, pending the new building work, to
remedy some of the glaring deficiencies of the old building; and
enquiries were set on foot to supply midday meals to the boys. Only
one local firm of caterers showed an interest, and this, G. P. Hawkins,
indicated that 'they would require more than a shilling a head' —
which was expensive for the time.

An additional expense was incurred shortly after this, in January,
1932, through the making-up of Glebe Road and Holbrook Road,
charges for which were met by the sale of a strip of land behind the
boarding-house, fronting on to Holbrook Road.

As architect for the new building the Governors retained Mr. W. A.
Forsyth (the first lay-out had been prepared by Mr. R. W. Forsyth).
His firm submitted two plans, a general one showing the whole
eventual scheme and a detailed one for the portion lying to the

north-east of the old building. Only this first instalment was in fact built. Several conferences with Board of Education officials were held and the scheme was approved, and a public announcement made at Speech Day, December, 1932.

On 22 February 1933, the Buildings Committee received Mr. Forsyth's completed plans, recommended the Governors 'to approve the proposed extension' and agreed 'that application be made to the Board of Education for their consent to the scheme, subject to the raising of the necessary funds in such a way as the Finance Committee with the Board's approval may decide'. On 17 March tenders were invited for the building, and on 31 July following — no time was wasted once a decision was made — the contract was awarded to Messrs. Sindall, who were in fact the second lowest in their tender. The work was shortly afterwards put in hand.

However, as so often before in the history of the Perse, a further financial crisis had developed during the period of all these promising developments. In October 1931, the very month in which the decision was made not to leave the Gonville Place site, the national economic crisis assumed such a grave level that the Government imposed a 10% reduction of all staff salaries, which the Governors could only accept. The Headmaster was asked to report on the staffing position and specify economies which might be made.

To achieve a reduction in teaching staff, a change in the house-mastership at Glebe Road was decided upon. Wootton had himself run the House from his appointment until February, 1930, when Mr. R. J. Gladden had taken over. In May 1932, the Governors were informed that there were vacancies for a Modern Language master (following de Glehn's retirement) and for a Boarding-house master. The Minute reads thus: 'In order to create a vacancy on the staff for the boarding-house master, the Committee authorised the Headmaster, as agent for and with the approval of the Governing Body, to give notice to Mr. Gladden and to Mr. Taylor to terminate their appointments at the end of the present term'. When Mr. Mansfield and Mr. Storr were appointed, the Headmaster stated, on 1 June, that 'as soon as he had received Mr. Storr's acceptance he should cancel the notice given to Mr. Taylor'. This was done. In informing Taylor, Wootton made the surprising observation that 'this sort of thing happens in many schools'.

In October, 1932, further staffing economies were ordered. The staff were obliged to work more periods in the week and the full-time staff was reduced to twelve. While the tenure of Parker-Smith was extended for two years, the services of one master in the main school and of one mistress in the preparatory school were to be terminated. The choice fell on R. J. B. Hicks and Miss Robson. At the same time poor 'Daddy' Broome, the Headmaster's Secretary, who also taught a little Art, had his salary cut from £150 to £100 and (in October, 1933) again to £50. In March, 1933, there was a further reduction: Mr. van Praagh, who resigned, was not replaced and Mr. Taylor was, for the second time, given notice. However, when Parker-Smith decided (after all) to retire, Taylor was once again reinstated. 'Parker' appears to have made a characteristically generous gesture in thus saving Taylor's post, and he did it modestly, so that the latter did not know at the time that he had been under a threat.

The national crisis was presently resolved, and, in March 1934, Wootton was the leader of a deputation of local representatives of the 'Joint Four' teachers' associations to the County Education Committee, which urged that the salary cuts should end and the scales applicable before October 1931 be restored.

During this period there was a good deal of illness, some of it nervous, among the staff. Cook and Bob Broome were away for longish periods, and Dagut and his assistant housemaster were kept away when Hillel House was put in quarantine. Among those who helped temporarily in taking classes were three Old Persean students, Harold Fleet, John Sharp and Frank Stubbings.

In February 1935 Hugh Lindeman was appointed to succeed Miss Burrows at the Prep.

XVI

REBUILDING IN PEACE AND WAR

Wootton now turned his undoubted organising ability to the task — made doubly difficult because of the financial stringency of the time — of raising funds for the new building project. He had a number of original ideas, thanks to which the money was raised, and a turning-point in the school's affairs once more reached. An Appeal, beautifully presented, illustrated the full scope of the plan, which was for a large courtyard group of buildings, with the old hall forming the central block. It was suggested that 'When Pendeen House, on the South part of the site, is removed and the final additions have been made, the completed building will be worthy of the particular use and character of the school and of its prominent position in the centre of Cambridge'. Two ideas now adopted deserve special mention. To promote the fund a society known as the 'Friends of the Perse School' was formed, and it was in its name that the Appeal was issued. The first Trustees formed a distinguished body: A. B. Ramsay, Master of Magdalen, G. H. A. Wilson, Master of Clare (and a former master at the school) Gavin Macfarlane-Grieve and A. A. Spalding. A major object of the society, was, of course, the raising of funds, and fêtes and other activities were regularly sponsored during the 'thirties and resumed in 1950.

A Parents' Committee of the Friends of the Perse was also formed. The idea of a body of parents interested in the school was an original one, and anticipated what is now standard practice in the majority of schools of all kinds. The School Fêtes which now began were valuable fund-raising events.

The foundation stone of the new block had been laid by the Master of Caius, then Vice-Chancellor, on 18 November, 1933; it was remarked at the time that this 'maintained the traditional connection between the school and the College'. It was formally opened in November, 1934, by the Rt. Hon. Stanley Baldwin, then Chancellor of the University, and afterwards Earl Baldwin. A further Appeal for funds to allow the full scheme to follow was issued at the same time.

The period that followed was perhaps the gravest in the recent history of the school. At one and the same time, in a desperate effort to recover its fortunes, plans were going forward for the rebuilding and money was being lost through a steady drop in the number of boys. The numbers were as follows: 1928: 336; 1929: 356; 1930: 335; 1931: 326; 1932: 308; 1933 (Feb.): 298; 1934 (May) 282. Numbers in the boarding-houses dropped still more seriously; in October 1933, there were only 16 boys in the School House, and 14 in Hillel House. This situation, whereby the fortunes were lower than ever but the responsibility of the expensive new building an embarrassment, was recognised in the letter sent to the Governors on 16 July 1934, by the Clerk, Mr. W. L. Raynes: 'In the last seven years the number of fee-paying boys has fallen by 18.63% and the fees by 14.6% and this means a somewhat reduced volume of work in collection. But there is much additional work in connection with the new buildings'. In the circumstances, Mr. Raynes agreed to a reduction of 15% in his fees, conditional upon an increase when the position improved.

The year 1934 had begun with a disaster affecting both the finances and the standing of the school. The Board of Education, as will be recalled, had, in Rouse's day, made a Special Grant to allow for experimental work in the teaching of Classics. Early in Wootton's reign, in October 1929, this had been reviewed at a special meeting of Governors and Inspectorate to consider 'the continuation of the Direct Method in a modified form . . . with a view to its being adapted to meet the circumstances, which were dependent on the staff available for teaching it'. The implication was, as often suggested in previous years, that the method needed a Rouse and an Appleton to be workable. After consideration, the Board wrote a letter in the following terms: 'The question is whether the circumstances of the school are now such as to justify the continuation of this grant . . . The Board do not feel justified, in view of the changes and the personnel responsible for the classical teaching, in continuing it after July, 1930'. The Inspectors made further enquiries during 1930, giving another chance for the development of experimental work; now, in 1934, they entirely withdrew the grant, adding a warning that 'unless there is a substantial increase in the number of qualified pupils entering the Science and Modern Studies courses next September they will have to consider whether they will be justified in recommending them for the purposes of grant'. It must be noted that, here, it was not the quality of teaching, but the number of pupils, which was thought unsatisfactory. The problem disappeared, when, in May 1935, it was announced that Advanced Course grants would no longer be given, being superseded by a new system of capitation grants; but the amount paid obviously still depended on the number of pupils.

A General Inspection took place in 1935, and the Report found, not surprisingly, that the standard of work in the school had fallen away, partly because of the departure of so many great figures of the past.

The 1934 wing was described as supplying 'only the most urgent requirements — new science laboratories, art room, dining-hall and kitchen'. A new staff-room was also provided; characteristically, perhaps, Wootton did not specify this in his announcement. The plans for further building provided for a new court, with further laboratories, rooms for Corps and Scouts, and a large gymnasium parallel to Hills Road. A further, smaller, court would eventually replace Pendeen House and the site of the huts behind it, and would also include a new dining-hall and kitchen, the 1934 suite becoming further laboratories and a lecture-room. The whole scheme would be completed by adding a storey over the cloakroom and the old staff-room, and converting the Armoury into a workshop. Wootton himself made the pleasant suggestion that the Jacobean hall from the old Free School Lane school should be dismantled and rebuilt in the extensions, but no details seem to have been planned.

The wing which was built survives today, along with many of the old class-rooms, as part of the present Local Examinations Syndicate Buildings; only the hall, the single attractive feature of the 1890 building, has disappeared. The 1934 wing cost £11,500 to build, and the Appeal asked for a further £40,000. A new library had been installed in what had been Turnbull's class-room, in July 1933. Shelves for this were presented by Girton College, through the good offices of Major Bowes. The old biology laboratory, below the new library, then became a prefects' room, and the old prefects' room an additional office — afterwards used as a Bursary.

Munich and the Second War prevented any further development of the rebuilding plan. When building was again a possibility the plan which realised Rouse's old vision was preferred, as will be described in later pages.

There were two changes in the office of Second Master during Wootton's reign. Robert Parker-Smith, who had been Rouse's deputy for most of his time, retired in 1932, when Léon Chouville was appointed. When Léon in turn retired, in 1938, the Annual Report of the Friends of the Perse (their fourth report) paid tribute to him, as follows: 'While we all regret his retirement, we must remember that he has left us with a great tradition and also a great responsibility for maintaining a high standard, particularly in the work of those boys who possess natural linguistic ability'. These words, which must have been written by the Headmaster, make a belated acknowledgement of the Rouse tradition, but end characteristically with the implication that staff and boys must be driven to continue on the right path. Chouville's departure was recognised as the effective end of the Rouse era, for he was the last of the old 'giants' to leave.

The new Second Master was, of course, Arthur Hawkins, of whom much is written in this book. He took office in 1938 and retired in 1964, having served as Acting Headmaster during the difficult period which was to follow.

We come now to the events leading up to the war of 1939-45 and to the story of the school in war-time. It so happened that a domestic crisis came immediately before the national one; for in the spring of 1939 the Headmaster was found to be suffering from a duodenal ulcer, and was obliged to enter the London Hospital for treatment. Characteristically he refused to have an Acting Headmaster appointed to control the school in his absence, though he did arrange for a temporary science master. Instead he wrote a letter setting out what he thought should be done, and sent a copy to each member of the staff. The following forms part of this letter:

'While I do not intend to run the school from my bed, I do not wish to lose touch with it entirely and so I ask you to send me a report once a week — not a formal report, but a chatty one. (Meaning a report from each Master!)

'Mr. Hawkins will naturally be Second Master-in-Charge, and will please exercise a general supervision and conduct prayers. He will prepare time-tables for absent masters. The use of the term 'Acting Headmaster' is generally restricted to an interim period between the departure of one Headmaster and the arrival of the next.'

The letter goes on to allocate duties to each of the senior members of the staff.

The staff, however, unanimously agreed that it would be impossible to run a school in this way; the letter was therefore ignored, and Mr. Hawkins acted as Headmaster during what proved to be the very difficult term immediately preceding the Second War.

When the Headmaster returned the war had just started, although it was for a time to be the 'phoney' war, with no immediate enemy action over this country. There was, none the less, much to be done as a matter of urgency.

One valuable effect of the war was to bring people in all walks of life closer together, and this applied especially to schools. Where a school was evacuated, or had received evacuees, a specially close bond was created. In a situation such as obtained at the Perse, the needs of Air Raid Precautions and passive defence brought together staff and boys, and sometimes parents and ancillary staff, and the result was a better understanding of one another. The Corps and Scouts found a more exacting role, becoming particularly aware of how they could help in an emergency, most of all in first aid. Within a short time of the outbreak of war in 1939 several rooms at the Perse were shored up with timber to provide shelters.

The tables in the dining-room were rearranged. Where previously the headmaster and the master on duty had taken their meal at a separate table, they now usually sat with the prefects. The conversations which then took place are recalled by some who were prefects at the time. They showed a charming side of Wootton, very different from the severe and distant headmaster of day-to-day life. He had, it appeared, a fund of humour which was normally suppressed, and a hearty laugh. He could joke about his daily medicines and the diet which, following his illness, he had to endure, including a milk-pudding as the invariable sweet.

Great was the joy of the table to discover in him a jolly sport, who in his youth had spent happy hours riding and tinkering with motor-cycles, including a big Indian, and indulging in various open-air sports, and to find that he was a film-fan.

On occasion he would discuss more serious topics; particularly schoolboy humour and practical joking, subjects which, it might have been thought, would not appeal to him. It interested him that in every school, and in society, there are always some who become the natural butts of the humourist. A religious man, he would speak also of the Cambridge churches, or comment on the sermons preached to the school in St. Paul's church. He was quite prepared to reminisce about his life in the army, his work as a headmaster, and educational questions such as homework, punishments and entertainments. He gave his young audience a detailed account of how he had converted the Governors to his view that the school should not move to a new site. Once, when discussing medical mistakes, he showed a spirit of tolerance and compassion and the detached fair-mindedness of the scientist. It became apparent that if only he could have relaxed sometimes when 'on duty' his health and the tone of the school would have gained immeasurably.

Wootton was always genuinely concerned about his pupils' welfare, and particularly in guiding them to enter the appropriate career. In November 1929 he spoke to the Cambridge Chamber of Commerce, of which he was a member, on 'Finding the Right Career'. His advice to boys about to leave school was always pertinent and helpful. Michael Goodchild recalls a talk he gave at the end of the summer term in 1943: Great was his hope that each one of us who had the vocation to marry would find the right partner and build up a happy home. He had seen the tragic results of far too many unions based merely on pretty faces or pleasant voices, and in so many cases of juvenile delinquency the root cause of the trouble was to be found in home conditions.

The Headmaster naturally felt that the coming of war had thwarted him in attaining his objectives in the school. He declared that he had had four main provisions in hand, and that, while progress had been made in all of them, the war had prevented their full implementation. The four were: (i) The improvement of the premises at both Upper and Preparatory schools; (ii) encouragement and possible enlargement of the Prep. school; (iii) provision of school dinners; (iv) securing the active cooperation of parents. Another idea was the introduction of the Tutorial system, which was approved by the most advanced thinking of the time. He had also had in mind the introduction of more practical work for the boys, including cookery as well as metalwork. But all the intended developments had perforce to be shelved. It is significant that the objectives named were practical rather than educational.

As in most schools during this period, approval was given to such work as boys could do without interfering with their education. During the holidays a number did harvesting and other work. At Christmas work at the Post-office was allowed. At the Head's own suggestion, a unit of the newly-formed Air Training Corps was established.

History repeated itself when it was agreed that, as in the 1914-18 war, free tuition should be given to refugee boys, of whom many came to Cambridge from countries overrun by the Nazis. A good number of Jewish boys from Central Europe were enrolled at Hillel House. Some boys also entered because their families had moved from London and other big cities. In consequence the decline in numbers entering was more than arrested, and the entry in 1940 'easily constituted a record'.

In 1940 there was great friction between the Governors and their Clerk, Mr. Raynes, who had resigned, through a quarrel over the collection of contributions made by parents towards the costs of the war-time Air Raid Precautions. His claim for additional payment to cover the work involved not having been met, he refused, in pique, to hand over the official Record Books when requested to do so. John Few, who had become the Governors' 'legal adviser', was then instructed to apply for a Court Order requiring the handing-over of the books; the year's Accounts were inevitably delayed. After three months of impasse, Mr. Raynes surrendered the books, without prejudice to his legal rights, and continued to demand payment of the sum claimed. The matter eventually seems to have lapsed by default. Mr. Few took over the legal work of the school, in January 1942 becoming the official Solicitor, and in April of that year, the Clerk.

At the same time, difficulties arose at the Boarding House. Mr. Storr, finding that he was now operating at a loss, asked for and secured a reduction in his rent, but urged that the Governors must, in the prevailing difficult circumstances, accept full financial responsibility for the House. Early in 1941 he resigned, stating that he would be willing to carry on 'if relieved of the present financial anxiety'. His request was granted at the ensuing Governors' meeting, and he continued as Housemaster, with the assistance of a Committee of Management.

The war news, following Dunkirk and the bombing attacks, became very distressing, even if the casualty lists were not as heavy as in the First War. Although Cambridge did not suffer greatly from the enemy's attentions, the Perse building was among the first in the country to be a target for fire-bombs, when, in January 1941, the whole of the school, except for the new block, Pendeen House and the outbuildings was so severely damaged that at first it appeared that the damage could not be repaired. Keith Barry recalls how this occurred 'just before the beginning of the Spring term, in the middle of a bitterly cold spell. The devastation was immense: no upper-floor class-rooms, no lighting, no heating, as much damage by water as by fire. We had a staff-meeting on, I believe, the Thursday, and Wootton announced, to our incredulity, "School will open on Tuesday". By the most stupendous efforts, mainly on his part, it did!'

Among the most serious of the losses suffered, much of the Players' material was lost, but a great part of the library and nearly all equipment of value was salvaged. At the time of the damage, the national scheme for 'fire watching' in buildings had not been introduced. In due course a scheme, with two shifts in winter, was operated at the Perse, with one master and three senior boys on duty at a time.

The successful continuation of school life, and the repair of the buildings, were achieved by the almost single-handed efforts of the Headmaster. A special War Damage Committee of the Governors was formed, with authority to act on its own initiative 'in cases necessitating immediate action'. An appeal for funds to cover the cost of repairs was put in hand, and this was drawn up by the Headmaster and signed by the Chairman, the Vice-Chairman and the Mayor. Correspondence with the Board of Education showed, however, what one would have expected would have been known already, that the Appeal was unnecessary and undesirable, since the War Damage Commission set up by the Treasury at the beginning of the war would meet all the costs arising.

Turning to the task of getting the repair work done, the Committee acted with great speed and managed to cut the red tape which abounded, so effectively that a licence for rebuilding was quickly obtained and Kerridge's undertook the work without delay. Damage to furniture and fittings was valued at £619. The Bank agreed to accommodate the Governors with a loan, approved by the Board, to provide the funds needed until the Commission could reimburse them; the limit was set at £7,500. The original estimate for rebuilding was £4500, in fact £5760 was paid. Additional sums were needed to repair Pendeen House and for the purchase of electric fires for drying out the buildings; the fires were afterwards sold off.

The provision of temporary facilities for teaching posed another problem, which Wootton solved in a few days, thereby once again demonstrating his tremendous capacity for hard work and single-handed, because never delegated, power of organisation. He drove his staff hard, but he drove himself harder. On this occasion he secured the use of the Technical College buildings, and the school functioned there except for science work and meals, which could continue in the undamaged part of the old building. He arranged all this, including complicated reorganisation of the time-table, and at the same time secured that repairs at Gonville Place should be treated as a first priority — at a time when the nation's resources did not allow much construction-work beyond the simplest patching-up. In this he was greatly helped by the Commissioner for the Eastern Area, Sir Will Spens, Master of Corpus Christi and a good friend of the Perse.

Largely because Wootton pursued the matter with the greatest vigour, the rebuilding was carried out speedily and the school returned united in November. Not only did the school suffer from the enemy's attentions. Wootton was himself 'bombed out' twice. His house in

Barrow Road — he had given up the Glebe Road boarding-house — was almost completely destroyed in 1942, and later on, when he had moved to a new residence in St. Giles' Vicarage, Castle Hill, bombs were dropped close by and further damage was done. He is said to have sent a question at this time to the popular radio 'Brains Trust' programme, enquiring about the superstition that 'tragedies happen in threes' and adding the wry comment 'I've just had my third tragedy'.

An opportunity of extending the Gonville Place site was lost when, in May 1944, the Governors were offered No 2 Drosier Road, at the rear of the school, but it was decided to take no action 'at the present time'.

The war caused serious disruption in all sorts of ways, and imposed obvious strains on every member of staff. Several masters were called up, including Goronwy Salusbury, who did not return to the school. After attaining the rank of Colonel in the Education Service, he returned to teaching in a large London comprehensive school, where he is remembered as an outstanding personality. Temporary replacements, not always of the best quality, enabled the school to continue.

Rising costs led to the introduction of a new scale of fees, even before the end of the war. In spite of this, the demand for admission, which had dropped at the beginning of the 'thirties, rose sharply, so that by September 1944 there was a long waiting list. By the spring of 1944, however, it was obvious that Wootton could not continue. He was chronically sick, and became so difficult that representations from the staff, through their representative on the Governors' board, indicated that his full return to the school was not acceptable. It was suggested that negotiations should begin to secure his compulsory retirement. This is what happened; it was not the first time, it will be recalled, that a Perse headmaster had been so retired. Interviews with Ministry officials led to 'certain steps' which provided for the granting of a gratuity and a very satisfactory pension.

On 24 January 1945 Wootton personally attended a Governors' meeting and tendered his resignation, pointing out that he did so on medical advice and that his ill-health was largely the result of enemy action. He 'expressed his regret at having to give up school-mastering at the age of 60'. His retirement had effect from the end of the following summer term, but he did not in fact return after that January meeting. Mr. Hawkins acted as Headmaster in the interim. Wootton's health had finally broken down, and he died in March 1947.

During the Second World War Old Perseans again played their part in many spheres of national service. At least 44 are known to have given their lives. The following decorations were won: George Cross, 2; D.S.O., 1; D.S.C., 1; M.C. and bar, 1; M.C., 5; D.F.C. and bar, 1; D.F.C., 6. Thirty-five were mentioned in dispatches and thirteen were awarded various grades of the Order of the British Empire. Two were awarded the American Bronze Star; one the French Croix de Guerre; one the Belgian Croix de Guerre; one the Chevalier of the Order of Leopold II. Among the staff who served under Wootton were several who deserve fuller notice. James Taylor, already mentioned as having had the unusual experience of having been twice dismissed as redundant and twice reinstated, was an excellent teacher of history and a fine influence in the school. He left to become an officer in the Army educational service, first at Woolwich and then at Sandhurst.

Harry Dagut (1929-44) took over Hillel House, and continued there the important work of fostering Anglo-Jewish relations in education and in life. He very quickly became devoted to the school and in every sense, a part of it, interesting himself in very many of its activities and helping to maintain its liberal traditions. A classical scholar trained at Manchester Grammar School and at Oxford, he had taken English as his special subject; his delight in literature and the theatre made him an admirable successor to Happold and a fine colleague for Caldwell Cook. He had, indeed, the gift for which both Cook and Happold, and pre-eminently Rouse, were renowned: that of imparting enthusiasm for the great writers and for the values they enshrine.

Dagut was a splendid teacher and interpreter, especially of Chaucer and Shakespeare, was keen on dramatic work of every kind, and trained his classes to write lucid and elegant prose. He occupied himself largely with the Upper School work which Cook found less attractive. Outside the classroom he interested himself enthusiastically in the production of the *Pelican*, in the Perse Players, and the Union Society and the Old Persean Society — in the last two spheres taking over the authority formerly exercised by Harold Cooke, handling it in his own distinctive way. His speeches at meetings of the Union were invariably both vigorous and witty. He added another society which has endured by creating the School Literary Society. As a teacher of religion, devoted to the ideals and finer values of Humanism, he exerted great influence both in the Jewish community and outside. He was a very fine House-master. On the games field, too, he had a valuable contribution to make, especially in cricket. The school suffered a sad loss when he died 'in harness'.

Vernon Boyle (1929-42) was the Art and Craft master, a kindly man, with an impressive moustache, who was popular with his colleagues and pupils. He did not get on well with Wootton, and retired sooner than he might have done. On retirement he returned to his native Devonshire, and gave himself over to work in praise of the county, giving talks on its countryside, people, folklore and especially its maritime tradition; the talks would be illustrated by his own sketches and by reciting poetry and singing songs, for he had a fine tenor voice. When he died in 1954, the *Devon and Cornwall Journal* published a profile in appreciation of a man of many parts who will be remembered as a fine artist (his watercolours had a lyrical quality and conveyed the spirit of Devon) and also for the verse he wrote, always in praise of Devon and the sea, and worthy to be included in a county anthology. For a short time the art work at the Perse was very capably covered by W. F. R. Rayner, who is remembered with affection.

Turnbull was succeeded as Senior Mathematics Master by James Buchanan, who is referred to below. The Classics department was taken over by a man who was over a long period to make an immense contribution to the life of the school, one of the best loved of Perse masters, Hugh Percival. Another mathematics master was George Braithwaite (1932-41), a Yorkshireman of sterling quality, whose work for the Scouts was also of special value. He was followed by Mary Beck (1941-44), a good teacher, a fine swimmer, and, above all, a very charming lady.

Three other masters of this epoch should have mention. C. H. Boutflower (1928-31) and R. M. Sibson (1931-34) were excellent teachers of Classics, who also helped on the games-field, and R. P. Ayres (1931-32), a scientist, although only briefly at the school, remained in contact, since he went on to the Leys and became Scout Commissioner for the district.

The most important recruit of the period was Keith Barry, the present Second Master, who joined in 1936, and has done so much in so many spheres to ensure the continuing success of the Perse that comment at this stage is almost impertinent. Percival and Barry covered the games organisation between them throughout the 'thirties, 'forties and 'fifties, while their work in the classroom kept academic standards as high as ever. With Arthur Hawkins they were the leaders of the staff during the Wootton period, and some of their comments have been quoted in making this assessment. Another classical master who taught the subject well and was popular with the boys was 'Jake' Bullock. 'Ferdie' Finch, the physical training master, did a great deal for the school in many ways, both in and out of class-time. When he rejoined the Royal Navy on the outbreak of war a serious gap was left, which was filled temporarily by two prefects, John Whitaker and Philip Jupp, who 'managed pretty well in trying to follow Mr. Finch's orderly sequence of exercises and vaults'.[66] Then a replacement was found, the first woman teacher, probably, apart from students, ever to break into the all-male ranks of the Perse staff. This was Miss K. E. Whincop, who, in spite of the difficulties her sex might be expected to occasion, quickly established her authority and became popular with the boys; those who were prefects at the time remember visits to her country home, where she kept a small-holding.

Those whose work continued into the next period of the school history are spoken of at greater length in following pages.

XVII

POST-WAR RECONSTRUCTION: STANLEY STUBBS

Another happy epoch in the history of the Perse began with the appointment as Wootton's successor of Stanley Stubbs, under whose direction the school fully regained its unique reputation, what remained relevant of the Rouse tradition was restored, and the great dream, nourished for so long by almost all but Wootton, of building a fine new School, was triumphantly realised.

Mr. Stubbs tells us how, soon after settling in his appointment, he went over to Histon to see his famous predecessor, who not unnaturally received him with some reserve. They talked on educational matters, and Stanley spoke of some of the hopes and ambitions he had for the Perse, both short and long term, which included the provision of new premises for both Upper and Preparatory schools. In showing his deep interest and approval, the Doctor wistfully recalled how he, too, had had such a dream, which was not fulfilled. Frequent meetings followed, and Rouse soon appreciated that here was a man who could continue his work. At the end of one early meeting he stood up like an Old Testament prophet and bade Stanley 'Go forth and prosper!'

There could not have been a better choice to make from the impressive list of 79 applicants for the Headmastership — which included several Old Perseans. Mr. Stubbs' early career and all-round experience had fitted him splendidly for the task before him. After leaving Newcastle High School, Staffordshire, where he had been a Senior Prefect, Captain of Cricket, Vice-captain of Rugby football and a sergeant in the O.T.C., he decided to enter local industry rather than to go to a University. He spent five years at the Royal Doulton Potteries, where at 23 he was Manager of the large U.S.A. Export department. This business experience was to prove invaluable in his efforts to put the Perse on its feet, materially and financially, as well as academically. However, the appeal of a career in education had become insistent, and he resigned his post to test the attraction of scholastic life. After a year teaching in a preparatory school he came up in 1930 to Emmanuel College.

At Emmanuel Mr. Stubbs took Second Class Honours in French and German, and was Captain of Association football. His student-teaching period was spent at Charterhouse. From 1934 to 1939 he was a Modern Languages and Senior German master, and Housemaster of Day Boys, at Gresham's School, Holt, from where he went in January, 1940, to the Headship of Soham Grammar School. At Soham he made a name for himself by his skilful direction during the difficult war years. He personally formed and commanded the School and Open A.T.C. squadron; and when an ammunition train blew up at Soham station in 1944 he earned the Regional Commissioner's commendation, as well as that of the County council, by his conduct as a Civil Defence officer. During his headship the Grammar School enjoyed a very good academic record and expanded to double-stream entry, and additional buildings were negotiated and provided.

Mr. Stubbs, like several of his predecessors, became Headmaster at a critical time in the school's history and indeed in national history. Just as Heppenstall, Barnes-Lawrence and Rouse in particular each found the Perse at a low ebb, and yet at a point where important educational reforms were being initiated, so Mr. Stubbs, beginning his work in September 1945, had to solve the many problems left by the war and at the same time to see that the school set its proper course under the Butler Act. His tenure of office was to cover the greater part of the period during which the Government authority — first as the Board of Education, then as a Ministry and finally as the Department of Education and Science — allowed some 170 schools to continue the special status of the Direct Grant; he fought valiantly throughout on behalf of what most sincere educationists at the time felt to be an admirable system.

The expression 'at a low ebb' needs, in this instance, some qualification. At his first Speech Day Mr. Stubbs was able to say that he had found the reputation of the Perse very high indeed, and that probably it was 'one of the best known of English schools outside our own country'. Yet it had suffered from the war and from the difficulties caused by Wootton's illness; it was not strong financially or numerically, much of the special quality of Rouse's day had been lost, and, in spite of all Wootton's efforts to improve them, its buildings and facilities still fell below the standard requisite for a school of its quality. Mr Stubbs saw at once that the task before him would embrace five stages, as he put it himself; they were Rehabilitation,

Reorganisation, Consolidation, Expansion and Fulfilment. It must have seemed that years would elapse before real progress would be made, but the new Head planned the school's progress so thoroughly and worked for it so energetically that the required improvements were all made, in logical stages, during his reign.

Mr. Stubbs stated his aims very clearly in his first Speech Day Report, pointing out the opportunities which the Direct Grant system gave: 'While it gives (us),' he said, 'the opportunity to cooperate fully with the forward movement in state education, we are also able to continue the wide outlook and varied intake, the individuality and character of the past, and to develop in freedom our own ethos and our own particular contribution of service to the community in our own way'. A week previously, similar feelings and philosophy had been expressed, striking a note of hope which in the long run events would not allow, when Leslie Symonds, the first O.P. Member of Parliament and the first Labour member for Cambridge, had 'expressed his personal belief in the Direct Grant system and in the fullest freedom and variety in education'. He was speaking at the first post-war Old Persean Dinner.

The first steps in rehabilitation lay in dealing with the remaining consequences of War Damage, both physically in repairs to the buildings and administratively in the final negotiations with the authorities concerned; and in reorganisation, the reform of the curriculum leading to the restoration of old standards in academic work and corporate achievement.

Obviously, the new Head could not succeed in this sphere except by the efforts of a dedicated staff, and this Mr. Stubbs had. It was by a superb team effort that in four years or so a level of attainment worthy of comparison with the 'great days' was reached. The year 1949 can be singled out as an outstanding one in the history of the Perse; it was the culmination of much happy and promising activity in a transitional period, as a glance through the pages of the *Pelican* shows. By March, 1946, numbers in the school had reached a record of over 500, and all vestiges of war-time difficulties had disappeared. Games, societies, the Corps, the A.T.C. and the Scouts had all returned to pre-war standards and were carrying out a full programme of activities. The Union Society had resumed regular debates and adopted a new constitution, with formal procedure on the lines of the early society. Music and dancing had begun to take a more prominent part in school life. Most notable of all was the revival of the Perse Players, whose report could say that 'with our post-war rebirth (we) hope for a return to the glories of the days of our founder, the late Mr. Caldwell Cook'. This was indeed achieved in full measure.

The happy connection with Dr. Rouse continued until he left Histon. Parties from the Classical Sixth went over regularly to take tea and talk Classics. When the Headmaster paid his visits he was usually accompanied by Mrs. Stubbs, who, like many an Old Persean wife, was received with characteristic courtesy. There was general sadness when the Doctor died, in 1950. A special number of the *Pelican* did honour to his memory and a representative gathering attended the funeral at Histon. The library of classical books he had given to the school — some 1400 volumes — was opened in the term of his death.

The first active reorganisation concerned the Boarding Houses, following a period of crisis. At the School House Mr. Storr resigned the Housemastership and Mr. Barry was appointed to succeed him, on the understanding that the Headmaster himself would be offered the post if it became vacant; he felt, very properly, that it would be for the good of the school if he could live in the main boarding-house. The year 1946 having shown a deficit of £100, in spite of the House being filled to capacity, fees were thereupon increased.

With regard to Hillel House, which, after the death of Mr. Dagut, had been run for a time by Mrs. Dagut with the help of a Tutor, and also for a time by Merton Dagut, despite the fact that he had been crippled by polio during war service, the Governors decided to approach the Jewish community with a view to continuing what had been, as was generally agreed, a very important experiment in Anglo-Jewish education, rather than taking over themselves and abandoning the Jewish connection. After some difficulty Maurice Wollman, then Senior English Master at Barking Abbey School and well known in the educational world, agreed to become Mrs. Dagut's tenant for five years, it being understood that the school took not responsibility, except for the control of entry. However, after only one term — a very successful one, it appeared — he intimated his wish to retire from the House, and its future once more came under the consideration of the Governors.

In October 1947, a joint committee decided to put in hand enquiries as to terms on which the Governors could acquire it, to operate on a non-denominational basis; the Headmaster gave his opinion that there would be sufficient boarders to fill a second boarding house. In April 1948, a special Governors' meeting discussed the question. It was made clear to Mr Wollman that it was hoped that he could continue as a teacher, although no special salary could be

offered, since the post of Senior English Master was already held by
Mr. Barry. He agreed to continue.

The Governors decided to ask Mr. Wollman to exercise his option to
purchase Hillel House from Mrs. Dagut and then sell it to the school
at the purchase price; the Ministry of Education concurred. In May,
1948, a circular letter was sent to all the parents involved, signed by
the Clerk, the Headmaster and Mr. Wollman. The purchase of the
House was completed in September. Ten of the former Hillel House
boys remained as boarders in the reorganised system.

Hillel House became the Junior House, for boys under 13, and was
later renamed Northwold House.[70] The Headmaster was now able to
take over the Senior House, while Mr. Barry moved to the Junior and
Mr. Wollman moved to Mr. Stubbs' former house, in a triangular
removal exercise.

In May 1946, the first steps were taken to provide a War Memorial
for those who died in the Second War. A joint committee with the
O.P.S. and the Parents' Committee issued an Appeal in February,
1947, and a Field Day fête was held the following summer to raise
funds. The memorial was to provide not only a suitable panel for the
hall but also further land on the Luard Road estate, where ground had
been bought as part of the memorial to the First War.

The panel was unveiled on 9th June, 1949, by that great colonial
statesman, Field-marshal Smuts, then Chancellor of Cambridge University. His visit was a red-letter day in school history, when 'his keen
wit and vitality charmed everyone'. After the ceremony he inspected a
detachment of the Corps and Scouts. In 1949 a further memorial was
commissioned, when a specific donation was made for the erection of a
formal entrance gateway to the playing-fields, from Hills Road. The
design for this, with wrought iron gates and brick piers surmounted by
carved pelicans, proved a notable addition to Cambridge art. The gates
were designed by Robert Hurst, O.P., and executed by Raymond
Lister; the pelicans were designed and carved by Mr C. J. Whitaker,
one of the finest local craftsmen in this sphere and the father of an Old
Persean.[66] Each block of Ketton freestone originally weighed a ton,
and after they had been roughed out by a mason Mr. Whitaker carved
them entirely by hand, using hammer and chisels, not pneumatic
tools. He was 82 years old at the time, and already had to his credit
carving work all over the country and fine restoration work, including
that of the Caius Gate of Honour. For the Perse he had already carved
the war memorial and the folding chairs which, in Wootton's time,
some Old Perseans had presented for use in the hall.

Subsequently, a plaque affixed to a pier set out, with dates, the history of the acquisition of the site.

The year 1950 proved an important one for the school in a number of ways. Modifications were then made to the Trinity Leaving Exhibitions scheme, which had lost value with rising costs; it was agreed that the Exhibition should become a biennial award of £50 for three years. At this time also preparations were made for the changes in public examinations consequent on the introduction of the General Certificate of Education.

An event of considerable significance was the introduction of Ballroom Dancing classes, which, conducted by Miss Stewart of the Girls' School, brought the two Perse bodies closer together. A class for parents followed the school period, and full-length Parents' Association balls at the University Arms provided a natural progression; later they were transferred to the hall of the new school, where they are today regular social occasions.

Most important of all was the General Inspection of the school, early in 1951, which produced a quite admirable Report, showing that the post-war rehabilitation and consolidation was now complete. The rising cost of living was reflected in a series of increases in tuition and boarding fees, from 1951 onwards; but there could be no doubt that parents sending their boys to the school were getting excellent value for their money, as was the County authority in respect of fees paid for its scholars.

This era marked also the beginning of an important connection with the United States which Mr. Stubbs was able to foster.[71] It began through his membership of the English Speaking Union and through Rotary, of which the Headmaster was a prominent local member. In 1947 a member of the Sixth form was chosen as one of four British schoolboys who spent a month in the States. Then, in 1950 and 1951, two American schoolboys were entertained at the Perse boarding-house, 'with friendship and enthusiasm on both sides'. In 1951 twenty sixteen-year-old Perse boys took the American College Entrance examination, an unusual type of paper in which they all did well. In 1952 and again in 1966 the Headmaster paid important educational visits to America.

The fourth phase of Mr. Stubbs' scheme, Expansion, could by 1950 be embarked upon; he began enquiries and negotiations, with support from the Governors, who largely came to share his enthusiastic persistence and cautiously to recognise that the possibilities he envisaged were increasingly practicable. Expansion of the estate had begun with the purchase of a strip of land between the playing-field and Long Road, which, bought with the approval of the County Planning Officer, preserved the privacy of the site for school use. Two further acres were added in 1952. A covered miniature rifle-range was, with the help of a grant from the Territorial Army, installed on the fringe of the field, also in 1952.

Now began a considerable programme of building development. The first large project was made necessary by the increasing need for a new preparatory department, which, had long been recognised, and now became urgent. It was pointed out that the lease of Bateman House — in any case an inadequate building for the school — would expire in 1963. Since pupils were normally accepted for a period of five years, action to secure new premises could not long be delayed. No suitable property was on the market, though the former Goldsborough Hotel, on Hills Road, was inspected and rejected. Plans were therefore considered for the erection of a new building on the school playing-fields.

However, it proved fortunate for the school that before further steps could be taken in this direction the perfect solution to the problem presented itself, in that Leighton House, a fine property on Trumpington Road, with spacious grounds, became available, freehold and with immediate possession. It had been built as his private residence in Victorian times by the celebrated local business-man, Robert Sayle, and had been occupied by a Government department during the war. The Ministry of Works had offered it to the County Council, which, fortunately for the Perse, was not interested. The Headmaster and the Chairman of the Accommodation Committee, having visited this property, were convinced that it was the ideal site and building for a Preparatory School.

The purchase went through with the minimum delay. The necessary conversion and adaptation were accomplished without a hitch, not a great deal of work being required, and valuable fixtures and 'chattels' were acquired. Surely the Headmaster did not exaggerate when he stated in his Report to the Governors that 'The purchase opens a new chapter in the history of the Perse'; he went on to express his gratitude to the Board for 'sharing his enthusiasm so practically' and for the encouragement voiced by many friends of the school. A nice little touch was given when Sayle's monogram 'R.S.' was adapted in the simplest way to the new use of the villa by striking the leg from the 'R'. The new school was opened for the Autumn term 1954, removal from Bateman Street proving a simple matter. The old premises were

Leighton House. The Preparatory School, 1954

sold to the Davies School of English. In 1976 a new Hall and block of rooms were built at Leighton House.

The most important building expansion of all was the provision of a new Upper School, which would realise the dreams of generations of Perseans. The project was first broached in the Headmaster's Report for Michaelmas, 1955: 'It seems that the time is now ripe for further consideration of a future building proposal; and at the end of term first steps were taken towards stating a claim on the new Industrial Fund [72] for Laboratory provision'. That fund would, of course, be of vital importance if the plan were to materialise. The following February the question of 'the future of the school site' appeared once more on the Governors' Agenda. An enquiry, dated 12 December, 1955, had been received from the University Board of Finance, acting on behalf of the Local Examinations Syndicate, stating an interest in the possible purchase of the Gonville Place site. This led to a discussion on 'the question of principle as to whether it was desirable to move the school from its present site to the Playing Fields in the Long Road/Hills Road area'. Mr. J. L. Brereton, Secretary of the University Local Examinations Syndicate, took part in the discussion, but retired when the question of price was explored.

The probability of a grant being forthcoming from the Industrial Trust was taken into account, and it was mentioned that the Ministry of Education had given the opinion that to obtain a satisfactory new building some £130,000 would be required.

The meeting resolved, with only one member abstaining, that the Governors should enter into negotiations with the University authorities with a view to the sale of the present buildings on such terms as would enable the school to be moved to the Playing Fields site. It was resolved that a sub-committee should discuss the plan with the County Education committee. A particular question of principle was whether the organisation should remain on the two-stream pattern; the meeting felt that it was desirable to plan for the existing size, but to allow for a possible future expansion.

In June 1956, a special Governors' meeting heard that the University had made a definite offer for the Gonville Place site, and that two (later three) other possible purchasers were in the field. In preparation for the Governors' meeting the following November, Mr. Stubbs issued a detailed Memorandum, setting out the advantages of a re-building scheme and the practical possibilities. The Memorandum justly asserted that 'The present opportunity is the chance of a lifetime, unlikely to be repeated in this century,' and that 'we cannot afford _not_ to go ahead with our plans'. It argued that the school, already as full as it could be, would continue to attract maximum numbers. Yet the accommodation had become so inadequate that 'the utmost ingenuity and courtesy are needed to ensure that efficiency is not impaired'.

The Memorandum then quoted the Report of H.M.I. in 1951, which had pointed out many defects in the facilities, including the smallness of classrooms, the inadequacy of the library and dining-room, the lack of a separate gymnasium and changing-rooms, and the unsuitable situation, on a site facing a busy main road.

The Headmaster's Memorandum went on to point out that to meet the needs both on the Gonville Place site and on the playing-fields — where adequate changing facilities were urgently needed — would probably cost as much as to build a new school; and rebuilding without removing would produce 'an architectural jigsaw, and reduce the playground to virtually nil'. Moreover, the growth in numbers in the school might well not continue 'if we fail to keep pace with modern standards of premises and amenities'. The Memorandum was considered at the Governors' meeting in November, and debated at some length. It was then proposed that the offer of the University be provisionally accepted; the amount likely to be needed for the whole scheme, over and above the proceeds of the sale, the grant from the

Industrial Trust and monies available from the Endowments, was estimated at £30,000.

At a further special meeting in December the Governors received a report of a visit paid to the Ministry in London by the Chairman (Sir George Thomson), when the opinion was expressed that a loan to meet the difference between building costs and monies available ought to be feasible. It was thereupon resolved 'that the Governors should proceed with the scheme to build a new school on the playing-fields site and that the Governors should obtain as soon as possible the names of architects to prepare plans'. Planning permission was to be sought forthwith and the agents were to prepare a contract for the sale of the old site to the University.

There was some opposition to the rebuilding plan, and arguments reminiscent of those advanced in Wootton's time were produced. In particular there was talk of the psychological advantage of retaining the school near the city centre, objection to the additional travel imposed on some pupils, and a fear that the Direct Grant might be withdrawn. When the decisive vote was taken, eight members of the Board voted for the Resolution, and eight, including the Chairman, abstained, none voting against. This red-letter day in the history of the school was, therefore, clouded by a certain lack of enthusiasm; but the vital decision was made and it was agreed that, subject to Ministry approval, the scheme should be proceeded with, and an Appeal for the needed additional funds be prepared.

Sir George Thomson later resigned from the Chairmanship, and was succeeded by the Master of Sidney Sussex, Dr. David Thomson. Thus: 'Not Amurath an Amurath succeeds, But Thomson Thomson'. Dr. Thomson had two sons in the school.

A month later, in January 1957, came welcome news from the Industrial Fund,[72] which was willing to award £20,000 and a further £1,500 towards laboratory equipment. The Trust made the condition that the contract for at least the Science Block must be accepted during 1957. At the same time the Clerk, Mr. F. W. Elworthy, an Old Persean who had succeeded Mr. Few, was instructed to approach the Cambridge Building Society with a view to securing a long-term loan for the building work; he would also commence negotiations with Barclays Bank, to the same end.

There followed a very active period of planning, the main burden of work falling on the Headmaster and on Alderman George Wilding, who had become Chairman of the New Building sub-committee which entered wholeheartedly into the very exciting work. The architects appointed were Robert Matthew, Johnson-Marshall and Partners, with Mr. S. A. W. Johnson-Marshall, C.B.E. (later Sir Stirrat) in charge. Mr. Johnson-Marshall paid his first visit to the site on 10 January 1957, and declared the proposition a practical one. At a special meeting of Governors on 14 June the architect presented his first sketch-plans and a model of the proposals, and explained how he had tackled the project. His ideas, subject to a few modifications and (at the Headmaster's insistence) some increase in the size of the class-rooms, were welcomed by those present, and detailed planning began. The general atmosphere of happiness was, however, much saddened when Alderman Wilding died early in 1958. Dr. David Thomson then took over the Chairmanship of the sub-committee. Others who served on it, and made an especially valuable contribution to the work, were Alderman Francis Doggett, also Chairman of the Accommodation Committee, which dealt with the maintenance of all buildings and grounds, and Cllr. S. A. Martin. A tribute should also be paid to the help given by the Old Persean H.M.I., Douglas Simmonds, and to Mr. Elworthy and his staff.

During the summer of 1957 the contract for building the new school was signed with Messrs. Rattee & Kett, and a full-scale Appeal for £50,000 was launched. An admirable booklet, printed free of charge through the good offices of Reuben Heffer, was prepared and circulated; the first term brought in many gifts and promises by covenant. Building work began promptly, and the Headmaster was able to report that his 'first cup of contractor's tea on the site was very sweet'.

The Parents' Association did great work in organising a series of fêtes, coffee mornings and other fund-raising functions, and donations to the Appeal fund, from old and young, old boys, friends, and anonymous donors, continued to come in well. An exciting day came in the summer of 1959, when the ancient ceremony of 'topping out', traditionally performed when the highest point of a new building has been reached, took place. The highest point of this new building was, of course, the Pelican weather-vane.

The New School from the Air

The Hall of the New School, showing the Galleries, Stage and (beyond) the Memorial Library

XVII

FULFILMENT OF THE DREAM: THE NEW BUILDINGS

It is generally agreed that Mr. Johnson-Marshall and his associates produced a highly successful design, in carrying out the exciting but extremely difficult task entrusted to them. Fifteen years of use have confirmed this. The Perse was the first public school to rebuild entirely since the late 'thirties, and many new ideas, both in design and in education, affected the plan, which might well serve as a model in school architecture. Mr Johnson Marshall had previously been Deputy Architect of Hertfordshire, one of the leading counties both in education and in architecture, and had gone on to the post of chief architect to the Ministry of Education; he was thus particularly well qualified.

The architect's brief implied the most economical design consistent with the purpose, but it was expected that the new school would have an individuality 'which would reflect something of the history and traditions of the school' (*The Times*). It was laid down that the hall should in itself be a worthy successor to the Jacobean hall of Free School Lane and the pleasant timber-roofed hall of Gonville Place; yet it had to serve also as a dining-hall and be linked with the gymnasium to allow a maximum auditorium for 900 persons. The remainder of the building had to be designed in wings enclosing small courts, allowing the possibility of extension. The best acoustic qualities were insisted upon.

The building's outstanding feature is, of course, the hall. From the exterior it seems that its roof gathers up the low-pitched slated roofs and emphatic gables of the wings into a neat flèche, surmounted by the pelican weather vane. The interior has a monumental effect, with its complex wooden truss roof supported only at the corners and enclosing fully-glazed curtain walls. Behind the stage — small, but capable of use in several ways, as the Perse Players have shown — is the library, on two floors, so that the upper room connects with the galleries running on either side of the stage. The gallery incorporates folding study-cubicles. When the curtains are drawn open there is a view from the hall through a glass screen and to the field beyond, which is as pleasing as it is unusual. Another unusual feature is the arrangement of the hall floor on two levels, the sunken centre for assemblies, and the sides and back for dining. African hard-wood floors are used throughout the building, those in the laboratories being of acid-resisting wood; but there are studded rubber floors in the vestibules and composition floors upstairs.

Special attention was given to the gymnasium — the first in the history of the school — and to the new Mummery, which had to be a great deal more than the 'drama-room' becoming standard in the state schools. The gymnasium, forming an extension to the hall, has its end wall used as a commemorative extension of the hall, carrying the war-memorials, the Fellowship board, the boards recording the names of Head boys of the school, and a selection of the Honours shields which adorned the old hall. There was room for a selection only; the discarded shields were, where possible, returned to the old boys or families concerned, and a new system, recording distinctions won in a hand-engrossed book, was begun. The equipment of the gymnasium is first-class, and changing-rooms, for games as well as for P.E. classes, are provided on each side, with cloak-rooms and toilets adjoining.

The new Mummery is notable, not only as a modern version of a Shakespearean stage, but because it allows the full use of lighting and music in a way that was not possible in Pendeen House. The 'tiring-house' is integrated, avoiding the awkward arrangement employing a cellar-room for the purpose. Caldwell Cook's furniture has been preserved, and seems no more out of place than his kindly ghost would be in these surroundings.

The class-room blocks are on two floors, grouped round central staircases. Science, with elementary and advanced laboratories, together with preparation-rooms and a lecture-room, is on the south. Arts subjects have their rooms to the north, with a well-equipped geography room. The class-rooms are perhaps a little on the small side, but large classes have never been Perse practice. The whole plan is compact and yet gives an air of spaciousness. The Sixth Form Centre is a well-planned addition, overlooking the playing-field on the north. It was presented by an Old Persean, Laurie Marsh, and officially opened by his wife Elizabeth in June 1971. On the other side of the playground/parade area are buildings for the Corps and Scouts, workshops, and houses for the caretaker and groundsman. The Scout building, to the south, was in part paid for by contributions from the Scout

Venturers' Fund and from the credit balance of the Perse Hostel Fund.[3] It was adapted in 1966, as a fitting memorial to Douglas Brown, to provide also an additional Mummery for senior forms. Its special value is in providing a more flexible area for English activities. Crate-platforms, screens and fairly elaborate lighting, together with facilities for film projection, allow sophisticated variations, and adaptable seating allows either formal or informal arrangement. Beyond the Corps building two covered fives courts were built in 1975 as a gift by Gavin Macfarlane-Grieve. Just to the north of the main building, the Macfarlane-Grieve pavilion, with its recent bar as a verandah-like addition, completes the site, and the surrounding playing-fields enhance the effect of spaciousness. A further rural touch is given by the vivarium and the ornamental fish-pools adjoining the main block.

The workmanship and finish of the building is extremely good, and the entrance, through the beautiful pelican-capped Memorial Gateway from Hills Road, is as delightful as it is impressive. Incidentally, the same architect, builder and clerk-of-works were responsible also for the rebuilding of the old site for the Examinations Syndicate, where a pleasant office building has replaced the Victorian school.

The removal from Gonville Place took place at Easter 1960. The end of the last term in the old buildings was marked by a special Thanksgiving Service in Great St. Mary's church on Monday 28 March, when the hymns sung included the Latin 'Veni, Sancte Spiritus' and the address was given by Canon A. E. Maycock.

In preparation for the removal — 'Operation Renaissance' as he called it — the Headmaster, with the Governors' approval, had purchased an ex-War Department lorry for a mere £125. Much of the scientific equipment was taken to the new site during the Lent term. Then, during the school holidays, a group of eleven boys, with assistance from two of the ancillary staff, who provided the drivers, made an excellent job of transferring all furniture and stores.

The school settled easily into its new surroundings, celebrating the move, and proving that no academic disruption had been caused thereby, in establishing a record that December by winning no less than nine Open awards at Cambridge colleges, in a variety of subjects.

The Opening Ceremony of the new school was held on Monday 3 July 1961, a beautiful, sunny day when, in the words of the Chairman of the Governors (Dr David Thomson, Master of Sidney Sussex) Princess Alexandra of Kent 'set the seal of Royal approval' on the fulfilment of Persean dreams. The long history of the school was recalled by the Princess, who felt that the founder and past benefactors

H.R.H. Princess Alexandra at the Opening of the New School, 3 July 1961.
Accompanying Her Royal Highness are the Chairman of Governors, Dr David
Thomson and the Headmaster, Mr S. Stubbs. Behind are the Memorial Gates,
with the fine pelicans sculpted

'as they watch over this new phase . . . will see the ancient traditions
flourishing in the new building'. The Headmaster remembered 'those
who are no longer with us, but who in spirit are surely about us and
rejoice', naming especially Dr. Rouse, Mr. Ramsay and Mr. Benians
and Ald. Wilding. He paid tribute to the many people who had worked
to make this red-letter day possible.

The Princess was met at the Memorial Gates by the Chairman, the
Headmaster and their wives, and inspected a Royal Guard of Honour
from the C.C.F. drawn up in the driveway. The hall and gymnasium
were filled to capacity and an overflow was accommodated in a
marquee at the rear; altogether some 1,900 were present.

After a short service of dedication by the Bishop of Ely and the Vicar
of St. John's, the Chairman and Headmaster welcomed Princess
Alexandra to the school at 'this very happy moment in its long
history'. After her brief, happily-phrased speech the Princess unveiled
a tablet which was afterwards placed on a pier of the Memorial Gates.
In the final speech of the ceremony the Head Boy, C. V. T. Walne,
hoped that on her tour of inspection the royal visitor would 'enjoy
seeing the school and grounds as much as we enjoy being here'. Those
involved felt that she did enjoy it, and she spoke personally to many of

the boys, who were charmed by her friendly interest and dignified informality.

At Speech Day, held the following day, the Chairman and the Headmaster added further apt comment on a development through which the Founder's charity had been honoured and enhanced.

When, in 1952, the Headmaster proposed that the Perse, like the colleges, should have its own flag to fly on suitable occasions, he was repeating an idea which sixty years before had been explored by Barnes-Lawrence, who had a special flag made when the Gonville Place building was opened. There is no record of the form the Victorian flag took. Mr. Stubbs, however, felt that the best design would be based on the Perse coat of arms. This had led to some research into the history of the arms, in which Messrs. H. T. Deas, G. M. Macfarlane-Grieve and C. E. Cope joined. Subsequently Messrs. A. F. Bottomley and A. M. Tupling made detailed research, including investigations at the College of Arms and the British Museum.

The researches showed that no grant of arms to the Perse family of Northwold is recorded at the College of Arms; records are, however, incomplete. The earliest positive evidence is given by the Heralds' Visitation of Norfolk in 1563, by the corresponding Visitation of Cambridgeshire in 1619, and by the book of arms compiled by Rouge Croix Pursuivant in 1621. The last-named, giving the most reliable evidence, is at the College, and it does show a trick of a crest (not the full coat of arms) belonging to John Perse. It may be assumed that this refers to John Perse of Northwold, and that, since a crest could not properly be used where no arms existed, a full grant had been made to him.

The Norfolk Visitation showed the arms as: *Sable a chevron ermine between three dragons' heads erased argent* and the crest as *a pelican argent membered sable vulning itself proper*. These are repeated in the Cambridgeshire record, and on Stephen Perse's tomb, except that the tomb shows the pelican as sable. It seems clear that Martin Perse was allowed to assume the coat; Stephen himself can have had no legal claim. Subsequent variations show some quite important changes: the crest may be on a torse argent and sable or on a mont vert, the pelican may be or and the field of the coat may be gules, and, most important, the dragons' heads may be shown as cockatrices'. The first version involving the cockatrices is to be found in a collection of armorial bearings made by Francis Whistler of Norwich in 1745-47. Griffins provide a further variation and the pelican has on occasion become a demi-pelican and even a stork.

There are obvious canting allusions. The pierced heart of the pelican alludes to the name Perse, and the sable of the field may be the nearest the Heralds could get to the very dark blue used as 'perse' in French heraldry. The punning motto, *Qui facit per alium facit per se*, different from that used by the family — 'En Dieu est ma fiance' — 'splendidly reminds us of the work that Stephen wrought at the hands of Martin . . . For, if Stephen was the school's principal begetter, Martin was the conscientious guardian of its early fortunes. There could hardly be a more gracious tribute to the spirit that attended the founding of the school'.[4]

It was with justifiable pride that the Headmaster was able, in December 1961, to report to the Governors on the growth of the Perse organisation under his direction. The school had for years been filled to capacity, the annual income and expenditure had more than doubled, and the assets had risen from £56,645 in 1945 to £253,366.

He went on to point out that the developments had meant increased pressure, because of the academic, administrative and social involvement, both on himself and on Mrs. Stubbs. They felt therefore that they could no longer give the time needed to take charge of the senior Boarding house. In any case, it had to be recognised that it had become normal practice in public schools to relieve the Headmaster of such duties and provide a separate official residence; when he retired, his successor would certainly expect a house to be available. Therefore, the one essential further building project called for was the provision of a Headmaster's house, for which a good site existed in the old orchard adjoining the Senior House, conveniently near the school.

The Governors approved, and, the Ministry having agreed to the financial arrangements proposed, the enterprise went forward without delay, the architect being Mr. J. T. R. Taylor. With the completion of this work, early in 1963, Mr. Stubbs' fifth aim, Fulfilment, was achieved. Changes in Housemasterships were made immediately, the Headmaster renting a house elsewhere as a temporary measure. Mr. Barry took over the Senior House and Mr. Symons the Junior House.

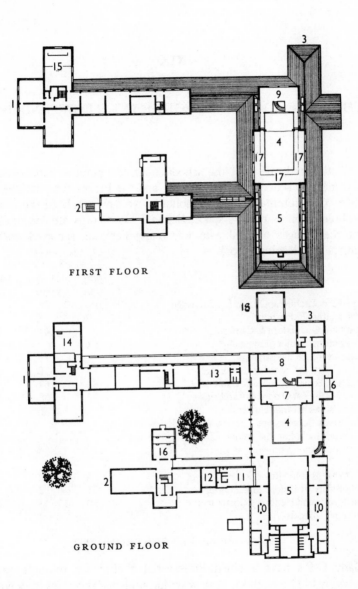

FIRST FLOOR

GROUND FLOOR

Plan of the New School

XIX

THE PERSE TO-DAY: DIRECT GRANT & INDEPENDENCE

On the academic side, the school could now point to achievements of which any school might be proud, and the Prospectus published in 1968 could summarise them as follows; we have tabulated the results in three columns to save space. Before 1906 records are incomplete, but these pages have shown how many Perseans achieved notable careers after leaving school.

	1906-1938	1939-1959	1960-1968
Open Scholarships at Oxford & Cambridge	105	28	17
Goldsmiths' Exhibitions	9		
Exhibitions at Oxford & Cambridge		41	28
Goldsmiths' Senior Studentship	1		
State and other Scholarships*		73	12
First Classes at Oxford & Cambridge	79	52	28
Second Classes at Oxford & Cambridge	84	161	155
Third Classes at Oxford & Cambridge	36	68	52
First Classes at other Universities		6	9
University Scholarships, Studentships, Medals or Prizes (including the second Chancellor's Medal for Classics—3 times)	19	38	42
Nobel Prizes	1		1
Fellowships of the Royal Society	4	2	
Fellowships at Oxford or Cambridge	11	12	4
Doctorates and Honorary Doctorates	10	8	17
Societies' Medals		4	3

*State scholarships were discontinued in 1962.

Many O.P.s have attained Professorial chairs; for example seven between 1931 and 1935. Peak years for academic successes in Scholarships and Exhibitions to Oxford and Cambridge were 1877, 1924, 1958, 1959 and 1968, in each of which seven awards were gained. This record was, as already noted, decisively broken in 1960, when no fewer than nine awards, all at Cambridge, were secured by Perse boys.

The proportionately higher achievements of the twenty years ending in 1959, and of the further eight years, 1960-68, show clearly what a magnificent academic standard had now been reached, making a notable school all the more notable. The record of distinctions outside the universities, detailed in the 1968 Prospectus, must be recognised as equally impressive.

What must be a unique distinction for a small school was achieved in 1952, when Old Perseans held the headships of four important University Colleges: Dr. E. M. W. Tillyard at Jesus, Cambridge; Sir George Thomson at Corpus Christi, Cambridge; Mr. Angus Macfarlane-Grieve at University College, Durham; and Canon Robert W. Howard, at St. Peter's Hall, Oxford.

During the period numbers in the school had risen dramatically. In 1930 the number of boys in the school was 333; in 1935, 288; in 1945, 482 and in 1961, 576. The Sixth Form had steadily expanded, from 57 in 1945 to 90 in 1950 and 120 in 1961 — a very remarkable tally for a two-stream school. For years the school had been filled to capacity; in 1953 327 boys sat the entrance examination for 50-60 places, and this pattern of five applicants for each vacancy, with a high standard of entry, had become a regular one.

In the number of awards at Oxford and Cambridge gained by public schools the Perse has, over the years, had a very fine record. *The Times Educational Supplement* in 1966 conducted a survey of such awards over eight years (1956-7 to 1964-5, omitting 1962-3). Manchester Grammar School emerged as the school with the best record; but since this is also the largest day-school in the country the absolute number of awards gave an unrealistic impression. A table was therefore prepared by the *T.E.S.* in which figures were adjusted according to the number of boys in the Sixth forms. Eleven groups were thus distinguished, and in nine of these Manchester Grammar School, even with proportionately adjusted figures, still headed the field. In the appropriate groups of schools with between 100 and 149 in the Sixth, the Perse, in 1956-59, took second place to Manchester, with an average of five Open awards. The Cambridgeshire High School was fourth in the same table, and the Leys was nineteenth. In the table for 1960-64, in the same group, Perse maintained its second place and the Leys were runners-up. The figures for the whole period showed a steady increase in the share of awards won by Direct Grant schools.

Such outstanding academic results have been possible only because boys of high intellectual calibre are brilliantly taught. Moreover, the

Mr Stubbs' Staff: July, 1969. Back Row: D. F. Maiden, A. B. Langlands, W. E. Kirby, D. H. Weigall, M. R. Ling, R. Wearing, N. J. Hutson. Centre Row: K. G. Sumnall, M. Seymour, J. C. Davy, J. R. Gerrish, D. Webber, M. J. Benton, K. G. Crook, D. G. Dunkley, G. Sudbury. Front Row: A. W. Billinghurst, S. S. Mitchell, K. Barry, V. G. Sederman, S. Stubbs, H. E. Percival, J. R. Tanfield, M. H. McFarlane, R. H. Whittaker teaching, as the examination results and Open awards show, is equally strong in the science and arts subjects. The most distinguished of the present school staff is probably John Tanfield, the Senior History master, whose lessons are characterised by lively discussion ranging over the whole field of human culture. His skill earned him the highest praise at the General Inspection of 1951. He is also a fine actor and producer, and his work in the Perse Players' public productions is noted on another page. He has been assisted by a series of sound historians; we should mention particularly Keith Symons, now Headmaster of Ryde School, who did especially valuable work in the sphere of British Constitution, and made major contributions in other areas of school life, especially in the R.N. section of the C.C.F.

The science department was headed by Arthur Hawkins, a first-class teacher who served a long and fruitful term as Second Master, thus continuing the remarkable series of Ushers and Second Masters who have served the Perse throughout its history. Incidentally, it was he who, having worked in the school, as man and boy, throughout his career, first urged that its history should be brought up to date, and there is much evidence of his perceptive research and memory in these pages. As a teacher of Physics he was thorough, understanding, but insistent on a high standard of work. For many years he was nicknamed 'Henry', a name obviously suggested by the Victorian music-hall song; this became 'Little Henry' or 'The Micro-Henry' — with a neat reference to the scientific unit and to his own small stature. As a young master he was on occasion mistaken for one of the boys. In Wootton's time his nickname became 'Oily'; this was an unfortunate name implying a characteristic which was not in his nature. His influence in the school was always good, and he was also a deeply religious man, prominent in the life of the church of Little St. Mary's. He played a full part, too, in the life of the Scouts and in every sporting activity, especially Athletics.

Among the most able of Perse masters was Alec Storr, who joined the staff in 1932 to teach biology. He also commanded the O.T.C. and was Housemaster at the school Boarding House, which he took over when Wootton relinquished it. The latter post he resigned in 1945, as already recorded; and he retired from the Corps in 1949 with the rank of Lt. Col., T.D. He continued teaching until his sudden death in 1955. Storr had a quiet yet firm manner; laconic in speech, he was seldom ruffled, never unjust, and always sympathetic to the problems of his boys. Outside the class-room, his main interest was shooting and he was largely responsible for the formation of the Rifle Club, whose work was greatly aided by the building of the new range. He was also a fine mountaineer, a former Secretary of the C.U.M.C., a member of the Alpine Club, one of the first to climb Mount Olympus. 'He loved the high and lonely places, and even more the effort of getting there, preferably by the shortest and most difficult route'. At Queens' he stroked the first boat for three years. He was also an excellent chess player, a County player for many years.

Among other excellent science teachers during this period we should single out Mr. F. C. Brown, an admirable Chemistry master, who joined the staff in 1945 and left in 1964 to join the Education department of London University. He had wide interests, including photography and cycling, and wrote the words of a new school song which, like a predecessor of the 'twenties, has not 'caught on'. In Barnes-Lawrence's time gatherings of pupils always sang *Dulce Domum*.

The Science department today, in the charge of David Webber, continues to produce excellent results, and a very high standard is maintained at 'A' level, and in University awards and degree results. The extra laboratory space in the new buildings has allowed an extension of science teaching. Whereas previously only one of the two parallel forms was able to study the three separate sciences up to 'O' level, it is now possible to offer the full syllabus to both. All boys now do Physics to 'O' level, about two-thirds do Chemistry and a half do Biology. In Chemistry the Nuffield Project scheme was adopted in the late 'sixties. In the Sixth form it has become possible to divide both the Physics and Chemistry 'A' level groups into two sets in each subject, and more recently the Physics has been extended to three sets. Chemistry embarked on the Nuffield Advanced Science Course in 1971, Biology in 1972 and Physics in 1973.

The Mathematics department has over recent years gone from strength to strength. James Buchanan, a sound head of department, left in 1957, to return to his native Scotland. He afterwards came back to the Cambridgeshire area to join the staff of Kimbolton School. The Senior Mathematics Master from then until July 1964 was Victor Sederman, who vacated the post on becoming Second Master in succession to Arthur Hawkins. He retired in 1972 and is now the school Archivist. The present Head of Department is R. H. Whittaker.

Mathematics has been given an increasingly important place in the time-table, and has provided a satisfying number of University awards, both in Mathematics and in Mathematics with Physics. Awards have mainly been at Cambridge, but more recently a greater proportion than previously have chosen Oxford.

Ordinary Level papers taken are Elementary and Additional Maths.

The alternative syllabuses in 'Modern Maths' of the School Maths. Projects have not been introduced, although the more able boys are instructed in 'modern' topics. Since 1972 another, less revolutionary, alternative, the 'Maths. in Education and Industry' paper, has been introduced for all candidates, at both levels. There has been a steady increase in the numbers going beyond the Elementary Maths. stage. In 1944 about eight from the top set took the 'Additional' paper. The number of sets in the Fifth form was increased from two to three in 1959 and since then it has been usual for the top two sets to present Additional Maths. at 'O' level. At 'A' level Mathematics has regularly been taken as a Single or Double subject, and here again numbers have steadily increased. A two-year course for Biologists not taking maths. as a main subject was provided in 1949. Statistics was introduced in the Sixth as an examination subject from 1970, and from 1972 a group mainly from the Naval Section has been able to present Navigation as an auxiliary examination subject. Mathematics at 'A' level is now available to any boy in the Sixth, irrespective of his other choices. All Sixth-form boys are now required to do some mathematical work, not necessarily for examination purposes.

Keith Barry, the present Second Master, is qualified in English and Modern Languages, teaching both subjects throughout the school. He well deserves the title of dedicated schoolmaster, since his contribution covers all branches of school life over a period of forty years. Himself a fine athlete and games player, he served for many years as a Games Master, his service covering the difficult war-time period. He has also commanded the A.T.C., helped in other ways with the Corps, been in charge, with his wife (a former mistress at the Prep.) of each in turn of the Boarding Houses, and has been a valued member of innumerable committees. Above all, he has been a stalwart member of the Old Persean Society throughout his time at the school, being Hon. Secretary for a number of years.

Under Mr. Barry's direction, as Senior English Master, the Perse has once again become widely known for its effective, sensitive and original work in this subject. Mr. Barry is well known throughout the country as a Chief Examiner for the Cambridge Board. The remarkable team he at one time headed at the Perse included Maurice Wollman and, most notably, Douglas Brown, an Old Persean who had received his early training under Caldwell Cook, and revived and enlarged the methods of the Play Way.

Like Cook, Brown disapproved of formal teaching of grammar and 'inactive' methods. Like Cook also, and like Rouse, he would have no

part in the teaching of Certificate examination work; he left the
preparation of examination candidates to his two colleagues, who
achieved excellent results without resorting to the dry methods practised in many another school. Brown's work, like Cook's, centred on
the Mummery. In the new school an entirely new Mummery was
possible, a real miniature theatre, in the design of which he foreshadowed ideas which were adopted in many other, more basic,
'drama rooms'.

Like Cook, Brown was able to turn a class-room lesson into a
memorable experience, for he did not depend on apparatus to arouse
the boys' interest. Another quality he shared with Cook was the ability
to keep in the background; he cleverly managed to give the boys the
impression that they were themselves providing the material for the
lessons and working out their own ideas. Whether he was taking a
poetry or composition lesson or producing a play, he suggested and
encouraged rather than intruding or ordering, and he intervened only
when it was necessary to decry inaudibility, to prevent mockery, to
keep the class on its toes. In consequence, the boys learned about
mime and movement, action and diction, poetry and drama by dis-
covering all about them for themselves and by developing their own
talents. The Mummery work, both drama and 'Speeches', was now
organised into Guilds, a more modern version of Cook's 'mistery'.
The increased facilities at the new school allow fuller use of lighting
and music, and the Masters of the Music can use the tape as well as
the record.

While the writing of original plays is no longer a feature of Perse
English, dramatic productions, in the Mummery and in the Hall,
reach a high level. Brown wrote a remarkable version of Sophocles'
Philoctetes, an essay in the philosophy of pain which proved sadly
ironical for Brown himself, since his life was to be cut short by a
painful disease. His early death was widely lamented, for not only had
his work at the Perse shown him as an ideal schoolmaster, but he had
become important in the world of scholarship. After a brilliant career
at St. Catharine's, with first class honours with distinction in both
parts of the Tripos, he had made himself an acknowledged authority on
Hardy's novels. On leaving the school staff he became a lecturer at
Reading University, and had been appointed a Professor at York
University, which his illness and death, at the age of 43, prevented
him from taking up. The gap at York was temporarily filled by another
Perse English scholar, Dr. Frank Leavis. The 'dialogue between music,
literature and education' which Brown had proposed at York has been

built into the academic programme there.

Brown's place on the Perse staff was for a time filled by Christopher Parry, another Persean devoted to the Mummery and all it stood for. He, in turn, left to follow a university career at Bangor. The work so firmly established has continued since, and English remains one of the most successful departments in a school which 'takes all knowledge to be its province'.

Another department which might truly be said to have gone from strength to strength is that of Geography. Parker-Smith set a high standard in his early work, relating the scientific side of the study to the wider interests of world culture, and F. V. H. Ramsbottom (1943-47) continued this. Since 1948 Malcolm McFarlane has made the subject a very live one, both inside the classroom, with the help of the well-equipped specialist room at the new school, and, most important, as a vital outside activity. His work in the Scouts and in the C.C.F. has complemented Douglas Brown's in showing the permanent values of the countryside and human activities. The amazing expeditions to sites all over Europe which have been inspired by Mr McFarlane's skill and enthusiasm are described on other pages.

Classical studies were directed from 1929 until 1970 by Hugh Percival, another long-serving member of the staff. His teaching was meticulous and thorough and he had a remarkable memory of all the boys who passed through his hands. His most notable scholar is Dr. Frank Stubbings, now University Orator and a Fellow and Librarian of Emmanuel, Hugh's old college. Hugh Percival's greatest work, how-ever, was outside the classroom. He took an active part in every side of school life, and was especially prominent as a Corps officer and as a Games master. Excelling as he did in all ball-games, and especially in Cricket and Hockey, and with a masterly skill in coaching and encouraging his teams, he, together with Keith Barry, who worked with him as Games master for a long period, did invaluable work for all school games.

The Modern Language department has continued to flourish in a way entirely worthy of the tradition established by de Glehn and Chouville. Two successive Heads of department have, sadly, died in harness, Mr. A. F. Mansfield and Mr. Stanley Mitchell. The latter, who was also distinguished for his long tenure of command in the Cadet Corps, was a particularly assiduous teacher and Housemaster, known for his meticulous attention to detail in everything he under-took, and for his loyalty and determination in seeing a thing through in proverbial Yorkshire spirit. Major Mitchell has been followed, both in modern language teaching and in the command of the Corps, by Tony Billinghurst, a brilliant all-rounder in work and sport. The present head of department is Michael Seymour, another good teacher who makes many contributions also outside the classroom.

The Art and Craft side of school activity was brilliantly served by Cecil Crouch, who was also gifted as a pianist, a teacher of ballet, as an admirable producer of the Perse Players, and in the organisation of many concerts and plays at the boarding houses and elsewhere. His productions owed to him their décor and costuming as well as their stage direction. The present Art master is R. Wearing.

Music plays an increasingly important part in the life of the school, the present responsible master being G. Sudbury. Choirs and orchestras, sometimes allied with groups from the Girls' School, have shown great promise and given great pleasure to their audiences on public occasions.

Religious instruction has, of course, always been part of the school curriculum. Stephen Perse, as a clergyman, laid down that all scholars must produce evidence of baptism, that prayers should be said twice daily, and that a memorial prayer for the Founder should be said at the beginning and end of each term. The Master and Usher were both normally in Orders, as were all the staff until this century.

In Victorian times the attitude to religion was, as has been noted, a narrow one, at its most bigoted in the administration of Allen. A liberal philosophy began to be expressed by Barnes-Lawrence and was extended by Rouse. The Doctor was a sound churchman; he was the son of a Non-conformist missionary and a missionary's daughter, but had himself joined the Anglican church. His sister had become a Catholic, and his life in India had made him tolerant of other faiths. He was highly sympathetic to Judaism, which led him to initiate the Hillel House experiment in Anglo-Jewish education. He was, in consequence, somewhat reticent in making any comment from the Headmaster's chair which might be thought denominational, even when he thought a misconception had arisen in some boys' minds. His school prayers, as has been mentioned, were very simple, and he limited his own religious teaching to the Greek Testament. His pamphlet *To Young Teachers* shows his own belief: he speaks there of the need for faith, 'an inward conviction that there is a God, that God is just, and, therefore, that it is worthwhile to persevere in our efforts at all costs because His purpose will be fulfilled'.

Religious activity became, in his time, largely a matter for societies, usually meeting out of school. The most important of these was the Bible Class which was started by one of the first Scoutmasters, Dr

Chris Mowll, brother of a former Archbishop of Sydney. This was held at Ridley Hall, and the theological students at that college took part, and later took over the running of the class. In the 'twenties it became a truly Persean organisation in that, although not officially approved by the school, it was entirely managed by Perse boys. Later it came under the aegis of the 'Crusader' movement, which was an influence in many public schools, but meetings were mainly conducted by senior boys and Old Persean undergraduates. The most notable leaders were Leslie Livermore, Geoffrey Rogers, Robert Sharp and Trevor Hughes. The classes always took a narrowly Evangelical outlook, and thus alienated some, but the influence exerted on a considerable number of boys was very great, and many who subsequently became clergymen or schoolmasters acknowledge their debt. Rouse, however, from time to time expressed displeasure, mainly because the movement seemed to him to lack breadth; he was more gravely displeased when some of the members in the Sixth form came to the conclusion that theatrical performances were often immoral and refused to take part in school productions, even of his Greek and Latin plays at Speech Day.

Among Rouse's staff were several who gave an example of practical Christianity which left its mark on many. We should name especially Parker-Smith, Hawkins, Berridge, Happold and James Taylor, all of them, as it happened, High Churchmen. Berridge and Happold, with their intellectual depth, extensive reading and interest in mysticism, were excellent teachers of Religious Knowledge, and their lessons became tutorials at which ideas were eagerly explored and exchanged, nearly everyone becoming involved. Berridge in particular, the son of a country rector, was a High Churchman in the true seventeenth century tradition, with a remarkable knowledge of the period and its divines. He introduced his classes to Hobbes, the Cambridge Platonists, the Little Gidding Fraternity, and, of course, our own Jeremy Taylor. Parker-Smith, as has been mentioned, edited a volume of Taylor's writing.

The Scripture Union, the S.C.M., and the Christian Union have also had their adherents, and the C.W.E.C. has, along with various other organisations, helped boys in their natural search for values.

A debt of gratitude is due to Wootton in that he made religion take a more open part in school life. He introduced a more lively form of Assembly and began a series of school Services which continues, the first of which, marking the end of his first year as Headmaster, was held in the chapel of his own college, Clare. During the war period, when a new significance was given to public worship, weekly services at St. Paul's Church were held on Saturday mornings, and these continued until the removal to the new school. Stanley Stubbs enlarged the system, arranging also termly and Carol Services in St. John's College Chapel. Preachers on these occasions were local and university clergy, and from time to time the Headmaster. The Perse also regularly attends the Christmas service which is also the final rehearsal of the famous King's College Carol programme, to which groups from all local schools are invited, the lessons being read by educationists.

Religious instruction in the school to-day continues to be a vital subject. The tradition, established by Rouse, of entry to the Perse being open to all races and creeds is maintained, and the American connection initiated by Stanley Stubbs has brought a number of American boys to the school, often temporarily while their fathers are in Cambridge on sabbatical leave.

The Preparatory School is an integral part of the Perse. The Headmaster is in charge of both, and he is responsible for all appointments, entries, organisation and administration. In effect the day-to-day running of the Preparatory school is as a separate Department with a Master-in-charge, at present Cdr. K. Sumnall, an ex-R.N. Instructor, and a specialist staff who are expert in the teaching of the 7-11 age-group and mostly have had N.F.F. training. The reputation of the Preparatory school is such that a high standard can be required of all entrants, and the great majority of the boys in due course pass, by promotion or scholarship examination, to the Upper School. The association between the two schools is close-knit and harmonious, and they share appropriate activities, matching Scouts with cubs, the *Pelican* with the *Little Pelican*, and combining at public functions. The *Little Pelican* deserves special mention, as a magazine of news and original contributions which shows the high standards of work and activity and reflects the ethos of a happy large family of 140 pupils.

The success of the 'Prep' is shown not only by its consistently excellent academic results but in that it has always been a happy community, thanks to a series of dedicated teachers who have continued the skilful and kindly work of Catherine Burrows, of whom something has already been recorded. The joint efforts of Miss Holden and Mrs Beacock and of Hugh Lindeman, who succeeded Miss Burrows, and involved himself fully in all the cares and occupations of his young pupils, gave them not only an excellent initiation to intellectual and physical effort, but also a sound moral basis for the lessons of life. Mr Lindeman showed himself the ideal Prep. school master, and the high esteem in which he was held was shown when he retired in 1963. Mrs

Edna Spence, who led the school for a time at this point, safeguarded continuity; her work for the Cubs brought out to the full the fine qualities of the movement.

Among the most loved and most talented of all the staff who have served the Prep. were Miss Bridget Carmichael and Miss Susan Taylor. Miss Carmichael, in specialising in the important sphere of introducing school life, its wonders and its demands in relationship to others, added almost motherly care and affection to her inspired teaching; her retirement in 1975 was marked by many expressions of affection and appreciation from old boys and parents. Miss Taylor's short stay at the school ended tragically when she was killed when a car collided with her stationary caravan in Sweden, in 1966. She had already made a great mark in teaching nature-study, taking full advantage of the opportunities offered by the spacious grounds of Leighton House. She initiated a number of projects concerning birds and trees, including bird-watching, the ringing of birds and charting of their territories and movements, and the study of trees. The boys were partners in all these activities and learned scientific method almost as a game; it was indeed the Play Way applied to science.

Something more needs to be said of the Perse Girls' School but this is not the place for a detailed account of the history of our highly regarded and successful sister school. To celebrate its seventy-fifth birthday a sketch history was published in 1956. A richly-documented field of research awaits a future historian, who will surely have the brotherly good wishes of all Perseans.

Co-education has never been a burning issue in the school's history. In fact until very recent times it has scarcely been discussed; there has rather been a general feeling of satisfaction with the degree of co-education made through harmonious cooperation between the two schools in activities and relationships. The newly rearranged County policy in education has left the Perse schools as almost the only single-sex schools in the area.

An earlier chapter has outlined the steps which led to the foundation of the school in 1881 and its transfer to Panton House in 1883. The first Headmistress was Miss Street, always addressed as 'Madam', and at the end of her twenty-eight years' reign the number of girls had risen to 200. Although primarily intended for day pupils, the school, like the boys' school, always arranged for a number of boarders to be taken. The administration has, from the first, been in the hands of a Trust, managed in accordance with the Scheme approved at the time of foundation; the Boys' school is represented by a number of its Governors.

The Perse pelican appropriately became the Girls' School crest, with the variant motto: 'Il faut savoir montrer l'esprit de son âge et le fruit de sa saison'. Succeeding Headmistresses were Miss B. L. Kennett (1909-26), Miss M. Cattley (1926-47), Miss M. A. Scott (1947-67) and Miss C. M. Bedson, the present Headmistress, who leads a school of 580 pupils in the Upper and Preparatory departments.

The administration of both schools is based on the Scheme of Government officially framed by the Board of Education and dated 1910, with amendments in 1918 and 1921. As a Direct Grant school it is also governed by the 'Direct Grant Regulations' issued by the Ministry, with periodic revisions.

The constitution of the Board of Governors at present includes representatives of the Cambridge City Council (6), the Cambridgeshire County Council (6), the University of Cambridge (2), Gonville & Caius College (2) and Trinity College (1). In 1976 a democratic revision has provided places also for representatives of the Old Persean Society, the Parents' Association, and the Staff.

The Governing Body is necessarily somewhat fluid in its membership, but in practice a solid core of long-serving members has ensured strong continuity in devoted work and service. The appointment of many Old Perseans to the Governing Body has also given a happy recognition of the interests of the school through the years, strengthened by the new appointment of a Society representative. In recent times three O.P.'s have been Chairmen of the Board, namely, Major G. Brimley Bowes, Dr. A. L. Peck, and the present Chairman, Professor J. C. Polkinghorne.

The business of the Governors is conducted through Standing and ad hoc Committees, which report each term to a full Governors' meeting. All meetings are attended by the Clerk to the Governors and by the Headmaster, who give professional advice. In recent years John Few and Frank Elworthy, partners in a long-established Cambridge firm of solicitors, have successively served as Clerks to the Governors. Financial matters and the annual Audit have been controlled successively by R. Chater Blows and his partner David Ruston. All four of these officers were educated at the Perse. Blows and Ruston have also acted as Hon. Treasurers to the Old Persean Society, which owes them a great debt.

Other persons involved in administration and advice are the Bursar, who is a member of staff under the authority of the Headmaster, and the Doctors who attend the Boarding Houses and advise on health matters.

Among Governors who have done outstanding work for the school in recent years, in addition to the Chairmen, special mention should be made of Ald. Doggett, Sidney Martin, Dr. Will Edwards (a former Headmaster of Bradford Grammar School), Ald. E. Halnan, Ald. E. O. Brown and Ald. P. F. Dennard.

Something must be said also of those who 'also serve' but not in the academic field. Apart from the secretarial assistants and domestic staff at the schools and boarding-houses, mention should be particularly made of the school's Bursars — two only, to date, H. G. Taylor and I. R. Yates — and of the Clerk's chief assistant, Norman McClement, who later became Mayor of Boston, Lincs., but retained his affection for the Perse to his death. Fine service was given by Robert McAndrew, ex-Royal Marine, who retired as Porter in 1976. At the boarding-house W. Dean gave exemplary service over many years. In maintaining the grounds and playing fields, the Wagstaff family have given many years; not only has Kenneth served as Groundsman, but also, for long periods, his brother, his father and his uncle have cared for our fields.

The future of the Perse, as of other Direct Grant schools, began to be threatened when the Labour Party declared its intention, on attaining power, of introducing a compulsory system of comprehensive schools throughout the country. This led to widespread debate, not only on the principle, but on details of the various possible schemes which might be implemented. The Headmaster gave the whole question very thorough consideration, and in January 1967, presented to the Governors a 'Memorandum on Secondary Reorganisation and the Perse Schools'; the Governors unanimously approved and accepted his findings, part of which should be quoted:

'In view of the present uncertainties, the practical and financial difficulties involved, we can still look only tentatively into the future. We seek simply to continue to serve Cambridge as we do now, with independence, responsibility and sincere cooperation; to maintain our high standards of quality; and to help parents in every way by direct and personal association. To do so, whatever variations in curriculum and age of entry might be possible, we should need criteria of admission which include genuine assessment of academic ability and aptitude'. . . . In view of the history and traditions of the Perse, 'it is unthinkable that we should allow our schools to decline into a mere neighbourhood unit in a comprehensive organisation. While we should sincerely wish to make our contribution to the provision of the L.E.A. we could make the value and quality of that contribution more high by offering something different and special in a genuine form of equality of opportunity for the ablest children'.

After considering possible patterns of organisation which the Authority might propose, dismissing the three-tier scheme and Sixth Form mass entry, and stressing the need for continuing the boarding houses and the preparatory school, the Memorandum reiterates the hope that 'a form of Direct Grant (call it Social Extension Grant) will be the integrating factor in bridging Independent and State Education.' A measure of administrative cooperation of a tighter kind with the Girls' school, possibly creating a four-stream 'quasi-coeducational' unit, could well prove useful. Closer attachment to the University might well be envisaged, and Mr. Stubbs' visits to America reinforced that idea. 'We would thus be taking advantage of our location in a University city to demonstrate the 'oneness' of education in a practical way'.

This was to be only the first round in a long and often acrimonious debate. It was another period in which the whole system and even the purpose of education was under review, and the Butler Act, the Fleming, Newsom and Plowden Reports and a series of Ministry circulars affected the future of the Perse, as they affected the whole country. The Perse was, as ever, anxious to play its part without betraying the principles of its founder and its tradition.

XX

THE CORPS, THE SCOUTS, THE PERSE PLAYERS
AND SCHOOL SOCIETIES

The Corps

The Corps and the Scouts have both played a vital part in Perse history. The Corps grew out of the Rifle Volunteer movement, which began in Cambridge as early as 1804 and by 1870 was well established, with units for both University and Town, each with its own shooting range, at Grange Road and Mill Road (later Coldham's Common) respectively. The movement spread to the public schools, the first school contingent being established at Rossall in February 1860. The Perse was not far behind, as is proved by the existence of two uniform badges, now in the archives, showing the crest with the words 'Perses School Drill Corps' over the date 1860. However, the early corps were not encouraged by the Government, 'disinclined to put rifles into the hands of school boys'. The first Perse unit did not survive, but Barnes-Lawrence and Rouse successively encouraged their Drill Class, Rouse naming it once again Corps, and organising a Drill Competition in his first term.

The first heyday of the Corps was during and immediately after the Boer War. The school Armoury was deliberately built in 1909 in preference to a gymnasium. Official recognition of the contingent came in 1905, and in 1906 rifles were supplied by the War Office, which were commandeered in 1914. The first uniforms (choice of design being allowed) were 'a useful Norfolk jacket and breeches of a neat and effective grey, with grey slouch hats and dark blue puttees'. There was some feeling against non-participants, who became known as the 'Squash Mob', which title remained in use until the 'twenties. In 1908 the unit became part of the O.T.C.

Regular training-schemes and camps were held, Rouse usually attending himself, and riding to the site. During the First Great War, when Rouse himself took a commission, it was customary to wear

Mr. Melville's Staff, 1976. Back Row: R. J. Revell, G. Sudbury, M. P. Nierinck, Dr D. G. Powell, R. V. L. Shannon, T. Jeffries, R. E. Smith. Middle Row: D. H. J. Baker, D. E. Roulinson, A. E. Piercy, Dr J. M. Parry, J. L. G. Pimbey, W. E. Kirby, P. F. Bradford, R. Wearing, D. J. Jones, C. A. Biddle. Front Row: M. Seymour, A. W. Billinghurst, M. H. McFarlane, K. Barry (Second Master), A. E. Melville (Headmaster), J. R. Tanfield, R. H. Whittaker. D. Webber, D. G. Dunkley.

uniform every day,[74] and a number of schemes in support of the war effort took place, while the 'Squash Mob' served as hospital orderlies. The commanding officer from 1902 until 1907 was Capt. F. M. Rushmore, afterwards Lt. Col. commanding the C.U.O.T.C. Capt. R. Parker-Smith was in command until 1922, except for a period when Capt. Ll. Davies took over; Davies was killed in the war. From 1922 Capt. F. C. Happold, D.S.O., was a competent but eccentric commander, introducing a uniform with shorts and purple puttee-tops which had an understandably short life. Shooting was always an important activity, the school entering some important competitions and awarding team colours. There was a miniature range under the Headmaster's classroom windows, and a larger range on the school field was excavated in 1909. At various periods there has been a contingent band.

In recent years two further officers have commanded the corps for the maximum period. Lt. Col. A. E. Storr was in command from 1932 to 1949, and Major S. S. Mitchell from 1949 to 1961. Both these officers earned the Territorial Decoration, and Major Mitchell was awarded the M.B.E.

In both great wars former cadets found that their training had equipped them for service, though it had not guaranteed commissions. In 1939 the O.T.C. became the J.T.C. and a parallel force, the A.T.C., was shortly afterwards created to cater for those interested in the flying services. The Perse unit was one of the first in the Cambridge area. After the war there was a further change of name, the new Combined Cadet Force incorporating the A.T.C. and providing a Royal Naval section. The Perse Naval Section, formed in 1949 has proved particularly successful and popular. The Naval and Air Sections together have provided valuable training in sailing and gliding, while the Flying Scholarship scheme allows cadets from any section to learn to fly solo in powered aircraft, bringing them within five flying hours of the Private Pilots' licence requirements. The R.A.F. Section has its own glider, which is housed in a hanger constructed in the 'twenties.[42] Shooting continues to be a major activity, a new covered range having been built in 1954.

The major annual occasion is the Inspection, when an important 'brass-hat' comes to review the work of the contingent. On two occasions Inspecting Officers have been Old Perseans, in 1948 Major A. E. French and in 1959 Lt. Col. G. T. Salusbury. In 1950 the Inspecting Officer was the son of an O.P. and was proud to see his father's honours shield in the hall. The filed official Reports speak of consistently high standards.

The peak in membership was reached in 1956, when there were 206 cadets in the corps. However, following the abolition of the Basic Training section, a defence economy of 1963, membership has been limited to the fifth and sixth forms; the unit has benefited from the change, there being now some 125 boys concerned, all seniors. Since Major Mitchell's retirement subsequent commanding officers of the Army section have been Captains J. E. Perry (1960-63), J. Symonds (1963-65), J. C. Davy (1965-68) and D. G. Dunkley (since 1968). The A.T.C./R.A.F. Section was commanded by F/O. K. Barry and F/Lts. V. G. Sederman (1945-58), D. J. Newton (1958-60), M. Seymour (1960-72) and D. E. Roulinson (since 1972). F/Lt. Seymour retired from the section in 1974, after 16 years' service. F/Lt. Roulinson, an Old Persean, was formerly a cadet in the section. The Royal Naval section was commanded at its inception by Lt. Cdr. K. N. Symons, who became Contingent Commander in 1961. In 1966 he was succeeded by Commander K. G. Sumnall, O.B.E., R.N. ret'd. Successive section commanders have been Lts. A. F. Crosbie (1970-73), R. H. Youdale (1973-75) and M. H. McFarlane (since 1975).

On Cdr. Symons' leaving the staff, he was succeeded by the present Contingent Commander, Wing Commander A. W. Billinghurst, who joined the R.A.F. section in 1953.

Today the activities of the Corps are varied, and offer great opportunities of training in leadership and team-work. The record of successes in proficiency examinations is very good; for example, recently seven out of eleven candidates gained Grade I passes at 'O' level in Navigation, in which they had been instructed by Cadet N.C.O.s as part of regular parade work. Field Days often take the form of cross-country and Night Exercises, or are extended to Field Weekends, enabling cadets to get further afield. Holiday courses provide exciting and rewarding training, involving initiative, campcraft, expedition training, life-saving exercises, mountaineering, sailing and canoeing, gliding, the ground-handling of aircraft, land-yacht operation and service engineering. Ambitious programmes of adventurous training, always popular with the boys, have been carried through since 1959, when the scheme was introduced. The courses have usually taken place in mountainous country, either in North Wales, in the Cairngorms, or abroad. An outstanding expedition was to Iceland in 1975. All these were led by Tony Billinghurst.

The Scouts

In Scouting, also, the Perse was among the pioneers. The movement, with its basis of training in citizenship and for the intelligent enjoyment of the countryside, was bound to catch the imagination of men like Green, Caldwell Cook, Macfarlane-Grieve and Rouse, and, in a later generation, Douglas Brown, Malcolm McFarlane and Tony Billinghurst. There are mentions of boy-scouts in the local press around 1908, but the movement was officially established in Cambridge only on 30 May 1910, when a meeting was held in the school hall for the purpose. A local Boy Scouts' Association was then inaugurated, and the Perse troop took the early number of 5th Cambridge.

The credit for the establishment of the Perse troop certainly goes to Green, a remarkable personality about whom something has already been said in these pages. He was, indeed, one of the founders of Scouting in Cambridge, and was for a number of years District Secretary, in which office he was indefatigable. He claimed to know practically every local scout, and personally issued all Badge certificates — applications for which, he once said, poured into his letter-box. He appeared at almost every camp or field exercise in the area, even when the Perse troop was not involved. Yet he does not appear to have taken out a warrant and certainly never wore uniform, though he always wore the Scout lapel badge. It was always he who carried out, at the school, the recruit's enrolment ceremony; it was he who, in those early days, provided the essential continuity of direction in the troop. The duties of Scoutmaster and Assistant Scoutmaster continued to be discharged by a series of undergraduates, who, as the *Pelican* of 1914 sadly observes, 'each year depart to take up their work in life elsewhere, and year after year we wonder if the new Scoutmaster will be able to uphold the great traditions of the Troop'. But they could, and did, always turn to Green, whose house came to be regarded as the headquarters and main meeting-place, for patrol-leaders, patrols and even for the whole Troop. Generous entertainment could be depended upon.

The first full-scale Scouting exercise in which Perse boys took part appears to have been one held at Madingley Hall on 30 December 1910. The *Pelican* reports that this heralded 1911, which was to be 'a great year for Scouting' and goes on to specify that the year was notable for 'B.P's Cambridge Rally, Windsor, Camp and the Concert, numbers increased, new Colours and more favourable conditions.' The list of events speaks for itself. The visit of the Chief Scout was to be the first of many.

Among the Scoutmasters to whose generous assistance the early success of the troop is owed are Mr (later Dr.) C. K. Mowll and his brother R. J. Mowll and Leslie Missen. Missen, while still an undergraduate at Christ's, found time to give regular help to the Scouts, and continued his interest for many years, even after leaving Cambridge. The greatest name in the troop over the next forty years was that of Gavin Macfarlane-Grieve, about whose work many pages could be written. He was concerned with every scouting activity, and his personal generosity enabled the troop to embark on a variety of programmes. His most important contributions were probably the visits to Scotland he organised, and the camps at West Runton, Norfolk, on a site which he procured, which became an institution over the years. At these Camps Arthur Hawkins always took charge of the catering, with assistance from a series of Old Perseans who came to look forward to that annual engagement. He afterwards retired to a bungalow nearby.

In the early days much help was given also by Caldwell Cook, Salusbury, Hambleton, Hicks and others. More recently the work of George Braithwaite and 'Jake' Bullock should not go unchronicled.

In the 'fifties and 'sixties there was a national passion inspired by the imaginative Duke of Edinburgh Award, for arduous expeditions of the 'Outward Bound' type. The Perse Scouts, and a number of individual Persean parties, were quick to adopt the idea and philosophy behind it, and to extend it in characteristically Persean ways. The various exercises undertaken always had a cultural, practical and intellectual value as well as being a test of initiative and endurance. While the Corps engaged in tough exercises in the mountains, the R.N. section practised sailing in the open sea, and the R.A.F. section undertook gliding, the Senior Scouts also achieved expeditions of major value. Through the development of Senior Scouting (1948-67) and Venture Scouting (introduced in 1965) opportunities were provided which the Perse Group took up with enthusiasm, under the leadership of Malcolm McFarlane, always assisted by Tony Billinghurst. McFarlane was Senior Scout Leader from 1948 to 1963, when, on his retirement, a presentation was made to him to which over a hundred O.P. ex-Senior Scouts contributed. In view of the difficulty of finding a successor he returned to act as Group Scout Leader until 1973. In 1974 he became an officer in the R.N. section of the C.C.F., and in September, 1975, he became commanding officer of that section. Christopher Parry was Senior Scout Leader from 1963 to 1965, when Tony Billinghurst, who had been an assistant since 1953, became Senior Scout Leader.

Senior Scout and Venture Scout camps, usually led by McFarlane and Billinghurst, have often, but not always, involved an element of geographical survey, as well as mountaineering. The important expeditions undertaken since 1951 were inspired by Maurice Dybeck, later

Warden of Brathay Hall and now Warden of Sawtry Village College. Among camps in the U.K. may be mentioned the two of 1953, that in March making a survey of Lake Bochlwyd and that in August undertaking a weather survey in the Cairngorms. In 1956 there was a corrie profiling exercise in North Wales, and in 1958 work involving bird-ringing was undertaken for the Scottish Nature Conservancy on the Isle of Rhum. In 1960 there was a survey of a corrie lake in Ben Eighe, in Wester Ross, and in 1962 a party worked on the Ffestiniog Railway. Three important expeditions travelled abroad: in 1956 a party made a Glaciological Survey, in support of the Cambridge University Expedition, at Austerdalsbre, Norway; in 1959 a climbing party went to the Central Pyrenees, scaling Vigemale and Mont Perdu (11,000 ft.); in 1963 a hut-tour in the Ötztal, Austrian Tyrol, climbed the Wildspitze (12,400 ft.) and other peaks. In 1961 and again in 1965 there were expeditions to the Lötschental, in the Bernese Oberland, and in 1967 the Ötztal was again visited, with the Stubai Alps. In April 1975, the Venture unit joined with the 7th Cambridge (Cambs. High School Venture Unit) to become the Cambridge Tithe Venture Unit.

In all these activities much help was given by Old Perseans. The school may feel pride in the fact that those trained in expeditions of this kind are always willing to return to help new generations. Indeed, but for the help of Old Perseans, parents, and friends without any actual Perse connection, the Scouts associated with the school could not have survived in recent years. Messrs. McFarlane and Billinghurst, because of their heavy involvement with the Corps and other activities, have had to withdraw: Tony Billinghurst resigned his Scout warrant on becoming Housemaster, but retains his connection with scouting as County Mountaineering Adviser. For a time the situation reverted to that obtaining in the early days of the Troop, when friends, many of them undergraduates, kept it alive by their efforts. Happily, the great traditions are being well maintained and the future of Perse Scouting seems assured.

Having been introduced to the skills and pleasures of mountaineering while at the school, a number of Perseans have gone on to achieve some note in this sport. Most notable was Robert Downes, who first visited the Alps with Malcolm McFarlane in 1948. From the Perse he went up to Clare to read History, and immediately joined the C.U. Mountaineering Club, becoming its Secretary in 1954 and President in 1955. The climbs he undertook in 1955 alone make an impressive list and he became well known in the climbing world. In 1956 he was invited to join an expedition to Masherbrum (25,660 ft.) in the

Himalaya. It was while preparing for an attempt on the summit of that mountain that he died of pulmonary oedema, in July 1957. He wrote well, and might well have become a noted writer on mountaineering.

A hut in the Peak District has been named after him. Others who should be mentioned in this context are Richard Johnston, who took part in the first traverse of Sukkertoppen ice-cap, in Greenland, with the Sandhurst expedition, David Chamberlain, who was in an Oxford University expedition to E. Greenland and Stephen Williams and Robert Squibbs, who, as undergraduates, were included in the Cambridge East Greenland Expedition. This party, led by Tony Billinghurst, made the second ascent of Pleintingbjerg (7000 ft.) by a new route on the east face. Another O.P., Stewart Watt, now works with the Danish Geological Survey Unit in East Greenland.

Among the many Perse societies the two most renowned have always been the Perse Players and the Perse Union Society. Both these are highly distinctive and are far more than the school dramatic and debating societies. The foundation of both goes back to the time of Barnes-Lawrence, but the two Cooks, Caldwell Cook and Harold Cooke, re-founded them and gave them a special quality which remains.

The Perse Players

The Perse Players, like everything else inspired by Caldwell Cook, had its own mystique and ceremonial. To belong to the Players in his day carried as much glory as membership of the First Fifteen. Leading members who had made a valuable contribution to its work (not necessarily as actors) were awarded a lapel-badge showing a pelican in purple enamel on silver. This was a personal award from Cook as President and was highly prized. When he first planned the society Cook put a notice in the *Pelican* of December 1911. This gives the founder's ideas so delightfully that it must be quoted: 'Their constitution will be quaint, their shows conducted with formal ceremony, and the whole tenour of their doings above the common. Their art, though simple and near to the interests of ordinary people, will be so far removed from the aimless vulgarity of present-day diversions as to seem in keeping with another more lovely age'.

The inaugural performance was on 18 June 1912, when a musical programme, arranged by the Master of the Music, Gavin Macfarlane-Grieve as a boy, was followed by a Prologue written and spoken by a very promising young man, Humphrey Devereux, who was destined to die in the war then closely at hand. Cook's prospectus made it clear that such a special prologue would be an essential ingredient of his programmes. There followed the first of several Perse Plays which were to follow in the ensuing years: blank-verse plays, written, acted and produced by the Players themselves. On this first occasion there were *The Cottage on the Moor* and *Thor's Hammer*. *The Cottage* told a story of Roundhead days; for the other Cook directed his young authors, as he often did, to Norse mythology. The performance was well received, the press waxing eloquent in the Master's own style, one writer declaring that the atmosphere 'helped to purge us of the commonplace', while the *English Review* spoke of 'a phenomenon, big with possibilities'.

Encouraged by this first success, Cook embarked on his ambitious appeal of 1913, to which reference has been made. When this failed so dismally, he turned to the more modest possibilities available in the Pendeen House Mummery and the school hall. The next two productions were *Baldr's Death* and *Freyr's wooing*, again from Norse myth, which critics found 'naively delightful'. That summer the corps of writers were embarking on an ambitious 'great trilogy, *The Twilight of the Gods*' which was unfortunately not completed. In the performances of the remaining pre-war years a similar pattern obtained, with Latin plays by Appleton added to the repertoire. In 1915 a group of Belgian refugees performed *Thor's Hammer*. Thus the war did not immediately interrupt the series, but Cook's departure for the Front did so, and it was only on his return that the Perse Players, in his stamp, really came to life. There followed frequent productions of plays of various kinds, especially scenes from Shakespeare, Miracle plays, mimed ballads, and, above all, original plays. Half a dozen plays of remarkable quality were produced by such groups, usually aged from twelve to fourteen. *The Cottage on the Moor* had been the first of these.

Perhaps the most effective of all such plays was 'The Fight of Finnsburg' produced in December 1923, by a third-year form. This was inspired by a passage from Beowulf, involving the so-called 'Finnsburg fragment'. The class read the Beowulf, and revelled in its plot and its language. It only needed a suggestion from Cook that in the 'fragment' was material for a play to get them going. They had been so well trained in the techniques of blank-verse that it seemed clear that that was the only possible vehicle. The division into scenes was soon made, and five boys each took charge of one Act.

Cook did not control or dictate, but was always there to advise, and when he did take a hand in shaping the work it was in the subtlest possible way. The class, and especially the five principal writers, lived and breathed a mixture of Beowulf and Shakespeare for weeks, and spent hours in writing and discussion, often in other boys' homes or at Cook's flat in Appleton's house. The production details were worked out in great detail, other members of the class taking over the staging and property arrangement until almost every boy was involved. Music was needed for a sad little dirge, and this was written by one of the principals (Cyril Peckett) and sung by another (John Morley). Thus Cook showed that he could 'awaken the creative artist by simply being one of a company which had become gay and inventive because of his own presence'.[49]

The final achievement was thrilling for the boys and impressive for the audience, and, although the play was never printed, it was certainly of a high standard; what matters, however, is that it gave a training and a feeling for language to its authors which nothing else could have given.

Some notable productions were plays written by individual boys; these were *The Death of Roland* by H. Richmond, in 1921, and *Knights and Squires* by Leonard Amey,[55] in 1926. *Paris of Troy*, by Peckett and Spry, which attracted comment because of its implied psychological analysis, was performed by Form IIIa in 1923, and again in 1928, after revision by a new IIIa. Two very talented young men, both of whom might well have become nationally known but for their early deaths, were Humphrey Jennings[75] and Donald Goring; both of them had a hand in writing and performing some of the productions of the 'twenties. Goring, who was Marius' brother, wrote in conjunction with F. C. Happold a blank-verse tragedy called *The First Born*, on the Passover story, and afterwards took a leading part in acting and producing *The Finding of the King*, in which Jennings did the décor and took another leading part. Jennings and Happold, with Broome, also offered *Le Théâtre des Souris Blanches*, a Christmas divertissement, which was acclaimed.

Speech Days were occasions for demonstrating the work of the school in its various departments, and served, very properly, to illustrate the use made of drama in teaching English, History, Classics and Modern Languages.

Sports Concerts, once or twice a year, struck a lighter note, but were the most usual occasion for performance by the orchestra and the notable solo-playing musicians. On three occasions Gilbert and Sullivan operas were chosen: each time the producer was Gavin Macfarlane-

Grieve, a great enthusiast for G. and S. *Trial by Jury* was done twice, once with *Cox and Box*, and a full production of *H.M.S. Pinafore* in 1924 was an immense success. *Cox and Box* was again performed in 1952 and the *Pirates of Penzance* in 1975. Among the light-hearted productions at Sports Concerts three were outstanding. In 1914 a play called *The Conversion of Palaiopaidagogos* was spoken of in the programme as 'an indescribable production in three acts written by and for members of the Perse School'. In 1923 a clever burlesque of some members of the staff described the loss and recovery of the detention book at Professor Denham's Pelican Academy. This was greatly appreciated by the victims as well as the audience, and Dr. Rouse congratulated Geoffrey Rogers on his impersonation of the head of the Academy. In 1928 the retirement of the Doctor was marked by a Persean revue in compliment to the second founder of the Perse; music was by Katie Goring, Marius' mother.

The private meetings of the Players were always stimulating. Such meetings, naturally held in the Mummery, were preceded by tea. Sometimes a play was acted through, sometimes there were dramatic readings, and sometimes a fuller programme was arranged, often to celebrate a festival, including Morris dancing, as well as poetry, music and drama. The main festivals which Cook liked to honour were Spring, or Daffodil Day; Shakespeare's birthday and St. George's Day; Midsummer; and Christmas or St. Nicholas' Day.

Public productions were of two kinds: the intimate performance in the Mummery and the formal presentation in the hall. By definition, the most important were entirely original, written, costumed and performed in the school, but there were also Shakespeare and other classical plays. In either case Cook's skill was especially seen in the technique he adopted as a producer. He hovered around, advising and suggesting rather than ordering, and the organisation was largely in the hands of the boys — who thought it was entirely so, but were in fact subtly guided by the great man's advice, often unobtrusively offered, or quietly hinted.

In the course of their public productions the Players have performed most of the important Shakespeare plays, as well as other Elizabethan, Restoration and modern plays. Cook produced *The Knight of the Burning Pestle* and Drinkwater's *X = O*, to name two widely different plays not of Perse origin. To name the various Shakespeare performances over the years would be to give a list of the bard's plays. There have been several productions of *Twelfth Night*, the *Dream*, *Richard II*, *Julius Caesar* and *Macbeth*; the most memorable have been the brilliant essays at the most difficult, *The Winter's Tale*, *The Taming of the Shrew*, *Romeo and Juliet*, *Coriolanus*, *The Tempest* and *Hamlet*. The finest individual productions were probably those of the last two named, in 1954 and 1949 respectively.

Caldwell Cook would be delighted if he could know how the Players, after passing through a comparatively undistinguished period in the 'thirties and early 'forties, reached new heights when they came under the direction of a succession of outstanding producers who have revived and continued his work. The first of these was James Buchanan; there followed Cecil Crouch, who covered music, costume and décor as well as productions, and John Tanfield, whose exciting and scholarly interpretations of a variety of difficult plays will long be remembered and made a considerable impact on the whole cultural life of the school. His production of the *Shrew* was a truly memorable occasion. Christopher Parry and Dr R. H. Pogson also made valuable contributions in recent years, and Douglas Brown's work in the Mummery was always in evidence. Parry demonstrated the work delightfully when, in 1965, he put on *The Festival of the Mummery*, followed by a performance of the *Philoctetes*, written by Brown and acted in his memory. John Tanfield's swan-song, an ambitious *Oedipus at Colonus* in 1970, was a milestone in that music played an integral part in the performance, and in that for the first time girls from the sister school took the female parts.

The productions of the Players have seen the first stage performances of several boys who were to become famous in the theatrical world or possibly in some other sphere. Frank Leavis, who was to become the formidable teacher and critic, first appeared as a memorable Macbeth. Marius Goring 'quite brought down the house' when he appeared as one of two golliwogs in *The Golliwog's Revenge*, a mime and dance to the music of Gounod in 1926. In 1929 Marius' presentation of the monologue 'Caliban upon Setebos' was justly declared a *tour de force*.

Another distinguished former Player, whose words have already been quoted in appreciation of Cook, is Spike Hughes, a many-sided personality who has done much to expound music of all kinds and has become a successful critic and script-writer. Yet another was Francis Baker-Smith, who became a B.B.C. producer, having first studied architecture, being the first to gain a Cambridge scholarship in this subject; there is a tribute to him in Spike Hughes' autobiography.[53] Marius Goring, somewhat their junior, brought credit to the Perse languages department as well as to Cook's English teaching when, in 1931, he toured France and Germany with the English Classical

Players, and when later, but still in his early twenties, he toured many European countries with the Compagnie des Quinze, acting in French. Having studied at Frankfurt, Munich, Vienna and Paris, he became known for his impersonations of continental characters. He was in charge of the wartime broadcasting programme in German, based on Bush House. Early in the 'thirties he had already made his name on the London stage, and an appearance at the Old Vic earned him, early, the distinction of figuring in a *Punch* cartoon — thereby especially delighting the Doctor. His first West End appearance was in *The Voysey Inheritance* in 1934, but he is perhaps best remembered for his delightful Celestial Conductor in the film *A Matter of Life and Death*.

Not a few of the Players appeared, in the 'twenties and since, in local dramatic productions, especially at the A.D.C. and at the Festival Theatre, of happy memory, under the brilliant management of Terence Gray and Anmer Hall. Some, notably John Farley Spry — later a Judge of Appeal in Central Africa and now Sir John — wrote poems and articles for the *Festival Theatre Review*. The outstanding theatrical name of a later generation, Peter Hall, first appeared in May 1946, as the Lord Marshal in a shortened version of *Richard II*; after he had attracted attention by a most promising performance as Marullus in *Julius Caesar* in which his appearance in a brief part was described as 'very moving indeed', he earned acclamation as Petruchio and Hamlet. The Third Player in that 'Hamlet' was Mel Calman, since noted as a cartoonist and illustrator. Hall first attracted wide interest by his exciting production of 'Cymbeline' at Stratford in 1957. He is now Director of the National Theatre.

Many interesting performances, often abbreviated Shakespeare plays, like the *Richard II* of 1924 and 1946 and the *Shylock* of 1968, and often performed by boys from junior forms, have prepared young actors for the world of the Players; above all, Douglas Brown's *Philoctetes* and Chris Parry's Festival of the Mummery have brought the Mummery methods delightfully into the public, or semi-public, eye.

The Perse Union Society

The Perse Union Society was originally founded, under the more modest title of the Perse School Debating Society, by the personal initiative of Barnes-Lawrence, in 1891. A letter to the *Pelican* in 1889 had suggested that 'it would be greatly beneficial to the speaking faculties of the school if a Debating Society were formed' and the idea

'Hamlet': 1949. The name part taken by Peter Hall

obviously appealed to the Headmaster.

The first meeting was held on Friday, 30 January 1891, when the motion was 'That in the opinion of this House ghosts do not exist'. It was proposed by G. B. Bowes, afterwards principal of the firm of Bowes and Bowes and Chairman of the Perse Governors, and was carried, 28-18. Debates continued to be held regularly, always immediately after school and either in the 'Big Room' of the new school or in one of the classrooms.

Dr. Rouse continued and encouraged the Society, often himself taking the Chair, and speaking on several occasions.

At first a member of staff always took the Chair, the highest office open to a boy being that of Vice-President. The first boy President appears to have been no less a person than J. M. Gray, afterwards Sir John Gray. Among interesting topics debated around 1907 — a particularly good year for the society — were the influence of the public-schools, the nationalisation of the railways and 'That this House would welcome a greatly increased tax on motor-cars' (which latter was lost). In 1910 a motion approving of mixed schools was carried, and Gavin Macfarlane-Grieve successfully proposed a vote of censure (passed unanimously) criticising the responsible master for not having spoken in any debate. In 1912 there were three innovations: an inter-form debate, an Old Persean debate, and a Visitors' Debate, at which the custom was started of inviting as guest speakers the President, Secretary and two other members of the Cambridge University Union Society. On the first such occasion Dr. Rouse took the Chair. The 1913 Visitors' Debate had as its guests, not Union officers, but 'a party of Presidents, ex-Presidents and Vice-Presidents of the Clare College Debating Society'.

The Perse Union Society was a continuation, in a more stately form, of the old society, which had flagged to some extent during the first World War, and had lapsed entirely between 1915 and 1917. It was, as has been mentioned, the particular brain-child of Harold Cooke, who was its first President. Through his inspiration the society became outstanding among English schools and renowned for an exceptional standard of procedure and oratory. Meetings were always held in the evening; the officers and principal speakers wore dinner-jackets and entered the hall, from the staff-room which adjoined, in procession. The hall was always lit by candles on the President's desk, the one used by the Headmaster at assemblies. An important rule was that the President on his inauguration delivered a Presidential Address — in a way analogous to the Prologues of the Perse Players — and these always reached a high standard and sometimes approached brilliance.

The inaugural debate of the Union Society was held on 13 November 1917 when the motion was 'That democratic systems of government during the present war have been weighed in the balance and found wanting'. Cooke was in the Chair and Rouse spoke for the motion, which was none the less lost. The first Visitors' Debate under the new title was on 22 March, 1918.

Among distinguished speakers at Visitors' Debates during this epoch were W. R. Sorley, W. F. Reddaway, J. C. Squire, G. G. Coulton and Gilbert Harding; the last-named is recorded in the minutes as having, even as an undergraduate, 'found time to disagree with almost everything'. Perhaps the most distinguished pair of visiting speakers of all were R. A. Butler (afterwards Lord Butler) and Selwyn Lloyd (subsequently Speaker of the House of Commons).

The Union Society has continued its activities without a break, although the formalities of Harold Cooke's day disappeared with his departure. A long series of masters have interested themselves in the Society, and many important topical subjects have been under discussion. In July 1942 the Jubilee of the Society was celebrated by a special meeting, when Major Brimley Bowes, who had taken part in the first recorded debate, in January 1891, spoke on the motion that 'Oratory is a doubtful blessing to mankind'. The debate was introduced by Mr. Wootton, who gave a brief history of the Society, and the chair was taken by Lord Porter, another distinguished ex-member. Incidentally, the motion was lost.

Other Societies

Only two other societies can boast a continuous or almost continuous life from the Rouse era until to-day. These are the Historical and Natural History Societies. To-day there are twenty or more school societies, including some unusual ones such as the Astronomical Society, the Contemporary Music Society, and the Perse Guild of Bell-ringers. From time to time there has been a flourishing Railway Society, of enthusiasts ready to travel to the end of the country to look over a locomotive works or a marshalling yard; Arthur Hawkins was prominent in this sphere. Societies devoted to Literature, Music and various Sciences have, with periodical gaps or changes, always flourished. The range of interests covered at various times by Perse Societies is immense, and probably greater than most other schools could show. Two gaps, which may be lamented, when the list from the 'twenties is compared with the present one, denote the disappearance of the Morris Dance Club and the Navy League.

All the societies, except for the old Union, which met in the evenings, meet after school, usually over tea and buns, to transact their business, which is often listening to an address by a member, one of the staff, or a speaker from outside, sometimes an Old Persean, often a university don; many highly distinguished scholars have from time to time honoured Perse societies by reading a paper.

Most important of all among the societies associated with the school is the Old Persean Society. Nothing shows the vitality of a school more than the strength and influence of its old pupils' association, and the O.P.S. must rank high among similar societies throughout the country. It has achieved so much that these pages cannot do it justice, and there is room for a book devoted to its history. From its inception it has worked to support the school, to help it in its difficulties and to secure recognition for its achievements. On several occasions, as has been shown, its practical help has been invaluable.

The Society owes its success over a period of ninety years to the devoted work of four men, Harold Cooke, Reginald Chater Blows, David Ruston and Keith Barry: the first three old boys of the school, the last-named a well-loved master. Cooke was also a part-time master, whose work has already been mentioned, and his ideas established a yearly pattern of activities which has since been followed.

The *Old Persean Chronicle* keeps members in touch and provides a record of members' activities, personal, academic and in all sorts of spheres, recording the many distinctions which Old Perseans have won and providing biographical sketches in obituary notices. When the time comes to publish a full record of the achievements of Old Perseans — something obviously beyond the scope of the present volume — the *Chronicle* will be invaluable. The annual Dinner brings all together, and there is also a London dinner whenever numbers justify it; the 1975 London dinner was held at the House of Commons, through the good offices of Mr. Brocklebank-Fowler, an Old Persean M.P. On these occasions notable old boys are invited as guests, and speak of their careers and reminiscences. The Headmaster reports on the school's progress. The toast of 'The Pious Memory of Stephen Perse' is always drunk, as a loyal toast second only to that of the monarch.

The President, always an old boy or a headmaster,[76] holds office for two years; when he is not a Cambridge resident a Chairman is appointed to conduct necessary business. The Annual General Meeting, in March, is regrettably always poorly attended, but other social functions usually attract large gatherings. Attempts to establish a permanent Club-room were made in the early days: in 1903 a room in King's Parade was open to members twice a month, and in 1906 there was a weekly club at the Dorothy Café. The first Dinner was held in 1901. To-day the Rugby Club provides a nucleus for meetings in the pavilion on the school field, thus reminding us that the first old boys' meeting, in 1884, was in the Football Room beside Parker's Piece.

Old Persean matches against the school have been an annual feature, usually in all three, and latterly four, of the major sports — cricket, rugger, athletics and hockey. Swimming matches have also been held, as well as tennis, and there is an important annual Club Golf tournament. By far the most important offshoot of the Society is the Rugger Club, about which something appears on another page.

An important kind of social work in which the Perse, like most public schools, has been concerned is in the establishment of a Hostel for London boys in need of sympathetic help. This was first opened at 2 Mecklenburgh Square, near King's Cross, in September 1937. Dr. Rouse, who would have liked to establish something of the kind during his headship, gave the scheme his unqualified, but necessarily remote, blessing. In the school the main worker was Gavin Macfarlane-Grieve; the real guiding spirit was John Illsley, who became the Warden. The President was Lord Porter, and other prominent Old Perseans made up the Council, with R. G. Heffer as Hon. Treasurer and R. M. Close as Hon. Secretary.

The premises were occupied jointly with the staff of another school mission, the Tonbridge School Boys' Club. Between 1937 and 1940 twenty-six boys passed through the Hostel, and there is no doubt that valuable contacts were made. It was intended, from the first, to limit the number of boys to seven, chosen from those who had appeared before magistrates and had been in trouble because of a bad home background or a complete lack of a proper home. Contact with the school was as close as circumstances allowed: John Illsley used to speak to the Sixth Form about his work, and parties went to stay at the Hostel for week-ends, while parties of Hostel boys came to camp at Toft and at Runton.

Unfortunately the Hostel was among the first victims of the 1940 'blitz'. When it was thus rendered uninhabitable the residents were evacuated to the country near Hitchin, and lived for a time in an old coach-house which had been used previously for week-end camps. The Hostel was approved by the Home Office in 1942 as suitable for boys on probation between the ages of 14 and 17, and later it admitted other boys whose home life had been unsatisfactory or were in the care of the Herts. authority.

At the end of the war, the Hitchin building had to close down. Efforts were then made to reopen in London, where obviously there was a greater need than ever for a hostel for homeless and delinquent boys. Illsley sent out an urgent appeal for funds. However, this clashed with the school's own appeal, at the time when the building of a new school was being actively pursued, and insufficient support meant that the project had finally to be abandoned. The cash in hand was first given to Winston House in Brooklands Avenue, but when this changed its scope the balance was handed over to the school to be used for youth work, and was quite appropriately put towards the new Scout building.

It is relevant to quote a part of Illsley's appeal, which eloquently and justly states the case for such a venture as this, and at the same time defines what its old pupils owe to the Perse:

From the Perse point of view it is vital. It seems to me that whether one's outlook be feudal or communistic, or anywhere in between, we cannot justify an institution which receives but does not give. I am acutely conscious of what I received at the Perse — not the instruction in French or maths, nor the opportunity to play games, but an outlook on life, the inspiration of a great headmaster, and no less of a great team of masters. We Perseans were, and I've no doubt still are, laden with the good things of life — things which are not in the market to be bought. These things are privileges, and with privileges duties go hand-in-hand; otherwise privileges must eventually fail.

XXI

THE RECORD OF GAMES

Compared with the major public schools, whose boys come to them only at 13+, the Perse is very small and it has not always been easy to field teams of high calibre. Yet the achievements in competition with other schools have always been creditable. Still more creditable has been the record of the 'ordinary' games, in which boys who were never in teams have acquired a measure of skill, kept fit physically, and above all enjoyed themselves in playing; for in games as in work the principle has always been that a boy's time at the school should be enjoyable.

As earlier pages show, the earliest sporting activities all took place on that remarkable public sports-field, Parker's Piece, which, in the second half of the nineteenth century, had become a nationally important ground for cricket, and was one of the places where the Town and Gown conflict does not seem to have raged, bringing the university, the town and the school together, usually amicably. It was particularly in the 'sixties that local cricketers made their names known internationally and the game had great popularity in Cambridge.

The annual calendar of school games includes a number of long-standing fixtures, notably with King's School, Ely, which goes back over a hundred years. Incidentally, the score-book of Bottisham Village Cricket Club records, in immaculate copper-plate, an early match between that club and the school on 4 July 1866. Bottisham then scored 95 and 42, and the school scored 57 and 81 for 1. The bowling analysis shows that five-ball overs were played at that time.

In the 'nineties another generation of equal stature arose, in Dan Hayward, an outstanding bowler, and the two legendary batsmen, Ranjitsinhji of the 'Gown' and Jack Hobbs of the 'Town', both of whom first played the game on the Piece. The Hayward family were great groundsmen and the elder used to 'do the pitch-making' on the Piece for both cricket and football and would do special work for the

Perse on occasion. The Perse groundsman O'Connor was also a distinguished player for local and county teams.

'Ranji', who gained his Blue in 1893, had, when practising here, the pleasant habit of placing a half-sovereign or sovereign on the bails and letting all comers bowl at him, on the understanding that any who knocked off the golden coin could keep it. Jack Hobbs was a local boy, who had first played at Jesus College — the only college which then had its own ground, where his father was under-groundsman.

Many local cricket clubs, now forgotten, flourished at this time: 'Ranji' played for the Cassandra and Hobbs for the Ivy, and other prominent clubs were the Camden, the Victoria and St. Giles'. Local institutions, such as the C.E.M.S. and the University Press, also fielded teams, and Old Perseans played in most of them, as well as in the O.P. Club team.

Perse boys of the time must often have watched first-class games on the Piece, and it must have been a thrill when, in 1893, the Old Persean First XI won the County Championship Cup — which was conspicuous at the ensuing Prize-giving. They had won four matches, and drawn one, losing none. There were two Old Perseans in the County team, Church and Gray, and Gray also won his Blue. In the same year the School First XI recorded ten wins, no draws and lost only one game. The Old Persean Cricket and Football Club had been re-established in July 1890, the original club of 1884 having, it appears, failed to survive.

Both School and Old Boys' sporting activities reached maturity in Barnes-Lawrence's time; but it should be remembered that his two predecessors, Heppenstall and Allen, had both understood the importance of games and done much to foster them. The pattern of games thus set continued. At first cricket was the strongest sport, but Allen made much of Athletics and Barnes-Lawrence introduced Hockey — which latter game was discontinued in Rouse's time, but re-introduced under Wootton.

Barnes-Lawrence, as has been recorded, felt very strongly the disadvantages and difficulties in using a public ground for games. His letter of appeal to the Master of Trinity has been mentioned. School teams were finding Parker's Piece so crowded that it was often hard to find a free pitch and sometimes play was difficult because players in other games impeded, or the pitch was invaded by 'townees' who were simply making a nuisance of themselves. The situation as it not uncommonly developed is described rather quaintly in the *Pelican* of 1897, when a game was said to have been played 'on a miserable little corner of Parker's Piece. As it was Saturday we were constantly annoyed by the inroads of strolling players'. We read also of Junior games actually terrorised by rough 'townees' who tried to turn the players off their pitches and if possible purloin their equipment into the bargain. In the days of the Gresham Road ground they would invade here also, and in 1890 it was proposed that, as a discouragement, 'Private' should be painted on the gate. Juniors in trouble naturally looked to the seniors, in the absence of a master, to protect them, and especially to the school captain. Quarrels were usually settled by stand-up fights between the rival leaders. Bernard Coulson recalls how his father on one occasion offered to fight a youth who was molesting the juniors, when his friend Percy Gray (afterwards founder of the well-known firm of estate-agents) pleaded, 'Let me fight him; you had a fight yesterday'.

In recent years cricket has flourished, largely through the tireless efforts of Hugh Percival and Tony Billinghurst. Hugh, himself an elegant batsman, ran the 1st XI almost single-handed from 1936 until 1952, when Tony, who is to-day the responsible master, joined him. D. J. Newton, joining in 1963, has also been of great help in the game. The school ground is now so well equipped and cared for as to be comparable with any in Cambridge, a city rich in fine cricket grounds. Always a superb batting wicket, it was originally rather open and wind-swept, but the nearness of the school and the maturing of trees planted when it was built, together with new sight-screens and the extension to the pavilion, have improved it greatly. A permanent site for the net wickets, established near the rifle-range in 1953, has been a further boon. Thanks to this training, the best years have been marked by hard-hitting, fast scoring batting, and accurate bowling.

Records show that in the early days of Perse cricket, when the school played colleges or village or town clubs, the side often included masters, so pre-figuring the Pelican C.C. founded by Mr. Newton in 1957, which continues to field sides composed of masters, Old Perseans and boys. Many school fixtures date back many years. These include King's Ely, Cambs. High School (now Hills Rd. Sixth Form College), Newport, Culford, Woodbridge, Ipswich and King Edward VII's, King's Lynn. Of particular interest, too, is the fixture with Newcastle Royal Grammar School, which made its first tour based on Cambridge in 1935 and, with some breaks, continues this. A growing number of schools are now also making cricket tours, either at half-term or at the end of the summer term, with Cambridge as the centre. These include Bradford G.S., Lancaster R.G.S., Cardinal

Allen's, Liverpool, Wrekin and Magdalen College School. In 1965 Haarlem Youth XI came over from Holland. Two important recent additions to the list are Cambridgeshire County (1956-76), which the Perse beat in 1958 and 1967, and the M.C.C. The latter fixture started in 1962, but it was not until 1975 that the school scored a victory.

The playing record and principal averages have, since the war, been published most years in Wisden's. The school now runs the following XIs: 1st, 2nd, 3rd, under 15, under 14, under 13 and under 12; all have regular fixtures. A run of successful seasons between 1955 and 1960, and again in 1967 and 1968, has led to the addition, or renewal, of some very interesting fixtures, including Bishop's Stortford, Chigwell, Kimbolton, Tiffin's, St. John's, Leatherhead, and St. George's, Weybridge. For the ordinary boy, what matters is that there has been an opportunity for all to acquire some prowess and competition experience.

A number of well-known players have played at the Perse. These include Jack Hobbs, O'Connor, J. G. W. Davies, M. R. Brearley (the last two playing for the M.C.C.). In addition to O'Connor, T. Jenner, the Australian test player, has helped with coaching; this was in 1974, when he also played for the Masters' XI against the school. Several O.P.s have played for Cambridgeshire since the war, some, like E. L. Kemp, H. A. L. H. Mumford occasionally, and others regularly, notably C. B. Gadsby and D. H. J. Baker (Baker is now a master at the school). R. M. Brooks has played for the Army.

About a third of the school fixtures are now all-day games. Obviously, in half-day games it is not easy to avoid a large number of draws on a good batting wicket such as we have.

Athletics became an important activity under Allen, an annual sports meeting being held on the Fenner's ground. Barnes-Lawrence continued this, apparently after a gap of one or two years, and in his time a full programme included those now outmoded events Throwing the Cricket Ball, Tug of War and the Obstacle Race. The Tug of War was by 1907 found 'a boring event'. Incidentally, in 1900 it was thought undesirable to include Weight-putting in the programme. The choice of events, of course, mirrored nationally-held views. There was a good standard of performances in these days, with some under 15 and under 12 events, as well as Open ones. Records were kept — how accurately it is hard to say — and that for the Quarter Mile, set by T. H. Brown in 1889 at 53 seconds, stood until 1957, when E. L. Kemp returned 52.6.

Fenner's was also used for occasional cricket matches, especially for the Staff v. Boys match, the first of which appears to have been in 1897. But cricket and football required their own ground, and the acquisition of the Luard Road field at the beginning of the new century made a profound difference. Cross-country running as a school sport goes back to the time of Barnes-Lawrence. It is not surprising that during this period cross-country runs were frequent, for the Second Master, Conway, was a cross-country Blue and President of the University Hare and Hounds. Paper-chases were much in vogue at this time. The Perse runs usually started from private houses on the Hills Road or the Huntingdon Road, where interested parents provided changing accommodation. The most exciting outing saw the capture of the hares by an irate gamekeeper before the hounds could catch up with them. The *Pelican* says that the hares 'met a pitchfork, a retriever and a keeper who proved deaf to all blandishments. It was vain for the senior hare to urge an experience of generations with the C.U.H. & H.' There were also runs when the trail was confused with other trails laid by the University club. Interest in this particular sport seems later to have waned, after Conway's departure, for the *Pelican* in 1904, when mentioning that such events still took place, sadly enquires, 'Why is it that the school no longer delights in paper-chases?'

The greatest age of Perse athletics was yet to come; more Blues have been won in this sport than in others. In the two major University sports, Rowing and Rugger, we may claim but one in each: A. S. Cohen in Rugger in 1922 and G. Paton Philip in Rowing in 1949. It is fair to observe that the Rowing record might have been very different had there ever been a Perse VIII.

Athletics received a great fillip through the work of A. J. B. Green, A. S. Mason and A. C. Hawkins, who, successively from 1908, developed the sport in a way typical of the Perse and well ahead of current ideas, though the system has since been widely used. During the second half of the Lent term athletics became the major activity for the whole school on games afternoons, and all the boys were expected to take part in as many events as they could, and to attempt to attain a 'standard' time or distance in each. The 'standards' were very carefully worked out by the masters, graded for age-groups and adjusted in the light of experience. House points were scored by each boy who attained a 'standard' by passing a test, and further points if, by passing an approved combination of tests, including some field-events, he qualified for an 'All-round badge'. A school list on which successes were marked was on display in the hall, with a red 'Q' to show the winners of badges. The record score for All-round badges was claimed in 1953, at 91. Athletics is a major activity during the season, in the Summer term since the move to the new school.

When Green, the originator, left, Mason took the system over and revised it with the skill to be expected of a meticulous scientist. In the 'twenties it was always Hawkins who acted as timekeeper, kept a general eye on all training, and wrote up the record sheet, which always aroused keen interest.

Cross-country had its own test, the course being from Granhams Road, Shelford, through Nine Wells to the school field. House teams were normally made up of the first six men home, and Kenneth Thompson wrote an amusing little poem beginning

I struggle blindly over muddy fields

and ending with a neat Alexandrine expressing effort:

'You're sixth man for your House; you've got to run again!'

There were not, as a rule, cross-country fixtures until the 'thirties.

In recent years school athletes and athletic teams have acquitted themselves well in inter-school matches and in the Cambridgeshire Junior championships, and track athletes have regularly appeared at the White City in the Public Schools Sports. Old Perseans have on many occasions become County champions, in all three areas: track, field and cross-country; many have represented the Eastern Counties, and a number have acted as officials. The national Secretary and Team Manager for cross-country is an Old Persean, G. Dunn.

School Athletics matches were the rule from the first, and when Green became Headmaster of Guildford and Mason of Hampton there were triangular fixtures which demonstrated the high standard attained in all three schools. Other schools with which regular fixtures have been held include the local ones, Bishop's Stortford, Ipswich, Felsted and Ely.

The school Sports have, ever since Allen established the meeting, been an important occasion in the calendar, though never, as at some schools, a kind of Headmaster's Garden party; the athletic contests were always the paramount interest. The school was fortunate in having access to the Fenner's ground, which was used almost every year from 1876 until 1960, when both the school and the C.U.A.C. moved away from the Gresham Road area. For many years the senior Mile race was held on Fenner's as a separate function, after school one non-games day. The system of Victores Ludorum was always maintained, and records were scrupulously kept — and regularly broken.

There is a popular annual match with the Old Perseans, one of a series of sporting fixtures which always excite interest.

Rugby football has, of course, for long ranked as the premier school sport. It was introduced by Heppenstall in the eighteen-seventies, when it achieved great and widespread popularity following the first inter-Varsity match of 1871. It had first been played at Rugby School in 1823. Under Barnes-Lawrence, a keen 'soccer' man, it took a secondary role, both codes being played until 1908. It was Parker-Smith who revived it, and he, along with Davies, Goodwin and Lyward, developed it in the school. In the earlier matches several masters, especially Goodwin, Gunn, Clayton and Parker-Smith himself, played for the school against men's teams; Davies broke a collar-bone in one game and in another Parker-Smith suffered a permanent leg injury. Some good early results included beating Bedford Modern 2nd XV 26-nil (Dec. 1910) and Bishop's Stortford, 31-5 (March 1911).

The most successful years in the early Rugger calendar were 1919-20 (when 13 out of 18 games were won, with one draw), 1921-22, 1922-23 (15 out of 21 won) and 1926-27. Old Perseans going on to the University did well. H. M. Woodhead claimed to be the first old boy to gain a Trial cap. In 1921 no fewer than four O.P.s appeared in the University Trials, and Cohen won his Blue.

In more recent years outstanding seasons have been 1940-41, 1947-48, 1950-51, 1951-52 (10 won, 1 drawn), 1956-57, 1958-59, 1960-61 and 1962-63 (12 won, 1 lost, 1 drawn). Following the very successful seasons of the Sixties, some important new fixtures were acquired, for example, with Oakham, Gresham's and Emmanuel. There have also been good results in the Seven-a-side game. In the Public Schools Seven-a-side Tournament the school has twice reached the last sixteen.

In Rugger the record of the Old Perseans is also creditable. The first old boys' team played in 1909, but a formal club did not develop, although various matches were played from time to time, and a match against the school was almost an annual event. There is a full description in the *Pelican* of the 1911 game, in which there was a Macfarlane-Grieve on each side and the O.P. team included R. Mayo. In the early 'twenties, the game enjoyed a new lease of life, corresponding with the successful period in school Rugger and with Cohen's Blue. From 1924 onwards there was a regular O.P. match against Cambridge Town (later City) played on Boxing Day; this continued until 1950. The club is strongly represented in the Cambridgeshire side.

It was only in 1949 that the Old Perseans established a more permanent club. It was at first known as the Perse Wanderers' R.F.C. and retained this name until 1957 when it felt sufficiently established to amalgamate with the Old Persean Society and take the name of O.P.R.U.F.C. At first the unofficial headquarters were at the 'Red Lion', Trumpington. From this period the club's fortunes were at first erratic, and it almost died in 1962 because of 'a gross deficiency in active interest'. However, since that year it has become a firmly established part of the life of the Society, largely through the efforts of a dedicated few under the guidance of Tony Billinghurst. In recent years two other teams have been fielded, one reviving the name of Wanderers and the other, an occasional 3rd XV, known as the Vagabonds. In addition to a successful calendar of games, the Club arranges many social functions, usually financially valuable. A great stride forward was made when the Governors gave permission for the Club to extend the school pavilion — by their own labour — and instal a small bar there; this helps to ensure continuity, and the O.P.S. committee now meets in the pavilion.

Among outstanding Old Persean players, too many to be fully named, mention should be made of P. J. Green (Bedford R.F.C.) a very promising player who was killed in the Paris air disaster of 1974. The *Cambridge Evening News* said of him that 'one hoped that one day he would win an international cap; no man would have worn it, figuratively speaking, more modestly. He upheld Rugby's traditions to the highest degree'.

Swimming has been an important activity from the time of Rouse onwards. He was very anxious that every boy in the school should be able to swim, and as an encouragement introduced the rule that non-swimmers should have white buttons on their caps. Medland, the porter, naively observed that this might help if a non-swimmer fell into the river, as those on the bank would know his incapacity from his cap! Certainly it was considered somewhat shameful to have to wear the white button and this must have led some to redouble their effort. There were periodically unannounced cap inspections, with a punishment for neglect of the rule. An amusing poem on the white buttons appeared in the *Pelican* in 1910. The school rented a swimming shed on the river, near the present Fen Causeway bridge, the area of which was doubled when the former Police sheds were incorporated. The first record of the acquisition of this little estate refers to it as part of Hell Meadow — a name which has long since gone out of use.

The first 'Swimming Master' was Llewellyn Davies, followed by Caldwell Cook. In the 'twenties swimming was a regular games afternoon activity, the three officials in charge being Caldwell Cook, Hawkins and Medland. Non-swimmers were taught by being suspended from 'the gibbet', a pole, held by the instructor, with a sort of harness at the end of a dangling rope, in which the boy was paraded like a captive fish. There were a number of inter-school fixtures. The annual swimming sports were, in those days, held a little higher up the river, at the Town sheds. When the new Jesus Green pool was built the sports were transferred there, and after the 'forties occasional use was made of the excellent facilities at the Leys school baths. The building of the Parkside pool provided an ideal, and more readily available, alternative, and the school swimming-place was abandoned; in any case, the river had by then become too polluted to be suitable for swimming.

Boxing has always been an important activity. The sport has enjoyed two particularly successful periods, thanks to the coaching of two very fine instructors, Costello in the 'twenties and Finch in the 'fifties. The outstanding O.P. boxer was certainly Douglas, 'Puggy', Simmonds, who boxed for Oxford. Undergraduates interested in Boxing have often helped to instruct, and to referee bouts, usually staged in the hall. Thanks also to Costello, Fencing was a popular pursuit in his time; he had been a fencing champion in the Indian Army and was a splendid coach. A number of his pupils did very well, notably C. L. de Beaumont, who won his national Cap in 1929, and was runner-up in the International Epee Tournament. He has been rightly described as the greatest name in British fencing in recent years. Among other good fencers should be named the Goring brothers; Marius made impressive use of his fencing skills in various stage productions.

Fives is another game which has always had its keen disciples at the Perse, good facilities having been available in the courts at Gonville Place, and even better ones in the splendid covered courts at the new school. The first inspiration for the game came from Barnes-Lawrence, who played well and encouraged the use of the courts as a play-time activity as well as for matches after school. His particular disciple was Harold Cooke, who played regularly on games afternoons while on the staff, and taught the game to a succession of boys. Caldwell Cook, Salusbury and Macfarlane-Grieve all played a good game, and it was his boyhood memories that led Gavin to present the new courts to the school. A little later Reg Chater Blows and Donald Hughes put up good performances for Old Persean teams. Fives has usually been included in the calendar of school versus old boys matches. During the Second War, however, the courts were out of use, having been sealed off as emergency sheds.

Badminton and basket-ball have attracted a number of adherents in more recent years.

Tennis, introduced in Wootton's time, following a nation-wide questionnaire on the attitude of the Public Schools to the game, has flourished, and regular fixtures are arranged. When to this list of games and activities are added those available through the Scouts and Corps — camping, mountaineering, sailing, gliding, orienteering, it will be recognised that a worth-while leisure pursuit is offered to every Perse boy, to supplement his class-work and help to complete his training for life.

Golf, though not a school game, is an important O.P.S. activity, and a number of Perseans, even while at school, have made a name for themselves on the links.

It would be interesting to compile a list of Persean Blues, and the result would be impressive and would cover a wide range of activities. For example, although Lacrosse has never been played in the school, Stanley Betts, Bishop of Maidstone and now Dean of Rochester, gained his Half-blue in this game.

Turning from the playing-field to the great indoor game of wits, a number of Old Perseans, following practice in school, have done well in Chess. Frank Lockwood played for the University, E. H. Church and Bernard Coulson between them have been the main inspiration of County Chess in Cambridgeshire for two generations, and Cyril Alliston is known as a redoubtable player. No doubt there are others.

XXII

EPILOGUE, AND PROLOGUE FOR THE FUTURE

When, in the summer of 1969, it was Stanley Stubbs' turn to retire, there were very many expressions of appreciation of all he had done for the Perse. Those who had worked with him and under him thought back over the years and were astonished at how much he had achieved. His interests were of the widest: in the school they embraced games, the Corps, the Boarding Houses, and as much teaching as could be arranged, principally the Headmaster's period with the Sixth Forms, which had so wide a scope that he called them 'Cabbages and Kings', but also some German and Divinity; and he was always the Careers Master, especially well informed on University entrance matters. Outside the school he was a prominent Rotarian, a Syndic of the Local Examinations Syndicate for twenty years, and well known in local and national education circles; his visits to the United States had done much to foster an understanding of the educational problems of the two countries, and allowed the Perse to cater effectively for American boys temporarily in Cambridge.

There would be much to remind future generations of Mr. Stubbs' work. The 'Stubbs-Perse Cup: for service' presented at annual civic parades of the Corps, marked his long service in the A.T.C. The position and prestige of the school, and the fine academic record, would mark his reign as successful, but above all the material achievements of building were such that his friends might say with Christopher Wren, *Si monumentum requiris, circumspice*!

Towards the end of the final term presentations were made to Mr. Stubbs, and to Mrs. Stubbs, who had shared so much of the devoted work he had undertaken. The Parents' Association gave a portrait to hang in the hall, in which the Headmaster's hand may be seen to be holding a paper carrying the plan for the new school. The Old Persean Society made a presentation to Mr. and Mrs. Stubbs at Emmanuel College, and the Governors made theirs at Christ's College.

Mr. Stubbs' successor, chosen from an impressive field of applicants, is Mr. Anthony Melville, who, like Dr. Rouse before him, hails from a distant part of what was once the British Empire, being an Australian by birth. Educated at Shore School, Sydney, and at the University of Sydney, where he gained a first class Honours degree in History and English, he came to Cambridge to extend his academic education, after a spell of teaching at Geelong Grammar School. He was an Exhibitioner of King's College, gaining a first-class with distinction in Part II of the Historical Tripos. Later he won the Austin Leigh Studentship for research in 18th century English history and also the Lightfoot Scholarship in ecclesiastical history. He then joined the staff of Haileybury and Imperial Service College, where he made a name for himself as a vigorous and thought-provoking teacher.

The final section of this chapter is written by Mr. Melville, who, after acknowledging his debt to his predecessors, speaks of the problems which lie ahead for the school, problems possibly as great as any of those which have been surveyed in the foregoing pages. However, the support of parents, Old Perseans and staff and boys will make a difficult task an exciting challenge, and the future of Dr. Perse's school must surely be assured:

The achievements of Stanley Stubbs' Headmastership justify us in seeing it as one of the most effective in the School's history. By 1969, the Perse was so securely established in Cambridge that it could envisage without fear the changes the second half of the 70s promised to bring. The demand for Perse places, and hence the school's size, started to rise during the war and the school now appears to have stabilised at about 580, with 420 boys in the Upper School and 160 in the Prep. These boys have become an academically highly selected group through the operation, not only of the Direct Grant system but also of the local demand for independent and academic education in an area where the population has grown rapidly. When the school was free from financial worry the step, which Dr. Rouse saw as vital and for which preparation had been made intermittently over 50 years in the accumulation of land to the south of Cambridge, was possible. Though this wise move to the new site was, as always in Cambridge, not taken without controversy, confidence in the survival of the school on its old and restricted sites of Gonville Place and Bateman Street would inevitably have been less. The re-building of the school on the Hills Road site and the moving of the Preparatory School to Leighton House equipped the Perse at last with the room and the buildings it needed.

The last seven years have been prosperous ones. Generous presents, like Laurie Marsh's Sixth Form Centre and Sir John Gray's bequest, enabled us to add to the school's physical resources, providing at the Upper School more privacy, comfort and opportunity for private study than ever before, and at the Prep a new Assembly Hall (which is also a gymnasium), a cloakroom, lavatory and form room block, not only increasing the size of the Preparatory School by taking more boys at 7+ but also very much improving its quality of life. Like all schools we have plans for the buildings of the future, but we are scarcely ill-equipped for the years to come.

During the 60s, as the tide of 'comprehensivisation' rose, it became clear that the Direct Grant system which had served Cambridge so well would be sacrificed to Labour's Left-wing were a Socialist Government to come to power, for such a move would be relatively cheap and apparently egalitarian. When the Governors, faced with the choice in 1975, ultimately made the formal decision to revert to full independence, it came as no surprise to any member of the Perse community.

Nevertheless, the decision was not reached without deep regret, for it was bound to restrict the school ultimately almost entirely to those who could afford the fees, while under the Direct Grant system for 30 years both the 24 annual Free Places at 11+ and the fee-assisted scheme allowed a much greater social mix than can exist in a future Perse School. When it was founded, the Perse was rich by the standards of the time but, as this record shows, that enviable position disappeared over the centuries. By the beginning of the 20th century (as today) the school's endowment was represented only in the land and buildings it owned, in contrast to many great Direct Grant schools like King Edward's Birmingham and Manchester Grammar School. There is no "foundation" to establish a Bursary system which can in any way replace the State's and there is a limit to what can be done from fee income. The Perse, alas, will be a less varied community when the Direct Grant has worked its way through and it will be further from its founder's wishes. But the alternative was the disappearance of all but the name of the school and that was unthinkable.

The future of the school rests upon demand for its places. The eagerness of parents to send their boys to the school (upon which all ultimately rests) has grown steadily, perhaps as a result of the comprehensive reorganisation of the Local Education Authority and the disappearance of its much-esteemed Grammar Schools. Both for educational and financial reasons, independent day school education has become more popular with parents who might once have thought in terms only of boarding.

All the developments of the past few years have gone in favour of schools like the Perse. We provide the kind of school parents recognise, with whose assumptions they can identify as a disciplined community with a common academic and moral purpose, conservative and traditional in many ways, but taking up new ideas when they have proved themselves and changing, not for the sake of change, but to meet new demands as they justify themselves. Almost every subject at the Perse is taught with a "modern" syllabus, but our aims remain recognisably the same. The distinctive emphasis falls, as it always has fallen, on academic excellence and the environment that favours it. The games, the plays, art and societies which flourish, perhaps more than ever in the school's history are seen not so much as the *esse*, but rather the *bene esse* of its life.

So long as parents value the kind of education the Perse endeavours to provide we should not be afraid of the future. The talents of the Staff, the loyalty of our Old Boys, the satisfaction of the large body of present and past parents, the esteem and respect of the Cambridge community are our most precious possessions and our best protection against the uncertainties of the next few years. The future of the school is bound up with the survival of independent schools in England as a whole, but our courage should not falter; in its traditions and continuity as well as its clear sense of purpose, we have the essential prerequisites for a new and challenging chapter in our history.

Headmasters of the Perse School

1618	Thomas Lovering
1637	Richard Watson
1642	Thomas Crabbe
1652	George Griffith
1687	Edward Sparkes
1727	Daniel Munnings
1728	Nathaniel Saltier
1732	Henry Goodall
1751	Roger Sturgeon
1760	Samuel Story
1765	James Cory
1767	Samuel Reeve
1768	John Franklin Squire
1768	John White
1776	William Bond
1776	Richard Fisher
1781	John Jelliand Brundish
1782	William Walford
1782	Thomas Cooke Burroughes
1786	Charles Davy
1791	John Drew Borton
1793	John Spencer Cobbold
1794	St. John Smith
1795	Benedict Chapman
1799	George Grigby
1802	William Gimingham
1804	William Wilkins
1806	Daniel Gwilt
1810	John White
1813	John Wilson
1825	James Bailey
1836	Charles Clayton
1837	Peter Mason
1864	Frederick Heppenstall
1875	John Barrow Allen
1884	Herbert Cecil Barnes-Lawrence
1902	William Henry Denham Rouse
1928	Hubert Arthur Wootton
1945	Stanley Stubbs
1969	Anthony Edwin Melville

NOTES AND REFERENCES

J. M. Gray's *History of the Perse School*, Bowes & Bowes, 1922, is referred to *passim*.

1.   On the Perse arms, see p.203.
2.   The observations of Dr. W. M. Palmer and Dr. Arthur Rook, both of whom made a close study of Cambridge medical personalities, are included.
3.   Chancery Proceedings, July, 1841: in the school archives.
4.   A. F. Bottomley, an Old Persean whose researches in this field are of the greatest importance.
5.   J. M. Gray thinks she was his niece; we take Bottomley's view.
6.   *Piers Plowman*, ed. Skeat, 1906.
7.   J. M. Gray, *Pelican*, Dec., 1965.
8.   The bequest of Dr. Mowse, an earlier Master of Trinity Hall (1552-3) had provided for the upkeep of the main highways near Cambridge, and was used to set up the famous mile-stones along the London road to Barkway.
9.   There is a photograph of this Court, before demolition, in F. A. Reeve's *Victorian and Edwardian Cambridge*, Batsford, 1971. William of Wykeham was the founder of Winchester College and of New College, Oxford. William Waynflete founded Magdalen College and Magdalen College School.
10.   Trinity boys later attended the Perse; see pp.76-7.
11.   Quoted in Vivian Ogilvie's *English Public Schools*, Batsford, 1957.
12.   Bowtell Papers: a very interesting collection of documents referring to Cambridge, amassed by the University bookbinder. Now preserved at Downing College.
13.   The founder of St. Paul's School, 1518.
14.   This limitation was intended to prevent the school from being swamped with non-foundationers, to the detriment of the 'free' scholars. From time to time the Trustees either enforced or relaxed the rule.
15.   Dr Rouse later insisted on this rule; see p.95.
16.   A further switch occurred later; the 1856 plan shows Wisken, as Usher, occupying the house to the south.
17.   Newport G. S. taught Hebrew. Any reference in these pages to Newport implies Essex, and quotes F. Thompson, *Newport Grammar School, Essex*, O. N. Socy, 1974. That school, like the Perse, was on foundation entrusted to the trusteeship of the Master of Caius.
18.   George Sampson.
19.   State Papers, Domestic, CCCXLVI, 429, 1636/7. The writer is therein indicated merely as 'Dr. E. M.'
20.   Richard Harraden wrote several delightful books, illustrated with prints, on the history and buildings of Cambridge. The reference here is to *Cantabrigia Depicta*, 1809. One of his prints is used to illustrate the use of the Free School Lane building by the Fitzwilliam Museum.
21.   There is a reference in Evelyn's *Diary*, 29 Nov., 1695.
22.   J. M. Gray, *Pelican*, March 1965, and the Rev. B. B. Edmonds, quoting Dr Robert Smith, in *Harmonies*. The organ-builder in question was Bernard (or Barnard) Turner, son of Henry Turner, a German immigrant, originally Tolner, who had founded a business with important University connections, including the care of the college organs of Trinity, Christ's

and Emmanuel. Bernard was organist of both St. John's and Christ's. His elder son was educated at the Perse and became a Fellow of St. John's. It is significant that the second son was 'educated privately' by his brother.

23.   Dr. F. H. Stubbings, Emmanuel College.

24.   At Magdalen College School there was a 'period of eclipse' in which feeling ran high between Town and Gown. See R. S. Stainer, *Magdalen School,* Blackwell, 1958.

25.   Dr. A. D. Harvey, of Wolfson College.

26.   J. M. Gray, *Pelican*.

27.   Dr. J. Venn. *The Perse School, Cambridge: Notes, 1619-1864, from the Admission Registers of Gonville & Caius College, 1890.* Venn was the historian of Caius College; he and his son, J. A. Venn, did much work on the alumni of Cambridge.

28.   The manuscript diary of Joseph Romilly, University Registrary 1832-61, preserved in the University Library, gives a fascinating picture of the time. There is a selection, ed. J. P. T. Bury, C.U.P., 1967. The author is grateful to Mr. P. J. Barnwell, of Downing College, who has drawn attention to other references not used by Bury. Romilly characterised Wilkins' design for a Fitzwilliam Museum as 'vastly heavy'.

29.   Peter Mason, junior, was also a noted pedestrian in an age when long walks were becoming a fashionable eccentricity. He walked to London and to Oxford, cutting across country when so disposed.

30.   This refers to the last years of Mason's reign, and to the scandal arising from the McDowall episode. See p.46.

31.   On Higher Grade schools see also p.62.

32.   Gray persistently misspells the name with one 'l'. The correct spelling appears on his prospectus and in letters in Trinity library. Harold Cooke noted the misspelling in his *Pelican* review of Gray's book.

33.   Barry's own parents were in business as drapers, on the ground floor of the very tall building in Sidney Street afterwards rebuilt as Lloyds Bank.

34.   E. E. Kellett.

35.   This prospectus proves the correct spelling of Pendeen. Spalding's *Directory* and the Perse Governors' Minutes concur.

36.   Girton College was originally founded at Hitchin under the title of The College for Women.

37.   J. W. Kirby, *History of the Roan School*, Blackheath Press, 1929. The Roan School, founded in 1643, has much in common with the Perse. A. J. B. Green (see p.244) was educated there, and the author spent eighteen happy years on the staff.

38.   Again Gray's spelling is at fault, giving the name as 'Laurence'.

39.   To mark the Queen's Golden Jubilee.

40.   Over what was afterwards G. P. Jones' shop. It was possible not many years ago to discern the name of the school painted on the brickwork above.

41.   Percy Copping, an O.P. afterwards Classical master at the City of London School, observed that its architecture was, for its time, remarkably restrained, even functional, 'avoiding altogether the major abominations of Victorian Gothic'.

42.   Designed by Shinkfield to be quickly erected and dismantled. The wood was subsequently used for the glider hangar on the playing field.

43. Harold Cooke.
44. Widdicombe and Wilson worked together, one year, as University Proctors.
45. Incidentally, a neat if obvious play on the name, suggesting 'purse'.
46. Arthur Hawkins.
47. Including Lord Porter and Sir Gilbert Wiles, writing in the *Pelican*.
48. Among portraits of Rouse should be mentioned the bust in Christ's College library by George Thomas (1928) and the painting at the school. The latter, painted by an Old Persean, H. G. W. Betteridge, who also painted the portraits of Jeremy Taylor and Edward Palmer for the school, shows the Doctor holding a paper with a plan for the new building of which he dreamed.
49. Dr. A. L. Peck, Christ's College.
50. A holiday was later declared. For the scene, see p.119
51. This corresponds with Ordinance 8 of Martin Perse's rules. It is to be noted that the parents, not the boy, are blamed.
52. This pamphlet does not seem to have survived.
53. Spike Hughes, *Opening Bars*, London, 1946 and *Second Movement*, 1951.
54. Caldwell Cook must have been in sympathy, but there is no record of his having visited Chesterton. For his Play Way work, see Chapter 11.
55. Leonard Amey, afterwards Agricultural Correspondent of *The Times*.
56. The Doctor preferred this word to 'educationist' on the grounds that the 'al' element always denotes a vague connection (as in 'historical'. The point is made in the *Oxford English Dictionary*).
57. The members of the Association took this Latin name (properly denoting inhabitants of Arles) from the English initials A.R.L.T.
58. The Doctor liked to take a share of Middle and Lower school teaching whenever he could.
59. Appleton illustrates this in *Latin on the Direct Method* by showing how he would explain the words *pignus* and *testamentum*.
60. C. W. E. Peckett, afterwards Headmaster of the Priory School, Shrewsbury.
61. Parry's work, and that of Douglas Brown, in continuing Cook's methods, are discussed in Chapter 19.
62. E. H. Warmington, afterwards Professor of Classics, University of London, Birkbeck College, and Joint Editor of the Loeb Classical Library. The author acknowledges valuable help given by Professor Warmington, especially in the writing of chapters 12 and 15.
63. A pleasant thread was woven into history when it happened that Mr. Mitchell, at Newcastle High School, Staffs., taught Stanley Stubbs, a future Perse Headmaster.
64. As a young master he was called 'Awkeye, no doubt because of his keen perception.
65. Canon T. L. Livermore.
66. Dr. J. H. M. D. Whitaker, afterwards a lecturer at Leicester University.
67. A letter in *The Times* in May 1976 pointed out that the Macfarlane-Grieve family could claim a remarkable spanning of the years, Gavin's grandfather having been present at the battle of Copenhagen.
68. Even when a school photograph was being taken, he personally arranged the boys, instead of leaving this to a master or to the photographer.
69. As G. T. Salusbury acidly observed, Wootton proved an excellent Head-

master 'in matters like keeping duplicate keys well greased'. Perhaps the Chairman of Governors had this in mind when he said that H. A. W. was 'a great expert in Natural Science and in the planning of buildings' — certainly an example of how the real point of a testimonial lies in what is omitted.

70.   Named in acknowledgement of the part played by the Norfolk village from which the Perse coat of arms originated. See p. 1.

71.   The American tours involved visiting a large number of schools and universities over a wide area, and examining in detail the equipment, curricula, examination system and educational philosophy of much of the huge country. It was with great pride and pleasure that Stubbs found the name and reputation of the Perse well known, and was able to make contact with a number of O.P.'s and others who knew the school well.

72.   The Industrial Fund, working on subscriptions from industrial firms, made grants to schools to allow for the building and equipment of science laboratories.

73.   For the story of the Perse Hostel see Chapter 20.

74.   For the story of the Doctor's uniform see p.92.

75.   Jennings would certainly have become famous had his life not ended tragically in a climbing accident on the Greek island of Poros, where he was filming, in 1950. He had already made a considerable name through his work at the G.P.O. Film Unit and elsewhere, and especially through the powerful film he directed about the martyred Polish village of Lidice.

76.   An exception was made when Louis de Glehn was elected President.

INDEX

259